Carried by a Magic Fan

Carried by a Magic Fan

Memoir of an Estonian Refugee Family

JAAK TREIMAN

McFarland & Company, Inc., Publishers
Jefferson, North Carolina

This book, published in Estonian as *Võlulehviku tuules*, was translated by Merike Pilter (OÜ Tammerraamat, 2018).

LIBRARY OF CONGRESS CATALOGUING-IN-PUBLICATION DATA

Names: Treiman, Jaak, 1943– author. | Pilter, Merike, translator.
Title: Carried by a magic fan : memoir of an Estonian refugee family / Jaak Treiman.
Other titles: Võlulehviku tuules. English
Description: Jefferson : McFarland & Company, Inc., Publishers, 2023 | Includes bibliographical references and index.
Identifiers: LCCN 2023015501 | ISBN 9781476691503 (paperback : acid free paper) ∞
    ISBN 9781476649818 (ebook)
Subjects: LCSH: Treiman, Jaak, 1943– | Treiman, Jaak, 1943-—Political activity. | Diplomats—Estonia—Biography. | Estonia—Foreign relations—20th century. | Estonians—Foreign countries—Biography. | Estonian American families. | Refugees—Biography.
Classification: LCC DK503.77.T74 V6513 2023 | DDC 327.4798092 [B]—dc23/eng/20230501
LC record available at https://lccn.loc.gov/2023015501

BRITISH LIBRARY CATALOGUING DATA ARE AVAILABLE

ISBN (print) 978-1-4766-9150-3
ISBN (ebook) 978-1-4766-4981-8

© 2023 Jaak Treiman. All rights reserved

No part of this book may be reproduced or transmitted in any form or by any means, electronic or mechanical, including photocopying or recording, or by any information storage and retrieval system, without permission in writing from the publisher.

On the cover: The memorial at Puise Beach is dedicated to those who left, many of whom started their journey from this spot. It is located a little less than 9 miles southwest of the town of Haapsalu (author's photograph). *Inset* The author sits with his parents at their dining table in their home in Sun Valley, perhaps in 1953. (Treiman family archive). *Background* © Igisheva Maria/Shutterstock

Printed in the United States of America

McFarland & Company, Inc., Publishers
    Box 611, Jefferson, North Carolina 28640
        www.mcfarlandpub.com

To Samantha, Avery and Zoe

People ask, "Why did you leave Estonia?" The will to live; the right to live a complete life! A person must be able to think freely, to criticize, to express oneself! And, no life can be complete if a person is not permitted to live according to her own beliefs, if a person is unable to develop one's abilities. Freedom is priceless. Living under dictatorial power destroys a person's life. For those and other reasons I and many others left.—Valli Treiman

I felt as though I was riding the wind, carrying us to unknown parts of the world.—Valli Treiman

Table of Contents

Preface to the Estonian Edition   1

Preface to the English Edition   4

Introduction   7

1. Mother's Time in Russia   11
   "How my father managed to feed me is still a mystery."

2. Upheavals   14
   "All citizens ... irrespective of their religion, ethnic origin, and political views, shall enjoy equal protection under the law and courts of justice."

3. Mother's Childhood, Estonia in the 1920s   23
   "Our sow and I had many conversations."

4. My Father's Family   32
   "Perhaps someday you will find this information of interest and be able to use it."

5. A Brief Normality   36
   "We savored the joy of living."

6. Foreign Occupations   42
   "Nothing in life remains constant..."

7. Two Weddings and an Exit   46
   "Alfred was a man of few words."

8. Back and Forth   50
   "I am left to speculate."

9. Escape   54
   "I heard the sound of guard dogs..."

Table of Contents

10. A New Life: Joys and Worries — 60
    "Freedom is priceless. Living under dictatorial power destroys a person's life."

11. Uncertainty — 72
    "…it is Sweden's wish that refugees return to their homes."

12. New York — 82
    "I will jump ship at the first opportunity."

13. America to Australia — 89
    "The passport control people even wished us a good trip."

14. Australia—Getting Started — 101
    "We moved five times during our first year."

15. Australia—Settling In — 107
    "More Estonians are coming to Australia."

16. Leaving Australia — 115
    "Go? Of course! America."

17. Establishing New Roots — 121
    "We arrived in Los Angeles on … Thanksgiving Day."

18. Restarting Our Business — 128
    "Father had put the fingertip in his pocket …"

19. Bridging Generations and History — 134
    "Even if you don't see my parents' actual words, they are still present."

20. Lessons Learned—University — 136
    "Don't believe what we say in public."

21. In the Army — 140
    "An education in the logic of the illogical"

22. Baltic American Freedom League — 146
    "Unity brings strength."

23. The 1984 Los Angeles Olympics — 155
    "A little too political."

24. America's Nonrecognition Policy — 163
    "The people of the United States are opposed to predatory activities…"

25. Appointment as Honorary Consul — 167
    "I Can Always Quit."

Table of Contents ix

26. Flying the Flag 173
    "Subtlety was not his strong suit."

27. Visitors and Guests 185
    "We were watching Estonia's rebirth."

28. Los Angeles Marathon: A Story in Four Parts 196

    PART 1. LOS ANGELES MARATHON 1987 196
    "'Estonia' was spelled perfectly."

    PART 2. LOS ANGELES MARATHON 1988 202
    "Please register me for the March 6, 1988, Los Angeles Marathon."

    PART 3. LOS ANGELES MARATHON 1989 206
    "...our parallel universes met."

    PART 4. LOS ANGELES MARATHON 1990 214
    Joy and Disappointment

29. Conversations with American Presidents 218
    "Mr. President, we have taken way too much of your time."

30. Reconnecting with Family 228
    "They were familiar strangers."

31. Independence Restored 237
    "...these ends required new beginnings."

Epilogue 241
Further Readings 249
Index 255

Preface to the Estonian Edition

My father was born in 1911. Russia's Prime Minister Peter Stolypin was assassinated; Italy declared war on Turkey; industrial unrest advanced across England and the continent. These events were precursors to the world war, revolution and civil war that my mother was born into seven years later.

My parents' lives spanned nine decades and three continents. They witnessed Estonia's independence, loss of independence and restoration of independence. They were among the refugees of World War II, the forerunners to the refugees of today. As did many of their compatriots they experienced much, including togetherness and estrangement, adversity and good fortune. My mother, father and many of their contemporaries led lives that bridged multiple generations.

The vignettes in this book are a glimpse not only into the life of one family but also offer a perspective into the lives of a generation of Estonians, separated from their homeland not by choice but by events beyond their control.

This book is based on my mother's recollections. Written in 2012 when she was 93, I had convinced her to enter an Estonian essay contest sponsored by the International Organization for Migration. The contest asked for recollections of "Living in a New Homeland." To her surprise, she won third place.

I probed what my mother had written, asked her follow-up questions and persuaded her to augment her text with additional information. I have now amplified her expanded text with portions of letters, transcripts of audio recordings of me "interviewing" my father and mother, some written recollections my father wrote as well as recollections of friends and relatives. Old photographs and memorabilia have helped jog my memory. Here and there I have added my own recollections.

The narrative in this book, as with all family stories, reflects not only my recollections but also the collective memory of many people. Memories, whether individual or collective, are tinged with time. I make no representation that all statements you will read are academically accurate. Dates may be off. Key actors may not be mentioned. Others perhaps do not warrant the space they have been accorded.

Events may not have happened exactly as set forth. My recollections, as my mother's, are colored by the passage of time, our respective vantage points and prejudices. They have all influenced the text you will read. Regardless, I believe this book offers a mirror, not only of one family's life but of the lives of countless others, Estonian and non–Estonian, who had their lives uprooted but continued to do what humans do best—survive, adapt and develop.

In compiling this book, I owe an obvious debt of gratitude to my parents—not only for the love, affection and support they gave me throughout their lives but also for being so frugal in what they threw away. While my mother may have tossed my extensive Australian comic book collection when we moved to America, she and my father nevertheless kept copies of many letters they wrote and the originals of what they received, even dating back to 1943–1947. Those letters have provided an invaluable insight not only into their lives but the lives of the Estonian refugees in Sweden, Australia and America.

The Uibo family, with my mother's eldest brother's son Mati as the superintendent of the family history, have identified old pictures, straightened me out on family history and provided me with countless letters and documents. Mimicking what appears to be a family trait, Mati has kept every letter that my mother and father sent him. I am grateful for the many times Ele Aruste, the daughter of my mother's youngest brother, has shared her recollections with me.

My mother's half-sister, Hilja, has been a fountain of information, allowing me to sit with her and record her recollections of family history. And amazingly, at some point during our conversation I realized I understood most of what she was saying in her Võru brogue.

On my father's side of the family Katrin Viilu faithfully journeys from Räpina to Võru each time I come to Võru, meets with me and offers conversation that always yields insightful tidbits.

The Baltic Studies Program of Stanford University Libraries, established through the generosity of the Kistler-Ritso Foundation, has been invaluable. Thanks to Liisi Esse, assistant curator for Estonian and Baltic Studies, and thanks also to Uve Poom, many old letters that would otherwise have been undecipherable to me were transcribed and made decipherable. Their help was immeasurable.

Jamie Hoehn, assistant archivist at the University of Minnesota's Immigration History Research Center Archives, was helpful beyond the call of duty in gathering material that I wanted to look at. Thank you, Jamie.

Preface to the Estonian Edition

There are countless people who have shared their memories and recollections. Of those, my former wife Jean, her sister Michelle and Michelle's husband Domenico have been particularly helpful. Thanks also to Maarit (Ritva) Poom for searching her parents' old letters for letters from my parents. Aivar Tsarski refreshed my recollection of the Los Angeles Marathon by sharing his memories and Eva-Maria Liimets and the Estonian Foreign Ministry archives provided me with background on the formation of the Los Angeles Honorary Consulate.

It has been a pleasure to work with Lea Arme whose editorial gifts have polished this [Estonian] edition and with Tiina Tammer and Tammerraamat. Their painless introduction to book publishing has been a joy.

Without the persistent prodding and assistance of my friend Margus Välja this book would never have been written. Once I finally began to write this book, without his patient, painstaking review of my disorganized photo archives this book would have been a book without pictures. These short sentences are an inadequate thank you.

I am conversant in Estonian because that is what we always spoke at home. I never received formal instruction. I have therefore had to write my portions of text in English. I needed someone to translate my English into Estonian. I was fortunate to have Merike Pilter as my translator. While I cannot write error-free Estonian, I do know if someone is saying something in Estonian the way I want it to be said. Merike has excelled in this.

Finally, the proverbial "last but not least." Thank you, Liisa, for asking incisive questions. Thank you also for listening to my many reflections about the Treiman family's foibles and adventures and each time, acting as though I was saying something fresh and new.

—Jaak Treiman, Los Angeles—Võru

Preface to the English Edition

In 2018 my book *Võlulehviku tuules* was published in Estonia. The English translation of that title is "In the Tailwind of a Magic Fan." The title summarizes my parents' life, a life they lived on three continents, each time initially earning sustenance by producing and selling "magic fans"—a toy they learned to make while refugees in Sweden.

The backstory of how the book came to be written and my gratitude to the people who helped me in that initial endeavor are set out in the preface to the Estonian edition, a translation of which appears immediately prior to this Preface. Without their assistance, this English edition would not exist.

Why publish an English translation? One catalyst was my daughter Samantha and my granddaughters Avery and Zoe. Samantha remembers my parents well; Avery and Zoe, not as much.

Growing up, Samantha watched me as I was engaged in Baltic activities. She participated in a good number of them. She heard many of the family stories directly from my parents and sometimes put the stories to practical use in the school papers she had to write. I wanted to give her something less ephemeral than hand-me-down stories about one side of her multi-sided family. I wanted Sam to have a permanent memory of some of the events she attended and some of the stories she heard.

Even though she is my oldest granddaughter, Avery's recollections of my parents are dim; Zoe's almost nil. I wanted both to know about my parents' life, not only as passed on by way of oral family stories but as a more permanent history lesson in my parents' own words. I hoped they could feel the immediacy of our family's immigrant and refugee experience to their own lives. Since neither Samantha, Avery or Zoe are proficient in Estonian (all my fault according to Samantha), this English translation of *Võlulehviku tuules* seemed in order.

I also wanted Samantha, Avery and Zoe, as well as others in their position, to read the story and be led to ask questions about refugee life and about the days when independence was restored to the Baltic States.

Preface to the English Edition

I felt unequal to the task of translating my mother's narrative and my parents' letters into English. Estonian is my mother tongue. We always spoke it at home. But I have never received formal instruction in Estonian. My Estonian literacy is inadequate for literary writing.

During the summer of 2019 my friend Liisa and I were in Estonia. We had dinner in Haapsalu with Merike Pilter and her husband Harles along with Margus Välja. As I explain in greater detail in the Preface to the Estonian edition, Margus is the person most responsible for my writing this book. Merike was the person Margus had persuaded to translate the text I had written in English for the Estonian edition.

During dinner we spoke about a possible English edition. Merike encouraged me to do the translation myself. She thought I was capable of translating my parents' Estonian into English. In fact, she insisted that I was the right person to do so. If I got stuck, she volunteered to help.

After more thought and with trepidation, I tested Merike's advice. She was right. I was able to translate my parents' Estonian into English—not as a professional translator but as a son who always spoke Estonian at home and who had a pretty good idea of what each of my parents wanted to say. The intent and meaning of what they said was never changed although on occasion how they said something was. Since they were my parents, I felt I had some leeway. I didn't think they would have objected to the few liberties I took.

Thanks to Merike's unstinting help, whenever I was stuck, she "unstuck" me. I am happy with the end result. Not only do I feel that I did justice to my parents' words, the process of translating was also a revelation. Children are inclined to hear but not always listen to their parents. I was no different, even when I reached adulthood. The process of translating my parents' words forced me to listen, really listen to what they were saying. I developed a better understanding of them.

A number of other people, some of them repeat helpers, also helped me complete this English edition.

Valdis Pavlovskis and Jaana Kõvatu improved the text by filling in details absent from the Estonian edition. They allowed me to insert some of their comments into the text. I appreciate my cousin Mati and his wife Ilme for continuing to feed information to Jaana to pass on to me.

A member of Generation Z, Royce Willis, read the entire manuscript and offered thoughts and comments worthy of a university professor. If Royce reflects the future, Americans and Estonians have nothing to worry about.

Aivar Tsarski continued the assistance he gave me for the Estonian edition by searching his family archives and letting me use a series of photographs from the 1989 Los Angeles Marathon.

Tiina Liiv patiently put up with changes I continued to make to the maps she so expertly drafted that show the Treiman family's route from Võru to Los Angeles and the stops in-between.

Maris Tippo, Ele Aruste and Cathy Hsia-Carmichael were generous in sharing their memories, which have been incorporated into the text.

I thank Mari-Ann Kelam, who is part of the story in this book, for her friendship over the years and for catching at least one of the mistakes in the Estonian edition.

I appreciate the time Tony and Danute Mazeika, Linas Kojelis, Elga Sharpe, Heino Nurmberg, Enn Auksmann, Anne Metsis and Ivars Miculs took to assist me.

Domenico and Michelle de Masi, Jean Ravin [Treiman] and Margus Välja spent inordinate time reviewing each chapter draft. They provided inciteful suggestions and commentary. And Domenico, I'm grateful for the additional incentive you and Michelle provided. I'm also awed at the time and energy you spent in searching for pictures of my mother making *pirukas*—pictures which unfortunately were so old the quality did not allow us to use them.

Merike Pilter deserves at least two if not more thank-yous. Not only did she help me with the translation, she also read each chapter revision and shared valuable guidance and insight. Both she and Margus continued to give me invaluable advice as I worked to include new photographs with new captions.

Katariina Välikangas-Dalloo, Irene Hodge, Roger Riske and LaNell Mahler Koenig deserve special acknowledgment for taking the time to read the entire text and then offering valuable feedback that appreciably improved the final product. In addition, Roger's suggestions on my "Further Readings" list were very helpful as were Katariina's comments as I struggled with the Introduction.

Whitney Wallace at McFarland has been a pleasure to work with. She has provided prompt help and useful guidance and done so with a sunny disposition.

And Liisa, thank you for the laughter we share, for opening new vistas and for continuing to ask questions and listen patiently.

—Jaak Treiman, Los Angeles–Võru–Saarikylät

Introduction

The Israelites journeyed from Rameses to Sukkoth. There were about six hundred thousand men on foot, besides women and children.

Many other people went up with them, and also large droves of livestock, both flocks and herds.

With the dough the Israelites had brought from Egypt, they baked loaves of unleavened bread. The dough was without yeast because they had been driven out of Egypt and did not have time to prepare food for themselves.

(Exodus 12:37–39)

The Book of Exodus contains perhaps the first, well-known description of people forced to leave their homes to seek safety elsewhere. Millenia later, in 1685, another group of persecuted religious believers fled from France to England and the label "refugees" originated.

Even though many historians have ignored the existence of refugees, an unknown number of millions of men, women and children have followed in the footsteps of the Israelites and Huguenots, forced to leave their homes to seek refuge elsewhere. Each of these refugees was "someone who is unable or unwilling to return to their country of origin owing to a well-founded fear of being persecuted for reasons of race, religion, nationality, membership of a particular social group, or political opinion" (United Nations 1951 Refugee Convention and its 1967 Protocol).

Refugees are a polyglot of humanity. They are a myriad of ethnicities, religious beliefs and political views. Just considering the last 100 or so years leaves one with staggering images—images of the sort that El Greco might have painted.

World War I produced a proliferation of refugees, as did the Russian Revolution and its aftermath. The carnage of World War II resulted in millions fleeing from the reach of Stalin, Hitler, Mussolini and Tojo. More recently, countless Uyghurs, Vietnamese, Cubans, Syrians, Venezuelans,

Afghans, Ukrainians and many, many more have become members of the corps of refugees.

This book recounts my family's history. It is the history of a refugee family—a microcosm of the refugee experience. The recount also serves as a description of the hopes, fears, tribulations and fates of many other refugees, including my parents' World War II contemporaries.

My parents' experience enables us to gain insight and appreciation of the hurdles today's refugees face. It may also help us see the contributions today's refugees can make, not only to their destinations of refuge but sometimes also to the homelands they left, if given the right opportunities.

Reasons for seeking refuge may vary and the details of a refugee's experience may differ. However, finding safety and new roots involves the same process, regardless of the geographic region from which the journey began or whether the journey took place in the past or takes place today, allowing that some refugees have the added challenge of facing racial, ethnic, gender or religious discrimination.

As I read my mother's narrative, as I study my parents' letters and as I recall my conversations with them, I am struck by the different stages of refugee experience. The stages I note start with what is obvious—the decision to leave, made either by the refugee-to-be or by a governing authority. For the refugee, it is not an easy decision to make. Not everyone can bring himself to leave home, friends and family, no matter how dire the circumstances.

Once the decision to leave has been made and whatever preparations are possible have been completed, the second stage begins—the trek to a destination. The destination is perhaps envisaged as temporary, perhaps as permanent—a view sometimes dictated by the refugee's belief as to how long he will be absent from his homeland.

Once a destination has been reached there is a third stage—the jolt of entering a new environment. New language, new customs, new foods, new laws, new culture—all must be adjusted to.

When the jolt has worn off the refugee enters the fourth and final stage—settling and adapting. She or he must settle into the new homeland and adapt to the new environment. This means, among many other things, learning a new occupation, mastering a new language and becoming part of a new and often lower, social and economic class, at least initially.

The stages seem self-evident, almost banal, yet they help me to better understand my parents. They can also help us to adjust our expectations about today's refugees, recognizing that a refugee is in no position to contribute to their new society until safety and stability are realized.

The stages a refugee passes through are not always clearly defined. One stage blends into the next. Backtracking takes place. The same stage may have to be repeated multiple times. A return to the homeland becomes impossible; what was a hoped-for permanent abode turns out to be temporary; new decisions and new treks may have to be undertaken in order to reach a permanent, secure home.

Throughout their journey, my parents and their compatriots experienced amity and estrangement, adversity and good fortune. They searched for, and many found, their own version of the American Dream. Their lives bridged multiple generations.

The first 18 chapters of this book disclose one portion of my parents' life, from childhood to being refugees. It is the story from which I identify the stages of the processes that a refugee's life entails. But my parents' story did not end when they settled in America.

My parents and their contemporaries had witnessed the birth and demise of a nation—Estonia. When they fled from Estonia, in addition to seeking safety and new roots, they wanted freedom and justice, not only for themselves but for Estonians and others who remained behind the Iron Curtain. The second half of this book describes how the refugees and their offspring sought to achieve those goals. In doing so, they complemented the pursuit of freedom and justice that took place within Estonia, Latvia and Lithuania.

In my mother's words, "We made time for political work. That was a very important part of our life. We had to let the world know about the injustice our country and people had suffered. Meetings on Saturday, demonstrations on Sunday, telephone calls during the week."

During the early years of our arrival in the United States the objective of most refugee political work was to simply keep the story of Estonia and the other Baltic States alive. Concurrently, within Estonia, active guerrilla warfare came to an end but passive opposition to Soviet rule continued unabated.

An oft-cited instance of passive resistance was cab drivers pretending they could not understand Russian, thereby forcing the few foreign visitors to speak to them in English. A small gesture that expressed disdain for the Soviet Union, approval of the Western world and was indicative of the national consciousness.

Following Stalin's death, changes began to take place inside the Soviet Union and its occupied territories. The terror of the Stalinist regime decreased but did not disappear. The secret police continued to be feared. Siberian prison camps received individuals rather than thousands at one time. Psychiatric prisons continued to house people the authorities feared but they became less pervasive. As the Soviet political system atrophied, its centrally run economy sank further and further into an abyss.

In the mid–1980s, within Estonia, Latvia and Lithuania, opposition to the Soviet regime became more visible, voices of dissent were heard, independence movements gained traction. At the same time, political activity by the Estonian diaspora intensified and complemented the vitalized opposition movement within the Baltic States.

The Estonian community in America, led mostly by the children of the refugees, broadened the scope of its political activities. They sought not only the continued acknowledgment by the American government of the illegality of the incorporation of the Baltic States into the USSR but, as opportunities presented themselves or as they were generated, they sought concrete manifestations of the nonrecognition policy. Shifting Voice of America broadcasts to Estonia, Latvia and Lithuania from the auspices of Radio Liberty, which broadcast into the Soviet Union, to Radio Free Europe, which broadcast into the Soviet satellite countries of Eastern Europe was one such successful move.

Information exchanges between the overseas Estonians and the dissidents within Estonia became more frequent. A larger number of the overseas Estonian community became politically active in demonstrating, writing letters and calling on local politicians, asking the U.S. government to provide greater recognition to the Estonian dissidents. Visits by Estonians living in America to see family in Estonia increased.

When Estonia regained independence, the surviving refugees had to make one more, final decision—to return or not? As my mother wrote, "Where do we belong? Is it where we were born, grew to adulthood and now, after many years, have returned? Or is it California, where we have built our lives? Life requires material as well as emotional support. We are attached to Estonia, our homeland, even as our day-to-day life is in California, where we live and also have roots."

1

Mother's Time in Russia

"How my father managed to feed me is still a mystery."

Mother: *I, Valentine, was born in Russia on January 21, 1918, in the city of Chudovo. My father was born in Võru County, Estonia, on August 13, 1877. His given name was Samuel Uibo.*

When he was 17, Father had to fulfill his military obligation. He served in the Tsar's army and was garrisoned somewhere around the Black Sea. His service lasted for a number of years. When his tour of duty ended, Father stayed in Russia, in Chudovo, and began his adult life. There was a

My maternal grandparents, Maria Uibo and Samuel Uibo, circa 1911 (Uibo family archive).

good selection of jobs. He bought a house and some land. All he lacked was a life partner.

Father went to Estonia to look for a wife. He asked his brother to help. Father's brother found a young, beautiful maiden. A meeting was arranged. Would father like her or not? Would she or would she not accept him as her husband? The girl's name was Maria Teder.

Before Samuel and Maria could meet, arrangements had to be made, agreements had to be negotiated. Father and the girl's father sat around a table, a bottle of kümmel in the middle. The sweet, colorless liqueur, flavored with caraway seeds, was the traditional drink used to seal successful dowry negotiations.

When the two men had settled on terms Maria was invited into the room. Samuel and Maria were introduced. Father said he fell in love with her from first glance. "When she entered the room, she was so beautiful, with her chestnut brown hair. I felt so lucky. I thought, please tell me that I am to your liking." With all parties in agreement the yet-to-be-opened bottle of kümmel was uncorked and wedding plans were made.

Uibo family, about 1917. From left: The first three people are possibly neighbors, names unknown. Next to them, Samuel, Aleksander, Maria, Kalju and Rosilda (Uibo family archive).

1. Mother's Time in Russia

After the wedding the young couple settled in Chudovo, a significant railway center. Father was the station master, controlling rail traffic in and out of the station and making sure that everything ran properly. Mother opened a sewing workshop where she made dresses to order.

A year later the family began to grow. For the first three births my mother returned to Estonia. The firstborn was a daughter, who was named Rosilda. Two years later a son was born, Kalju. Within the next two years another son was born, Aleksander. Then, after two more years I, Valentine, was born. I was born in Chudovo. Because of the Russian Revolution it was impossible for Mother to travel to Estonia for my birth.

I was six months old when Mother was stricken with cholera and died. Father was left alone with four children. I required milk. Money had no value. Food could only be obtained by bartering. Father went to the countryside and exchanged my mother's fur coat for a liter of milk. When he returned home, he discovered the milk had been half diluted with water. How my father managed to feed me is still a mystery.

The peace treaty between Estonia and Russia declared that all Estonians living in Russia could return home if they did so within one year. My father packed our belongings and with his four children, began the journey home. I think I was one or two years old. We traveled by train to Narva. In Narva we were quarantined for two months because of the typhoid epidemic ravaging Russia.

2

Upheavals

"All citizens ... irrespective of their religion, ethnic origin, and political views, shall enjoy equal protection under the law and courts of justice."

My mother wrote her narrative when she was in her ninth decade. Still possessed of a clear mind, she transcribed childhood images of her father, the only parent she knew, as well as fleeting, handed-down images of the mother she never experienced. She begins her narrative with an account of how her father came to live in Russia and what he did there. As with all histories, perhaps especially family histories, my mother's

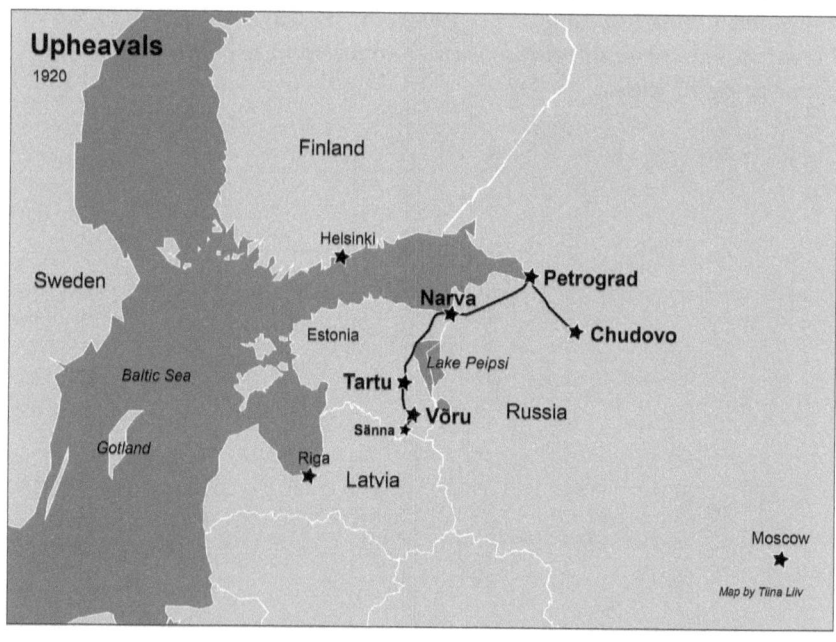

The 1920 return route to Estonia taken by Samuel and his children (Map by Tiina Liiv).

2. Upheavals

narration is tinged with time and colored by the collective memory of other people in her life.

When she tells us about Samuel's early life, my mother offers her recollection of the Uibo family history as it has been passed down over the years. History books and archival records offer a few gentle modifications of some of what she relates. Historians tell us that Samuel would have begun his mandatory service in the Tsar's army at age 20 rather than 17 as my mother writes. His period of active service would have been six years plus an additional nine years of reserve obligation.

Regardless of the exact dates, Samuel would have been discharged from active duty around 1903. He settled in Russia, within Novgorod Province in the city of Chudovo, a rail center located about 370 miles northwest of Moscow, 80 miles southeast of St. Petersburg and 250 miles northeast of Võru, Estonia.

My mother writes that Samuel was the Chudovo station master. Here, family history and my mother's recollection of that history diverges from what was the probable reality. A document filed in the Estonian National Archives suggests that Samuel had a different occupation. When he and his children returned to Estonia in July 1920, Samuel completed an entry questionnaire. On it he identified himself as a blacksmith employed by the railroad. His income came from making "handcrafts."

My mother may have romanticized how my father Samuel and his brother discovered Samuel's bride-to-be. Perusal of a genealogy chart indicates that Maria was in fact Samuel's brother's wife's sister—a description that may leave one tongue-tied but a relationship that presumably eased the brother's task of finding Samuel a prospective bride. Given that relationship it may not be unreasonable to speculate that Samuel and Maria had met at some earlier time.

Samuel and Maria's marriage, perhaps a case of instant true love but nevertheless still sealed at the bargaining table, was followed by the births of my mother's siblings: Rosilda on February 5, 1910; Kalju on July 19, 1911; and, less than a year after the start of World War I, Aleksander on March 19, 1915. Then, in the midst of the revolutions and chaos that were the offspring of "the war to end all wars," my mother was born on January 21, 1918.

Echoing a narrative she felt compelled to tell and retell throughout her life, my mother explains that Maria traveled to Estonia for Rosilda's birth, for Kalju's birth and for Aleksander's birth. However, the fury of the Russian Revolution made it impossible for Maria to travel from Chudovo to Estonia for her birth. My mother was always keen to remind that one's place of birth did not necessarily determine one's nationality.

My mother alludes to the devastation and turmoil existent when she

Top and Right: Following Estonia's successful war of independence, Estonians returning to Estonia from Russia had to complete an entry questionnaire. Samuel listed his occupation as blacksmith (item 8); said he was employed by the railroad (item 9); and identified making handcrafts as his primary source of income (item 10) (National Archives of Estonia).

was born. Six months after her birth Maria died from cholera, one death among the 500,000 who died in Russia during one of a series of cholera pandemics that continued to 1925.

My mother mentions Estonia becoming independent only in the context of the Uibo family's departure from Russia. Perhaps a bit of historical

2. Upheavals

content will help paint a more dimensional picture of Estonia in general and the era in which she began her life in particular.

During the third millennium B.C. the ancestors of modern Estonians were already living in the region now occupied by the Estonian state. The first known description of those people as Estonian was by the Roman historian Tacitus in AD 98. In the 800s the area described by Tacitus was invaded by the Vikings. The Danes were the predominant power throughout the 1200s. In 1285 Tallinn became a member of the Hanseatic League, later joined by other Estonian cities. In the following century it became part of the Teutonic Order.

Strategically located, Estonia's west coast bordered the well-traveled

Baltic Sea. The Gulf of Finland buffeted its north coast. In its early history the gulf was the artery for ingress and egress to the Neva River and its tributaries, a waterway trade route to the Byzantine Empire and the Black Sea. Later, the Gulf of Finland was the entry route to St. Petersburg. Imperial Russia, the Russian Bear, stood on Estonia's east flank.

Until the 1600s, Estonia's history was a history of invasions and conquests. That is when Sweden became a long-term landlord. Swedish rule continued until 1721 when Russia defeated Sweden and imposed its sovereignty over Estonia. The German Baltic barons were the landowners and effective authority for many centuries regardless of who exercised formal control over the region.

A national self-consciousness, an awareness of being Estonian, had simmered in the 1850s. It reached a boil in the closing decades of the 1800s as Samuel and Maria grew up. By the time my maternal grandparents were born, Estonia's epic poem *Kalevipoeg* had been written (1861); Estonia's first Song Festival had been sung (1869). The precocious Lydia Koidula had already published her poetry—poetry that stirred a national consciousness.

> To the last hour of my life
> I will cherish thee, my land,
> My Estonia in its bloom,
> Dear and fragrant fatherland!
> The praise of mead and stream,
> And thy soothing mother tongue,
> To the last hour of my life
> Shall be spoken, shall be sung.
>
> Dearer is the gentle peace
> Of thy bosom, Mary's land,
> Than the glamour and the bliss
> Found upon a foreign strand.
> Yet I often find the tear
> Welling in your saddened eyes;
> Take thou hope, Estonian land.
> Better times shall yet arise!
> For the future that shall come
> Shall transform our hope to sight;
> Firmly walk! Keep head erect!
> Time will put all things aright.
> (E. Howard Harris, *Literature in Estonia*)

In the late 1880s, the Tsar's attempt to Russify Armenia, Ukraine and Azerbaijan as well as Estonia and other non-Russian parts of his empire collided with the aspirations of the people living there—subjects who were becoming increasingly aware of their own distinct identities and who did not want Russian culture and language imposed on them.

2. Upheavals

Talk of national autonomy, freedom of the press and the right to use one's own language in education could be heard throughout the Russian empire. In the case of Estonia, there were demands for the right to speak, write and learn in Estonian, a Finno-Ugric language with a Roman rather than Cyrillic alphabet. Later, this talk would be followed by demands for national self-determination.

As Samuel completed his tour of active military duty, anti–Tsarist discontent morphed into physical turbulence. Tsarist blunders such as the Bloody Sunday Massacre of unarmed demonstrators at the Winter Palace (1905) and Russia's ignoble defeat by Japan in Manchuria (also 1905) catalyzed outbreaks of worker strikes, peasant uprisings and military mutinies. Russia's Social Democratic Party split into Bolshevik and Menshevik factions foreshadowed further splintering of Russian society even as the Tsar vacillated toward democracy.

Within Russia, amid World War I, a century's accumulation of frustrations exploded. The Alexander Kerensky-led Provisional Government replaced Tsar Nicholas II and assumed power in March 1917, but the Lenin-led Bolsheviks toppled it less than a year later. A civil war followed.

Because of military battles and skirmishes, peasant uprisings and worker strikes, rail traffic through the Chudovo station became infrequent. Even when trains arrived, finding work connected to the railroad was futile. Samuel struggled to support his family. The January 25, 1919, issue of *Railway Review* magazine described conditions:

> For several weeks after the Bolshevik revolution the railroad men worked on as if nothing had happened. The sympathy of most of them was with the Kerensky government, and so the time came when the Bolsheviki decided to clean house and install their own men. A frightful period ensued with disastrous wrecks, in one of which four hundred were killed or burned to death, and then a compromise was reached whereby the former operatives were retained under a soviet form of government. Committees of the workers at each station chose the stationmaster and the other officials. These committees took out of the station master's hands the decision of all important questions and tied him down to a mere course of routine duties.

The year 1918 marked the end of World War I but not the end of Russia's Civil War. That war continued in its own muddled, bloody way until 1922, further complicated by the intervention of a potpourri of British, French, Italian, Japanese, Greek, Romanian, American and other troops. Neither did the conclusion of the world war end Estonia's war of independence.

Within the turmoil of war, revolution and pestilence, Maria gave birth to my mother. Less than five weeks later, on February 24, 1918, the Salvation Committee of Estonia's Provincial Assembly issued a declaration proclaiming the birth of Estonia as an independent country. To secure that independence, Estonia's nascent army fought both Russian and German forces.

The Assembly's February 24 declaration, its "Manifesto to All the Peoples of Estonia," referenced Estonia's national epic *Kalevipoeg* [the youngest son of Kalev and Linda, he was only known as Kalevipoeg-Kalev's son] and declared that:

> Never in the course of centuries have the Estonian people lost their ardent desire for Independence. From generation-to-generation Estonians have kept alive the secret hope that in spite of enslavement and oppression by other nations the time will come in Estonia "when all splinters, at both ends, will burst forth into flames" and when "Kalev will come home to bring his children happiness."

The Manifesto recited the principles that should govern life in Estonia. The first four were:

> 1. All citizens of the Republic of Estonia, irrespective of their religion, ethnic origin, and political views, shall enjoy equal protection under the law and courts of justice of the Republic.
>
> 2. All ethnic minorities, the Russians, Germans, Swedes, Jews, and others residing within the borders of the republic, shall be guaranteed the right to their cultural autonomy.
>
> 3. All civic freedoms, such as the freedom of expression, of the press, of religion, of assembly, of association, and the freedom to strike as well as the inviolability of the individual and the home, shall be irrefutably effective within the territory of the Estonian Republic and based on laws which the Government shall immediately work out.
>
> 4. The Provisional Government will be charged with the immediate organization of the courts of justice to protect the security of the citizens. All political prisoners shall be released immediately.

Finnish volunteers aided the Estonian fight for independence. The Estonians also received a modicum of help from the Russian White forces. Estonian supplies were replenished by a British naval squadron, which also turned over two captured Russian destroyers. Most of the local Baltic Germans also supported the independence movement.

Following a decisive Estonian military victory over the Bolsheviks, the Tartu Peace Treaty of February 1920 formally ended the Estonian War of Independence. In addition to renouncing "forever" any claim to Estonian soil and agreeing to pay reparations the Soviet government agreed that Estonians living in Russia had a one-year window to repatriate to Estonia.

Taking advantage of the window of opportunity, after many years away, Samuel repatriated to Estonia in the summer of 1920, accompanied by his children, speaking broken Estonian and bringing with him

2. Upheavals

not much more than his knowledge of blacksmithing and skills in making "handcrafts."

They travelled by train from Chudovo to Petrograd (now St. Petersburg and prior to that, Leningrad) and then to Narva, the town in northeast Estonia that shares a border with Russia. There the American Red Cross was at work, trying to stop a typhoid epidemic in western Russia from spreading into Estonia. According to my mother's narrative, Samuel and his children were quarantined for two months. A contemporaneous *Esthonian News Service* report says that each refugee was quarantined for five days and then "turned over to the civil authorities for help in reaching their destinations." It may be that my mother was referring to the total time she and her family spent in Narva.

A report published in the summer of 1920 in the bulletin of the American Red Cross Commission to Western Russia and the Baltic States, described their work in Estonia and in Narva in particular:

> It is in its work against the typhus epidemic that the Commission performed its greatest service.... It did mean the actual delousing of more than 9,000 persons; the disinfecting of 80 hospitals, and the organization and maintenance

The Narva River marks the Estonian-Russian border in one section of northeast Estonia. On one side is Narva Castle, built by the Danes in the early 1300s and acquired by the Teutonic Order in 1346. Across the river is the Ivangorod Fortress, built by Tsar Ivan III in 1492. From 1918–1922 a typhus epidemic that killed two to three million people swept Russia. The American Red Cross established a quarantine camp adjacent to the Narva Castle walls in order to prevent the epidemic from spreading into Estonia. Samuel and his children passed through this camp when they returned to Estonia (American Red Cross, photographer / Esthonia News Service / Library of Congress).

of a sanitary cordon between the district of Narva in the northeast of Esthonia, seventy miles from Petrograd, and the rest of Esthonia. Only in this drastic way could the entire country be protected from disease....

The Esthonian Government adopted the mobile sanitary squad idea and has put 80 groups of 4,000 men in the field. They work in the small towns and villages where the danger of typhus brought by individual refuges crossing over from Soviet Russia is a standing menace. These outfits work with supplies furnished by the American Red Cross Commission [quoted in *A Question of Trust: The Origins of U.S.-Soviet Relations, the Memoirs of Loy W. Henderson*].

3

Mother's Childhood, Estonia in the 1920s

"Our sow and I had many conversations."

Mother: *After our family cleared quarantine, we continued our journey to southern Estonia, specifically, to Sänna in Võru County. Father's brother had found a place for us to live—a building that used to house the Sänna justice court. It was located on the main road connecting Rõuge and Võru, less than a mile from the Sänna manor. Father had a chance to buy the building, and did.*

Father made his living as a blacksmith, hammering out knives, forks, spoons, dishes and buckets for the neighborhood. Since he brought very little with him from Russia, he also made our dishes, spoons and forks. Father was not a businessman. If someone asked him how much something cost, he would often dismiss the question by saying, "Well, who cares about price?"

Groves of birch trees grew on each side of the road. Across from our home was a massive, brick building, used as a cooperative grain storehouse. It belonged neither to the manor nor the municipality. Farmers stored a portion of their crops there as a communal backstop to crop failure.

The nearby Pärlijõgi—Pearl River—separated us from the large farms and from the Sänna schoolhouse. In the spring, when the snow melted, its waters swelled so that even the bridge, elevated high above the river's usual level, was flooded.

Our home, the converted village courthouse, was rectangular with a long hallway, an indoor privy instead of an outhouse and four rooms, one of which had served as a jail cell. The former jail cell was a small room. It had a tiny window, a stove for heating and a bed. Next to it was a room that father made into his workshop. Then, there was a room that had an oven for cooking and a storage area for firewood. It was also where a spinning wheel and a loom were kept.

The last room was large. It had two beds, one for father and the other for my sister. My brothers slept on the floor. The room also contained a

The 26-mile long *Pärlijõgi* (Pearl River) begins in Latvia, flows through Võru County in southern Estonia, and empties into the *Mustjõe* (Black River). My mother spoke of it often, with love and affection. Parts of the river still retain its old charm and beauty (author's photograph).

large, brick stove used for heating and for baking bread, biscuits, potatoes, roasting short ribs and doing everything else that required baking.

In addition, the stove was used as a cure for common illnesses. If you had the flu you would lie on the warm bricks and drink strong herbal tea. That did not always work. I remember once when I was sick and neither the heat from the stove or the tea had helped. Curled up on a bed, I felt as though the walls of our house had collapsed on top of me. I couldn't breathe. I was suffocating. I don't know how long my delirium lasted. Then, suddenly the walls straightened and I began to breathe normally. I opened my eyes. Father was standing next to my bed, tears in his eyes. When he saw that my eyes were open his face lit up with a big smile.

For stomach aches we were given a teaspoon of sugar that had been transformed into medicine with the addition of three drops of liikva.* Sweets of any kind were a rarity. It was no wonder that I went to father more than once, complaining of a stomach ache.

---

*A compound spirit of ether consisting of one-part diethyl ether in three parts alcohol. Also called Hoffmann's Anodyne or Hoffmann's Drops. *Wikipedia*.

3. Mother's Childhood, Estonia in the 1920s

At night we gathered in the family room and an oil lamp was lit. One of us was chosen to read aloud from a selection of books borrowed from the school library. I still recall some of them: James Fenimore Cooper's Leatherstocking Tales about the lives of American Indians, Kitzberg's stories about Estonian village life and Toots' tales.* There were others. Folk tales, historical novels and Estonia's past were all included in our nightly readings. After a story was read, there would be a discussion. Sometimes father would play his kannel [a classic Estonian zither-like instrument] and teasingly sing an old Estonian dance song, "A Russian from Savikoa woos my daughter." I didn't like the implication that I would marry a Russian from Savikoa.

An elderly woman who was my caretaker lived in the room that was the former jail cell. Everyone called her Holy Mai. She and I were inseparable. We went everywhere together. We slept in the same bed. Even though I did not understand what I was reading, at night before falling asleep, I read the Bible aloud to her. For a reading light we used a small lamp that Holy Mai and I called "snot nose." It had a short extension or tail. We hung the lamp by jiggling the tail into the cleavage between the wall's wooden planks. This freed my hands to turn the pages of the Bible.

When it was time for me to go to sleep Holy Mai would, from the next room, interrupt our nightly family readings and discussions by pounding on the wall. I hated that! Sometimes I had to leave in the middle of a lively discussion. To get to my bedroom I had to pass through two pitch black rooms. The way was familiar but scary, so I shut my eyes and ran. Sometimes I ran into a wall.

When I was about six, I no longer slept with Holy Mai. But I still went to her room every morning to say hello. One morning I walked in, wide-awake with a smile on my face. I was stunned. Holy Mai was dangling from the rafters. She had hanged herself. I have never forgotten that sight. For a while, I had frequent nightmares. As the oldest, Rosilda looked after us from that time on. Kalju helped with the housework.

When we arrived in Sänna, disease was everywhere. Between 1920 and 1922 countless people died from smallpox. My earliest childhood memories are filled with images of people burning with high fevers, their bodies and faces pockmarked with blisters, the few survivors carrying with them permanent, deep scars etched on their face and body.

Funeral processions to the Rõuge and Võru churches passed our home, two or three each day. Whenever a procession passed the nearby grove of birch trees, mourners would pause, pick a tree and carve a cross into its

---

*Joosep Toots—a colorful, fictional character created by Oskar Luts (1887–1953). An inquisitive boy who gets into a series of predicaments. Think Pippi Longstocking with a dash of Tom Sawyer and Harry Potter.

spotted, white bark. There were countless crosses. Some ninety years later I looked for those cross-etched trees. I could find none. They had all been cut down.

Death came to a boy who lived at our neighboring farm. The burial did not take place for several days. We and other village people went to his house every night until the burial. I did not want to go but each night I was brought along. We sat around the boy's lifeless body and sang religious songs. I prayed no one else would die. Eventually there were fewer and fewer cases of small pox, the number of funeral processions decreased and life became normal.

My brother Kalju was always cheerful and he had a sense of humor. Sometimes he would have fun at my and Alex's expense. Once when a spring thunderstorm had just passed, water was still streaming downhill along our road. I was collecting pretty stones. I saw a frog. It didn't move. I asked Kalju why the frog wasn't moving. With great solemnity my older brother told me to open the frog's mouth and blow into it. He promised that if I did, the frog would wake up. I did as he told me. I opened the frog's mouth and I blew and I blew. The frog never moved.

During the summer all farm children worked. This is how families made ends meet. As the youngest in the family, it was my job to look after our neighbor's baby. At the time, I was five years old. The baby was swaddled inside a basket that was attached to a flexible alder branch. The alder branch was fastened to the ceiling. When the baby cried, I had to rock the swing up and down. I found this really boring.

Looking after chickens and pigs was a lot more fun than babysitting. I especially liked looking after the pigs. Pigs are very intelligent. If you put a pig into a pen, she remembers where she entered and she knows where to go to get out. Cows and horses will run around a fenced-in area and not know where they entered.

Our sow and I had many conversations. She always agreed with me. When I complained about something, she was on my side. Her calm, affirming grunts in response to whatever I said told me that here was someone who understood me. I also played games with the pigs. I would see who was the smartest. How long did it take the sow to sneak into a potato field to steal potatoes? Could I stop her before she did? At other times, the sow was tired and would go to sleep. Then, I would put my head on her stomach and we would sleep together.

In the fall the pigs were killed. That was heart wrenching. Their final sounds, their death cries, broke my heart. The pigs were my friends.

From age seven to 15 I herded cows for neighboring farmers. On my first day a farmer's wife gave me a cloth bag that contained a spool of yarn and knitting needles. By the end of summer, I was expected to have knitted

3. Mother's Childhood, Estonia in the 1920s

a pair of socks. Unbeknownst to the farmer's wife, I added a book and magazines to the bag. One of the magazines came once a month and contained exciting stories, often serialized. I couldn't wait for each new issue.

Some romanticist once rhapsodized that nothing compared with a childhood spent herding cattle. I would not agree. Each day began at 4:00 in the morning. While still in the blissful rapture of sweet sleep, cows had to be milked. I sat on a stool and squeezed their teats. The milk streamed into my pail even as my head rested against the cow's stomach and thoughts of sleep swirled through my head.

After milking, the cows had to be herded to pasture. Every cow had a name, usually one that was descriptive. Kirjak, Mustik, Sarvik—a spotted cow, a darkish cow, a cow with horns. If the cows were grazing quietly, I would sit on a rock and read. Sometimes I would close my eyes. I remember one time I lay down on a rock and fell asleep. I slept a deep sleep, as though my head were resting on a feather pillow. When I awoke, the cows were gone. I panicked. Where was Kirjak and Mustik? They were the leaders.

My legs wobbled. I could hardly run, but run I did. I thought the cows might have gone through the forest making their way to a nearby oat field. I was right. I found the animals grazing peacefully. I sometimes still have nightmares about waking up to a field empty of cows. By 11:00 a.m. the horse flies would attack the cows and the cows would either bolt for the forest or for home. No force on earth could stop them.

When summer ended, I had to return the knitting bag with the knitting needles, the remaining yarn and the finished socks. I only had one quarter of one sock finished. The farmer's wife said nothing except, "How do you know you will marry a man who will be rich enough to buy you socks?"

One of our neighboring farms was the large Matson manor. They had 12 children: eight boys and four daughters. The youngest boy was my age. His name was Verner—Verner with the runny nose. He was known for not being able to take a practical joke. He got mad. If you wanted to play a trick on Verner you had to first find a hiding place so you could take cover when he reacted.

Usually, Verner and I got along well. He needed a playmate as much as I did. We didn't have toys so we invented our own playthings. Our property had an open pit that contained blue clay. Verner and I used that blue clay to make whatever our imaginations conjured. Pine cones and pretty stones were also favorite toys. In the winter we played cards using old Russian rubles as our money. The rubles were worthless and plentiful.

Verner, who was four months younger than my mother, was shot and killed by Soviet troops during World War II. My mother would not find out until nearly fifty years later.

Mother: *Father was a passionate fisherman. Regardless of his daily*

The Eomoisa Mill, next to the Pearl River, and remnants of its adjoining dam, where Samuel began many of his fishing treks, still stand (author's photograph).

work he always had energy for fishing. He was master of the Pärlijõgi—Pearl River, and its banks. When it wasn't fishing season Saturdays would be spent sitting on our front door steps, surrounded by tackle and dozens of fishing rods lined up along the old courthouse wall. He would work on them with loving care, occasionally casting a smile in my direction. When spring came, and the Pärlijõgi was running high on the banks and flowing with full force, Father was ready with his fishing gear.

Sometimes Father let me come along on his fishing trips. I went with him as far as the Eomoisa Dam, not far from where the Eomoisa family mill was located. I had to promise to be very quiet so as not to scare the fish—fish don't like the sound of people talking. Father would begin by fishing close to the dam.

Usually, he caught some fish right away. I took them home with me. These fish were beautiful. They were called "iherus" in the Võru dialect or, in literary Estonian, forell—trout. They had rainbow-colored stripes along their sides. I have never seen fish as beautiful as the trout from the Pärlijõgi. Their meat was yellow. They tasted delicious.

Northern Estonia does not have rivers or lakes with trout. When I lived in Tallinn that did not stop me from trying to find trout whenever

3. Mother's Childhood, Estonia in the 1920s

I hungered for fish. My friends laughed and told me I was persnickety because I was not satisfied with any other fish.

Father began his fishing treks at the Eomoisa Dam. Once I returned home, he would continue from there, fishing along the banks of the Pärlijõgi. He would walk through the night until he reached the point where the Pärlijõgi and Mustjõgi—Black River—met. Then, toward morning he would come home. He told me that fish won't bite after sunrise. He would bring a mess of fish with him, not in a bag but hanging next to each other strung on a wire or rope.

The route my mother outlines would be about a 20-mile roundtrip walk interspersed with some serious fishing along the way. It is possible Samuel did this during the course of one night but it may also be that my mother was, with the passage of time, attributing additional powers to him.

Mother: *Father loved to talk about the music of the night: As night fell there would be the sound of an instrument resonating from somewhere in a distant village; there would be the mischievous chatter of young people talking among themselves; the beat of distant dancing and singing; and dogs barking and barking. These sounds would be followed by the stillness of a summer night, and then at dawn, by the song of the nightingale—"Öö pikk, öö pikk, lazy girl, bring a whip, plaks, plaks" later joined by the sound of cuckoos cuckooing. Father loved to evangelize about how he watched the fish play in the water. I doubt if he actually wanted the fish to swallow his bait. He could have written a book about his experiences walking and fishing at night. He was a romanticist.*

On Sundays we attended church services at the Rõuge church, about six miles from Sänna. We went there on foot, walking barefoot. When we reached the base of the hill on which the church stood, we put on our shoes. We always sat in the first row. After our long walk it was nice to sit and admire the different colors formed by the rays of sunshine that streamed through the church's stained-glass windows. Sometimes I became drowsy but the minister's angry voice kept me awake.

The pastor was always angry with the young people who, during his sermon, would mill around the church. For the young people, going to church was an opportunity to mingle and meet. After the service, going home was usually more fun for me than going there or listening to the sermons. Often someone would invite us to ride on their wagon. I was grateful. For a six-year-old, Sundays were long and tiring.

Fall came. Leaves turned to gold. Morning frost covered the ground. Herders returned to being school children. Cows stayed in their barns. They were fed there. My friends the pigs were killed. Their meat was salted and their blood kept in cold cellars until Christmas when it would be used for blood sausage. Roast pork and blood sausage—without them Christmas would be incomplete.

The first day of school! I felt important. My chest filled with excitement. For my winter clothing I had Father's Russian era suit jacket for a coat and on my head Mother's bearskin hat. Instead of gloves I had Mother's muff tied around my neck with string so I could put my hands in it. I saw that the other girls were dressed differently. That didn't bother me too much. When the warm days came, I only needed a dress. I didn't need the fur hat or the muff. Father's suit jacket was replaced with a sweater.

I didn't like that my dress was sized to give me room to grow, especially as to its length. The other girls wore short dresses. Mine was long. When the other girls ran or played you could see their panties. That was nice. I came up with a solution. At home I found some string. Half way to school I tied the string around my waist and used it to pull up the hem of my dress. That way, when I ran or played, my panties were also visible even if they weren't made of lace.

My mother makes no further mention of her childhood education except a statement, made without explanation, that "The Rõuge school was a boarding school. We lived there during the week, went home on Saturday and returned on Sunday." The Rõuge school would have been a six-year "Higher Elementary School." The school in Sänna was, in all likelihood, a four year "Village School." A typical girl's education would have been six years so it seems reasonable to assume that she completed the last two years of her education at the Rõuge school. After that, as she describes later in her narrative, she attended vocational school in Antsla, 15 miles distant from Sänna—close to home in today's world, not so close in my mother's world of the time.

Mother: *All of us had to look after ourselves. Of my siblings, my sister Rosilda, more than 10 years older than me, was only able to attend school for four years. She worked on several different farms. My brother Kalju was the only one who was a business person. He knew how to take care of himself. One job where he earned good money was that of log driver, dislodging logs as they were floated downriver. The work required nerves of steel. One day he came home and told us that he had bought a house. He was still young when he made the announcement. His son Mati lives there now with his wife Ilme.*

My brother Aleksander went to high school thanks to a middle-aged couple with no children. They were related to us from Mother's side of the family. This couple lived about eight miles from us in Varstu. They told Father they would like to give Aleksander an education. They proposed that they adopt Alex and he would live with them. Father did not agree to the adoption but did permit Alex to live with them. They sent Alex to school in Võru.

3. Mother's Childhood, Estonia in the 1920s

For the rest of us, attending Võru high school, the only high school in the area, was an insurmountable challenge. In order to attend school there, one had to have an apartment in town. That was expensive. In addition, there was the cost of food and school supplies. Father did not have enough money to educate us in Võru. Even getting there was problematic. Travel was by horse. It was too far to walk. Father did not have a horse, much less a car. But the Varstu relatives found an apartment for Alex and he could therefore attend high school there.

4

My Father's Family

*"Perhaps someday you will find this information
of interest and be able to use it."*

My mother grew up in Sänna, a hamlet populated by 50 or so people. Eleven miles away but light years distant, my father, Alfred Treiman, was born and raised in Võru, a town of 5,000—small compared to Tallinn but a metropolis compared to Sänna. The paths of the Uibo and Treiman families did not cross while my parents were growing up although one is tempted to speculate whether my father's uncle's future wife may perhaps have been in Narva with the American Red Cross while Samuel, Rosilda, Kalju, Aleksander and my mother were there in quarantine.

For years I had asked my father to tell me about his relatives and to talk about his life prior to World War II. For reasons known only to him, he was always reticent. Then, in 2004 as we celebrated my mother's 86th birthday, my father relented and answered some of my questions. I tape-recorded his answers. A year and a half later, on June 3, 2005, on his own initiative, my 93-year-old father sat at his desktop computer, composed a three-page letter and emailed it to me. The letter began, "*Dear son Jaak. Here is some information about me and my kinsfolk. Perhaps someday you will find this information of interest and be able to use it.*"

My father left one other writing that addressed our family history. When I was 13 or 14, around 1956 or 1957, the local Boy Scout Council asked me to submit a short biography. Why, I don't remember. I asked my father for help. On the back of our company letterhead my father typed a compilation of our family history. It was a little more than three pages long. He wrote it in Estonian as though I were the author. Presumably I then translated it into English and gave the English version to the Boy Scouts as the requested biography.

Here and elsewhere in this book I have melded what my father told me in 2004 with information contained in his 2005 letter to me along with some excerpts from his 1950s compilation.

4. My Father's Family

Father: *I was born on August 22, 1911, on Karja Street in the town of Võru. My father's name was Rudolf (Rudi) Treiman. As fate would have it, he was a soldier in the Tsar's military. He served in the First World War as a member of the Russian army's artillery forces. Most of his service time was spent in the Rumanian region.*

At the outset of Estonia's War of Independence my father, along with many other Estonians who found themselves in the Tsar's military service, returned to Estonia and joined the fledgling Estonian army. My father was stationed in Northeast Estonia, on the front near Narva.

Regime changes took place in Russia during and after the revolution—changes that were also felt in Estonia. There was the Kerensky period followed by the Bolshevik seizure of power. This was followed by the Russian Civil War, with the White forces and their different factions fighting Trotsky's Red forces even as some German troops remained in Estonia. Each group had their own printing presses and issued their own currency. The Estonian army fought each at various times.

Even though I was a young boy, I remember one time when Russia's White forces were camped in our area. I was standing in the park on the shores of Lake Tamula, that large body of water on the southeastern side of Võru that is one of the town's defining features. A flock of geese were flying overhead. The soldiers were having fun shooting at the geese. They kept missing. The son of the owner of Jääson's sauna was with me. He got so mad at the White soldiers that he went over and berated them. They stopped shooting.

*From that same time period I recall a battle where the Russians [**presumably the Red forces**], stationed near Haanja's Munamägi—Egg Mountain, were firing shells toward Võru, about ten miles distant. Not one shell came close to hitting their target. An Estonian armored train parked on the tracks near Lake Tamula returned fire. I don't know if their aim was any better.*

My father was a part-time fisherman and a part-time cobbler. As a fisherman he netted fish, usually from Lake Tamula and then sold his catch. I fondly remember my father bringing home a bucket of crayfish whenever he returned after a day of fishing.

Father had three brothers: Richard, Jaan and Eduard Treiman. Before Estonia became independent Richard lived in Ukraine where he owned a stationary store. He returned to Estonia. After 1918 he lived in Võru where he worked as a city manager. The Võru tennis courts and sports field were established through his initiative. Richard was a passionate fisherman. He also designed and built fish hatcheries. He operated and maintained a small hatchery at the Võru electric power station.

Richard's wife Linda, whose maiden name was Uibopuu, which means "apple tree" in the Võru dialect, was born in America. Her father was an Estonian gold miner who took part in the Alaska Gold Rush. During Estonia's War of Independence Linda came to Estonia as part of the American Red Cross contingent that provided assistance in Estonia. She did some Red Cross work in Võru, where she met Richard. They married. Linda's father also returned to Estonia. He lived in Otepää.

Jaan Treiman owned a farm in Koristaja in the Tartu region. That branch of the Treiman family had many children. Unfortunately, I know nothing about them.

Eduard Treiman had some run-ins with the authorities at the time of the Tsars. After he had served a prison term, he was exiled to the Ural Mountains. During Russia's first occupation of Estonia during World War II I received a letter from him. That was the only communication we had.

My mother was born on January 10, 1885, in Haanja. Her name was Elfriede Treiman (Naba). Since my father spent most of his time at the front, mother was the person who raised me.

As a soldier in the Tsar's army, my grandfather Rudi was often absent from home. Consequently, he did not play a significant role in my father's life. In addition, he and Elfriede divorced, another reason for the lack of connectivity with my father's life. My father never mentioned the divorce. I did not find out until I was compiling information for this book. It appears that for most of my father's younger years Elfriede was his primary caregiver and that Richard and Linda filled the paternal role.

Father: *Mother was very entrepreneurial. During Tsarist times she made her living by washing the clothes of the Russian soldiers stationed in Võru. Later, after Estonia gained independence, she operated a booth at Võru's open air market. Later she ran a small general store in Võru.*

Mother had a happy personality but during the last few years of her life she suffered from many diseases. She died an early death on August 2, 1936, only 51 years old.

Mother had two sisters. Leena Kodusaar lived in the Räpina parish of Võru county in the village of Võõpsu. One of her sons, Kalju Kodusaar, continues to live there. He is a good singer and the leader of the local choir. Leena's daughter, Õje Veeroja, lives in Võru. She is married to a man who is an expert beekeeper. He is an all-around good person. They have a daughter, Velli, and a son, Imre, who also live in Võru.

Grandfather Jakob Treiman was also a Võru resident. He lived on Karja Street. He was married to Lisa whose maiden name was Hain. Grandfather sold sauerkraut to the Tsarist military stationed in Võru. He rented a large plot of land where he grew cabbages. In the autumn the cabbages were harvested, their roots and dirty leaves removed. They were then taken by wheelbarrow to a shed where they were chopped into small pieces.

The small pieces were placed in large barrels. Salt, cranberries and sometimes carrots were added. The barrels were then stored in a cellar where the cabbage fermented and became sauerkraut. Each year he sold his entire stock to the Russian military. Grandfather supplemented his cabbage income by tarring roofs.

I went to school in Võru. The first school I attended was a three-grade level grammar school known as Sirk's School, named after its headmaster. The school had three principal teachers: Sirk, Lepp and Sepp. Sepp was also the priest for the local Russian church. Next, I attended Võru's Higher Elementary school, located on Jüri street, across from Võru high school. The headmaster was named Korol. During 1943–1944 he fled from Estonia. He lived in America and was 103 when he died.

I remember a teacher named Kõpp, who taught Estonian. He liked to smoke. He would roll a cigarette during class and would smoke it. We had a gymnastics teacher named Harik who told everyone that "Treiman is clumsy." I was not so clumsy that the next summer I started to play soccer. Soon I was on the Võru city team. I think I was about 16 or 17.

After I completed the school on Jüri Street I joined the Boy Scouts. Soon I had the title of Young Scoutmaster. Later, for a few years, I was the official head of the Võru Boy Scouts. At the same time, I became active in the Young Men's Christian Association. I participated in the association's annual school held in Tartu. Just before World War II began the YMCA had decided to send me to England to pursue further studies. The war eliminated that opportunity. About the same time, I organized a section of the Võru Estonian Youth Sport League.

5

A Brief Normality

"We savored the joy of living."

Global events buffeted my parents' lives, yet neither makes more than a passing reference to them. Perhaps even in retrospect, my mother and father thought most of the events were too distant, too much beyond their control. They may not have seen the relevance to their lives of a meeting in Paris or a war in Spain. My mother alludes to "dark clouds" but neither of my parents mention global events unless they felt a direct impact, such as my father's reference to the Great Depression.

On August 27, 1928, my father was a member of the Võru soccer team; my mother was herding cows in Sänna. Concurrently, the General Pact for the Renunciation of War, also known as the Paris Peace Pact or the Kellogg-Briand Pact, was signed, generating international optimism, at least among those whose voices were heard. France, the United Kingdom, the United States, Germany, Italy and ten other countries renounced war as an instrument of national policy. Thirty-two additional countries, including Estonia and the Soviet Union, ratified the treaty before its July 24, 1929, effective date. Additional countries signed later, ultimately bringing the number of signatories to 63—the most ratified treaty in history up to that time.

The optimism generated by the Kellogg-Briand Pact was short-lived. The American stock market crashed in October 1929, signaling the start of the Great Depression. Few countries were unscathed. Totalitarian regimes flexed their power.

Japan invaded Manchuria (1931). The Spanish Civil War (1936–1939) previewed the coming world war. The *Anschluss*, Germany's annexation of Austria in March of 1938, forecast the Soviet Union's future territorial ingestion of a portion of Finland and all of Estonia, Latvia and Lithuania.

International conferences generated headlines but accomplished nothing. The now infamous Munich Conference in September 1938 quixotically promised "Peace in our time" by trading Czechoslovakian land for

5. A Brief Normality

a fascist's hollow promise. Czechoslovakia was neither invited to the conference nor consulted.

Hitler and Stalin became allies in August 1939. The terms of their partnership were spelt out in the Molotov-Ribbentrop Pact and its secret protocols, where the symbiotic twins privately divided Europe, labeling their respective bounty as areas of "spheres of influence." Poland was partitioned, the bulk ceded to the Third Reich. Estonia was earmarked for the Soviet Union.

In September 1939, as my mother managed a canteen in Ravila, and while my father studied at Tartu University, earning his keep as a taxi driver, the Soviet Union pressured Estonia into entering a mutual assistance pact. The pact allowed Soviet military bases to be established in Estonia. Within weeks, bases were set up and occupied by Soviet troops. Then, in the summer of 1940, shortly after the end of Russia's Winter War with Finland, the Soviet Union fabricated excuses and successfully invaded Estonia.

The Estonian government was forced to resign. Rigged elections followed. A puppet government was installed. The "people's assemblies" then asked that Estonia "rejoin" the U.S.S.R. Moscow promptly agreed. Estonia became the Estonian Soviet Socialist Republic, one of the Soviet Union's constituent republics. It was now privy to Stalin's reign of terror.

In 1941 Estonia suffered its first wave of mass deportations. From a population of a little over 1 million, about 10,000 persons were secretly classified as "enemies of the people." One night in June all were seized and railroaded in cattle cars to prisons in the nether regions of Siberia and Kazakhstan.

From my father's recollections and my mother's narrative, we can follow how their lives shifted from normality to a survival mode.

Father: *In 1931, when I turned 20, I had to fulfill my military obligation. I began my service in the Estonian army assigned to the communications battalion in Tallinn. When I completed that training, I was sent to the military school in Tondi, Tallinn. I graduated from there as an ensign (an officer's rank, one below a lieutenant).*

I was discharged from the army around 1932. There was a worldwide depression. Initially I worked at Judeik's sawmill, then at a real estate agency and finally with the Võru County Economic Department. The department's director was known to everyone as "Old Man Antso." It was there I learned to type with ten fingers.

My mother died in 1936. With financial help from my uncle Richard and his wife Linda, I enrolled in Tartu University. I studied economics. Thanks to additional financial support from my uncle, I bought an old 1932 Ford which I used as a taxicab. That is how I earned my keep while going to school.

My mother's narrative resumes from the time she began vocational school. The year was 1937. She makes no mention of the raging Spanish Civil War. The *Anschluss* was still a year away.

Mother: *After I completed my Higher Elementary School in Rõuge, I enrolled in the Antsla Home Economics School. I no longer lived at home so I was no longer in close contact with my family in Sänna. My father had remarried. They had a daughter, Hilja, who was born in 1932 on November 8.*

The Home Economics School was a private boarding school for women. Classes were held in the Old Antsla Manor House which had been remodeled and converted into a school. The school prepared young women not only to manage a domestic household but to use those skills outside of the home. I was 19 years old.

I did not have money for the tuition. However, a friend, an older lady who knew the school's director, suggested that I be allowed to attend on a loan. The director agreed. As part of my loan agreement the school promised to find me a job if I successfully completed my course of study. I agreed to repay the loan from my salary at the rate of 20 kroon a month.

I completed my courses. The school found a position for me in Tallinn as an assistant to the manager of the kitchen that serviced the Ministry of Economics. The manager, Miss Oja, was a former teacher at the Antsla Home Economics School. She took me under her wing. She helped me professionally and personally. I was a young girl who had grown up in the country. For me Tallinn was huge, full of revelations and surprises. Miss Oja was like a sister to me.

I had a fulltime job that I loved. I received a monthly wage. I was discovering Tallinn. I was

During Estonia's first period of independence, all males were required to perform one year of military service. My 20-year-old father received his basic training in communications. He then successfully completed Officer Candidate School, graduating as an ensign—the equivalent of a second lieutenant in the American army (Treiman family archive).

5. A Brief Normality

Takso O-160 *Telefon 229*

Rõõmsaid pühi
ja
hääd uut aastat

soovib

Alfred Treiman

My father was self-employed as a taxi driver while he attended Tartu University. During Christmas, he used a business card that wished everyone a "Merry Christmas and a happy new year" (Treiman family archive).

This Uibo family photo was taken circa 1938 in front of the old residence that was formerly a courthouse. My mother no longer lived at home. Front row, from left: Samuel, step-sister Hilja and Hilja's mother Minna. Back row: mother's siblings: Aleksander, Rosilda and Kalju (Uibo family archive).

happy with my life. After a year Miss Oja felt I was ready to manage a similar kitchen on my own. She had a friend who taught at the horticultural school in Ravila. The friend told us about an opening for a manager at a canteen on the campus of the Ravila folk university. I applied for the position. I was hired. My pay was 50 kroon a month.

The horticultural school and the folk university were part of the same campus. The designation "university" (ülikool) is misleading. The "rahva ülikool" (folk university) offered non-academic credit courses like those offered in America by some community colleges. These classes are sometimes referred to as "continuing education" or "adult education." Organizations such as the American YMCA have similar offerings. The classes are of limited duration and are taught by people with expertise in the subject matter but who generally are not academics.

My mother, wearing one of Estonia's most popular folk costumes, one associated with the country's third largest island, Muhu. Although Estonia is only as large in land area as New Hampshire and Vermont combined, each of its four regions—Islands, North Estonia, South Estonia and West Estonia—has their own distinctive folk costume. There are also over 100 parishes. Each parish adds its own unique patterns to their region's folk costume (Treiman family archive).

Mother: *Once again, I was in the countryside. Ravila is in Harju County, about 25–30 miles southeast of Tallinn. On the road to Tartu from Tallinn there was a bus stop at the small town of Kose. Those going to Ravila got off the bus at Kose and then traveled another one-or-two-miles, either on foot or by horse until they reached Ravila.*

Even though Ravila was in the country, instead of my small, childhood hamlet of Sänna with always the same small group of people, I now mingled with many people, a portion of whom were constantly changing—students from two schools, of which there were about 50–60, four permanent teachers and the head of the horticultural school. There was a lot of work.

My apartment was very nice. It had an open design. It was on the second floor, with a view into the garden. But, perhaps the nicest thing about the apartment was that I didn't have to pay monthly rent. Lodging was included as part of my wages, as were meals.

5. A Brief Normality

I could now spend more on myself: a new dress and a skirt and jacket combination. I paid the seamstress who made these clothes in advance. She didn't ask for it but I felt better knowing I wasn't in debt to anyone. I felt like I had millions but I was prudent. I paid my school loan. I never over-spent.

Ravila, beautiful Ravila! When I was there Ravila mirrored the vigor of youth. Young men and women, each with plans for the future, each with plans grander than the next. All of us took pride in our work. We savored the joy of living.

6

Foreign Occupations

"Nothing in life remains constant..."

My mother's carefree days ended while she was working in Ravila. In 1939 she transitioned from the youthful joys of anticipation to the concerns of adulthood. Although she doesn't mention them, the German *Anschluss*, Germany's annexation of Austria, took place a year earlier, followed by the infamous Munich Conference. The Stalin-Hitler Non-Aggression Pact was signed in August 1939. Political turmoil that Winston Churchill called *"The Gathering Storm"* and my mother described as "dark clouds," impacted my mother's life as they did my father's.

Mother: *Nothing in life remains constant, so also it was with the Ravila community. Dark clouds began to move toward us from the east. The Estonian government is engaged in negotiations with the Russian Communists. Are these rumors?*

Russian troops arrived in Tallinn. People visiting Tallinn returned home with bad news. Not only were there military restrictions on movement but only homogenized thought was permitted. Out of fear and a sense of self-preservation people socialized only with their own small select group. General trust in each other disappeared.

I remember traveling from Tallinn to Ravila. As my bus passed through Lasnamäe, Russian tanks could be seen everywhere. The Russian occupation had begun. Passengers in the bus were worried and quiet. Many had tears in their eyes. There were security stops on the streets, deportations, imprisonments, killings.

The folk university was a school with patriotic spirit. The school's leadership was in the forefront of those the Communists eyed with suspicion. Many of them disappeared without a trace.

A girlfriend of mine in Tallinn suggested I get a new job in the office of the Tallinn Pediatric Outpatient Clinic. I applied and was hired. In Tallinn I lived in a small room at 8-2 Köleri Street. The children's clinic was on Niguliste street. There were six of us who worked there.

6. Foreign Occupations

The Russians settled in comfortably. The troops brought their families. The Russian women brought their children to the clinic. To treat them properly we needed information. They had to fill out forms, which were all written in Estonian. The Russians did not know Estonian. We did not know Russian. To our distaste, we were required to take Russian language courses. The head doctor was ordered to have everyone at the clinic attend a workers' meeting once a month. The meetings were held under a banner that proclaimed, "Workers of the world, unite!."

It was a terrible time. A person couldn't be real. One had to be either silent or lie. Who is or isn't your friend? A young man invited me to dinner. I accepted. We talked about this and that. My younger brother had warned me to be careful about what I said. His warning was correct. When it came time to pay the young man said, "Now we have equal rights. Each will pay for themselves." I paid for my dinner. Now I knew who I was dealing with—a Communist.

Bombings. The German army was closing in. Anti-tank trenches were being dug near Lasnamäe—deep trenches which it was hoped the German tanks could not cross. Every office was required to send at least one person to help with the digging. My office sent me. The clinic's head doctor, Dr. Püümets, heard that I had been sent because I was the youngest person in the office. He complained that I had been treated unfairly and sent a car to bring me back to the clinic. The trench was dug without my help. Within a couple of days, the Germans had captured Tallinn; their tanks came from a different direction.

While my mother's passage about splitting the cost of a dinner date should be read in the context of the days' social customs, her narrative describes the Soviet occupation and its impact on her. In the meantime, the occupation's effect on my father triggered an increased level of political activity, often with other members of the Tartu University student society he had joined, EÜS Põhjala.

EÜS Põhjala or "Estonian University Students Society, Nordic" was, and still is, a student organization that traces its origin to 1884. Organized by Estonian students in St. Petersburg to further Estonian culture and identity, many of Estonia's founding fathers were members.

During World War II about 100 of its members escaped to the West. Those who escaped formed their own chapters in Sweden, Canada, America and Australia. In Los Angeles, my father and three of his contemporaries who were also members kept Põhjala alive in California by holding periodic meetings. Membership was replenished with offspring. Members who remained in Estonia continued their activities in secret.

Father: *When the Russians first occupied Estonia in June 1940, I was beginning my third year at the University of Tartu. Following the* *occupation, the curriculum consisted of nothing but courses on Leninism and Stalinism. It made no sense to continue with my studies.*

The authorities considered me to be a member of the working class, pursuing studies at the university. It therefore wasn't hard to get a job at the People's Department for Trade. The Department was located at the nationalized EÜS Põhjala house. Several Põhjala members had obtained jobs there under the new regime.

I worked as an inspector. Initially my job was to calculate allocations of how much of a given item or product a person in a particular region could use—effectively, to draft rationing schedules. Often, we would be ordered to report at odd hours, even at night, to draft "extraordinary" plans. More than likely this was done to test our dedication. The actual allocations always came from Moscow. I was also required to inspect inventories of the larger stores throughout Estonia to see if rationing schedules were being maintained.

The work that my friend from Võru, Arvo Horm, and I did for the new "Greater Homeland" [**Stalin's Russia, to which Estonia was annexed in August 1940**] *ended with the mass deportations of June 14, 1941.*

Although he doesn't mention it, my father's benefactors, his uncle Richard and Richard's wife Linda, were among the roughly 10,000 victims of the 1941 mass deportations to which my father refers. By happenstance my father saw them from a distance after they had been seized and packed into cattle cars. He often recalled, sometimes with tears welling in his eyes, how helpless he had felt, wishing he could do something, *anything*, to save them.

Father: *I left Tallinn and drove to Võru. Together with several companions I hid on Roos Island until the Germans arrived in July 1941. Horm went to Viljandi and hid there. During the German occupation I was chairman of the office responsible for repatriating properties that had been nationalized by the Russians. I got that position on the recommendation of another freedom fighter and member of Põhjala, Jonasse. In the meantime, Horm had arrived in Võru from Viljandi. Together we planned our next steps.*

Mother: *A new occupier—the Germans. They were received as saviors. But not for long. Except for the uniforms and the language there was no difference between the occupying forces. Tight restrictions over movement and thought continued, the shortage of food saw no change, a disregard of basic human rights and an absence of personal liberty continued unabated.*

When the Germans arrived, I still lived on Köleri street. From time to time the Russian Air Force dropped reminders of their continued interest in Estonia. It was November 1941. Night. I had just fallen asleep. There was a giant crash and then a bang. A bomb landed next door. The building in

6. Foreign Occupations

which I lived swayed and shook and its windows fell out. I pulled my blanket over my head. I was afraid to see what had happened.

My building withstood the bomb blast. As for the building next door, there was only a hole.

My father was in Võru when the German occupation began—my mother in Tallinn. Notwithstanding the 160-mile gap, their paths would meld.

7

Two Weddings and an Exit

"Alfred was a man of few words."

Mother: *Private cars had been conscripted for military use but bus transportation in Tallinn was still available. One day I walked a friend to a local bus stop. A man known to my friend was there. The man's name was Alfred. My friend introduced us. We had a polite, perfunctory conversation and departed. I returned to work at the Niguliste Children's Clinic.*

A few weeks later Alfred was in town and visited me at the clinic. I had night watch duty and could not leave. Alfred was a man of few words. He said nothing more and disappeared. About 45 minutes later he returned and presented me with a large, delicious sandwich. My co-workers started to laugh—love travels through the stomach.

Sixty years later my father, "a man of few words," offered his version of meeting my mother. He volunteered a compact recollection. He amplified his breviloquence by offering a retrospective statement about the consequences of that meeting.

Father: *In Tallinn I met a very nice and cheerful girl who would become my son Jaak's mother. She would care for my son and bring herself and my son to the free world. Her entrepreneurial spirit and grasp of survival realities were the keys to the success of our future ventures—ventures that did not have the benefit of seed capital.*

My mother mentions, without detailing, their wartime courtship and their sudden, civil marriage, accelerated no doubt by her pregnancy. Following the civil ceremony, she moved to Võru feeling that she was among strangers. Three weeks later a church wedding was celebrated to solemnize the earlier civil ceremony. My mother's siblings, Rosilda and Kalju, were present. Most of the other attendees were my father's friends, strangers to my mother.

Mother: *Alfred lived and worked in Võru but he found opportunities to visit me. One visit changed my life. On Monday, December 14, 1942, Alfred and I registered our marriage with the Tallinn city government. The*

7. Two Weddings and an Exit

witnesses were a married couple who were friends of Alfred. We were now husband and wife.

Following the registration process Alfred returned to Võru and I remained in Tallinn until December 19 in order to finish my work at the clinic. On December 20 I traveled to Võru as Alfred's wife. Everything was strange—even Alfred, whom I really did not fully know.

A marriage isn't real unless there is a church wedding. We had our church wedding on January 9 at the Pindi church, about 10 miles from town. After the ceremony a sled took us home to Kasarmu street 2a in Võru. A thick layer of snow covered the ground. I was wrapped in a sledding blanket. On the way, the driver intentionally drove the sled into a ditch. This was an old wedding tradition. The bride had to struggle out of her coat. At home a bountiful wedding table waited for us. Where the food came from, I don't know. There were about 30–40 guests, most of whom were strangers to me. The next day was spent cleaning up.

Now everyday life began, bringing with it serious issues and an unknown future. I was three months pregnant. Alfred was often gone until late at night. I knew something was being planned. It was no use asking. I could only guess. The Germans were mobilizing former Estonian officers. Neither Alfred nor his friends wanted to be part of the German army. There was only one choice. Alfred had to leave. Before he left, Alfred and I calculated when our child would be born. Our calculation was exact.

Our April 8, 1943, farewell was wordless and short. As he passed the window Alfred raised his hat. So began a time of waiting—not knowing what each day would bring. I was questioned by the Germans and placed on their watch list. Acquaintances and guests from our wedding party

Married in a quiet civil ceremony in Tallinn during the German occupation, Alfred and Valentine Treiman pose for their wedding picture on December 14, 1942 (Treiman family archive).

More than a decade after my father passed my mother's window in Võru, raised his hat and waved a wordless goodbye as he left for Sweden, he raised his hat again, I imagine in much the same way. This time the raised hat was by way of a greeting while in the snowy mountains of California (Treiman family archive).

avoided me. There were two families who were the exception. They weren't afraid of my friendship although the Germans were watching me.

Father: *My friends and I left Estonia to avoid being drafted into the German army; we had a naive belief that we could explain to the Western allies the dangers posed by Russia, whose return to Estonia we anticipated; and we wanted to try to maintain the continuity of the Estonian state.*

As my father explains, he and his friends had three reasons for leaving Estonia:

One. To avoid being drafted into the German army. Since my father had graduated from military school as an ensign, he was classified as an officer. This made him subject to German mobilization orders. Neither he or his friends wanted to be part of the German military.

Two. They wanted to warn the Western allies about the danger that Russia posed. To that end, they would write papers, distribute flyers and publish newspapers. They sought to buttress their arguments with facts, witness my father's later assignment to return to Estonia from Sweden and bring back supporting material, including statistical books, from the Tartu University library. (I still have two of those books, *Eesti Statistika 1938* and *Eesti Arvudes 1920-1935—Estonian Statistics 1938* and *Estonia in Numbers 1920-1935*. One day I will return them to the library.)

7. Two Weddings and an Exit

Throughout his life my father lamented his and his friends' "naive belief" that they could successfully warn the West about the dangers of Communism and the Soviet Union.

Three. My father and his friends wanted to maintain the continuity of the Estonian state. I never heard my father address this point as a reason for leaving Estonia. I assume what he and his friends had in mind was that if the war ended badly, they would establish a government in exile. In fact, one of the friends he left with later became Prime Minister of the Estonian Government-in-Exile.

With my father gone, my mother, pregnant and having been questioned by the Germans, was an outcaste. Two unidentified families plus her brother Kalju and her sister Rosilda were her support. Her father Samuel could no longer help. For the past two years he had been ill with tuberculosis. He was dying.

My parents' plan was to have my father return and bring my mother and by then, the new-born me, to Sweden with him. While my parents' decision to leave Estonia was bilateral, their motivations differed but were not mutually exclusive.

My father, the pragmatist with a touch of idealism, gives three specific reasons for leaving Estonia. On the other hand, my mother, the idealist who would demonstrate large measures of pragmatism throughout her life, speaks throughout her narrative in more general terms. Her lodestar was freedom, the right to choose, the right to think independently and make individual decisions.

8

Back and Forth

"I am left to speculate."

In a 2021 *Estonian World* online article, "Remembering Estonia's WW II refugees," Tania Lestal recapped the war-time exodus from Estonia. "Estonians started fleeing to Sweden already in the spring of 1943, but the exodus intensified in August 1944 and achieved its peak from 19-23 September 1944, when it became clear that the German front was collapsing and the Soviet military forces were about to occupy Estonia again. The overwhelming majority of Estonians did not favour any occupying force—the country had simply been sandwiched during the Second World War between the Nazi Germany and the Soviet Union."

My father escaped before the exodus became a torrent. By the end of the war about 25,000 Estonians had fled to Sweden, another 40,000 or so had made their way south, ending up in German displaced persons camps and the rest to such far flung places as South Africa, Morocco, Argentina or whatever other place would take them.

Father: *In early spring 1943 I left my wife and unborn son Jaak in Võru, to the grace of God, and drove to Tallinn. My intention was to return for them soon. We found a possible escape route to Finland. An Estonian Transport Ministry truck took us from Tallinn to Loksa, a small town located on Hara Bay, which opened to the Gulf of Finland. There were 13 of us, mostly University of Tartu students. We hid next to a haystack and waited for the boat on which our trip to Finland would begin. The person responsible for our crossing was a boatman named Nikkar, also referred to as a Black Captain. Because the occupying German authorities considered all crossings illegal, boatmen carrying refugees were frequently called Black Captains.*

Nikkar finally arrived in his motorboat and took us from Loksa to a small, nearby island. He left us there to wait for his return. When he came, we again boarded his motorboat. This time he took us far into the Gulf of

8. Back and Forth

Finland. There we were met by a sailboat captained by a man who was about 60–70 years old.

We settled into the new boat and sailed to Finland without incident. Once inside Finnish waters we transferred to a Finnish patrol boat which took us to Helsinki, in secret. We were jailed for the night, but all the cell doors were left unlocked. In the morning we were free to go.

One of my compatriots on the boat was Heinrich Mark, who would later become Prime Minister in the Estonian exile government. Heinrich had developed earlier contacts in Finland. One of those contacts, a Finnish member of Parliament named Huittinen, sheltered us in his home in Helsinki.

Within a couple of weeks, we were able to sail to Sweden—with the approval of the Swedish Embassy but without formal Finnish permission. In Sweden we settled into the Kummelnäs refugee camp, located on an island in Stockholm's archipelago.

My father probably stepped onto Swedish soil in late April or early May 1943. The Swedish embassy in Helsinki had issued entry visas to my father and his companions. When they arrived, at least one refugee camp was already in existence. Although little seems to have been written about them, the Swedish camps appear to have provided refugees a large amount of freedom, with opportunities for outside employment and unfettered ingress and egress.

In a November 15, 1944, letter my father refers to having earned 100 kronor digging ditches while living in the refugee camp. For him and the other refugees, lack of money was a constant problem, sometimes exacerbated by the time spent on refugee activities. My father writes about having to turn down an offer for gainful employment because of his anticipated return trip to Estonia to carry out some political tasks and to bring my mother and me to Sweden.

By the time my father arrived in Stockholm, or at least shortly thereafter, the rudiments of an Estonian political organization seem to have been in place. According to my father, his return trip to Estonia was organized by "the local [Estonian] political people." From that same November 15, 1944, letter, it seems that his trip was among the earliest of such missions. A number of similar secret forays, carried out by different people, followed.

My father received word of my birth in late July. If my mother's recollections are accurate, my father is mistaken that his return trip took place in late fall. It probably took place in late August or early September.

Father: *By late fall 1943 a secret, return trip to Estonia had been organized. The boat crew consisted of Aleks Soom, Siniveer and me. We took a supply of saccharin to use as money. Each of us had specific assignments.*

FISCHER-BERUFSSCHEIN
KALURI KUTSETUNNISTUS Nr. 1853

Hiermit wird bescheinigt, dass _Suursaar_   _Johannes_
Käesolewaga tõendatakse, et
(Familienname — Perekonnanimi)   (Vorname — Eesnimi)

geb. _22. aug. 1909_ wohnhaft _Tallinn_   _Köie 5_
sünd.   elukoht
(Gemeinde — vald) (Dorf — küla) (Gehöft — talu)

ist auf Grund der Anordnung zur Sicherung der Versorgung mit Fisch u. Fischereierzeugnissen in das amtliche Verzeichnis der Berufsfischer eingetragen worden.
on kala ja kalasaadustega varustamise kindlustamise määruse alusel kantud kutselise kalurkonna registrisse.

Art der Berufsausübung _Selbständiger Fischer_
Tegevusliik kalandusalal _Iseseisev kalur_

Berufsschein ist gültig bis _31. märts_   194_4_
Kutsetunnistus on kehtiv kuni

Reval _5. juuli_ 1943.
Tallinn

FISCHEREIABTEILUNG   EESTI OMAWALITSUS
DER ZENTRALVERWALTUNG DER LAND-   PÕLLUMAJANDUSE KESKVALITSUS
WIRTSCHAFT DER ESTNISCHEN VERWALTUNG.   KALANDUSOSAKOND.

Once my father and his companions entered Estonian waters on their return trip to Estonia, they altered their boat to look like a fishing vessel and disguised themselves as fishermen. Among my father's memorabilia I found this certificate, issued on July 5, 1943. It certifies that "Johannes Suursaar" is a commercial fisherman. I suspect my father used "Suursaar" as part of his traveling persona, as he tried to avoid German occupation troops (Treiman family archive).

 Siniveer was to obtain important military information and then transmit that information through the existing Finnish-Estonian line of communication. I was to take important political papers from Sweden to Estonia and to bring other essential papers back with me. I also had to deliver a radio transmitter to Tallinn and make it operational. While in Tallinn I was to contact the leadership of the Estonian Consumers' Co-Operative.
 In addition to those tasks, Horm gave me some letters for people at Tartu University. Horm and I had also prepared a list of other materials to bring back if possible, including statistical information. Finally, I was to bring back to Sweden professor Ronimois as well as Horm's wife and my wife. While in Estonia, I added the university student Madis to the list of people to bring back to Sweden.
 We left Sweden and sailed to the island of Hiiumaa. There we altered our boat to look like a fishing vessel and disguised ourselves as fishermen. From there we sailed to Tallinn.

8. Back and Forth

I completed my Tallinn assignments and went to Võru, to bring my wife and newborn son to Sweden. In this I was not successful. To this day she and I have a difference of opinion as to why this was so. I returned to Sweden having completed all my tasks except bringing my wife and son with me.

Mother: *Our son was born in the Võru hospital, about half a kilometer from where we lived. When I felt I was about to deliver I walked to the hospital. The doctor examined me and sent me home. In his opinion it would be another two weeks.*

I returned home, pausing along the way when the pains got to be too great. The contractions became stronger and more frequent. I retraced my steps to the hospital. When I arrived, the contractions were stronger and stronger. Nurse Toover, a large woman, pressed my stomach. I asked her, "What if it doesn't come out?" She replied, with a laugh, "Where else can it go?" She was right. Soon I saw a big, beautiful, baby boy. I immediately named him Jaak.

Later, Alfred, who was in Sweden, said that he knew about Jaak's birth the next day. The underground lines of communication were very efficient. Secret missions between Sweden and Estonia with their special tasks were well organized. However, some failed.

A little more than a month following Jaak's birth, toward the beginning of September, the exact date I don't remember, Alfred walked into my room at twilight. I was amazed. We were together for a few hours. Jaak slept the entire time. Alfred left at dusk. Jaak and I remained.

My father, having heard of my birth, returned to Estonia tasked with certain objectives. One objective was to go to Võru and bring my mother and me back with him to Sweden. What happened during the few hours they spent together remains a mystery. My father offers no explanation concerning his sudden departure except to say, decades later, that he and my mother continued to disagree about the reasons for his departure without wife and child. My mother's narrative describes what happened but not why. When I was young, I was told that when my father arrived, I was too sick to travel. Later, I was told that my father's presence had been reported to the German authorities and he therefore had to leave quickly. I am left to speculate.

9

Escape

"I heard the sound of guard dogs..."

My mother, shunned by Alfred's friends, feeling abandoned, under surveillance, a target of sexual advances by the local German soldiers and nursing a three-month-old baby, prepared to join my father in Sweden. The journey would be dangerous. First, she would have to circumvent internal travel restrictions and get from Võru to Tallinn. Once in Tallinn, she would have to find passage across the heavily mined, combat-roiled waters of the Gulf of Finland. If she successfully navigated those perils

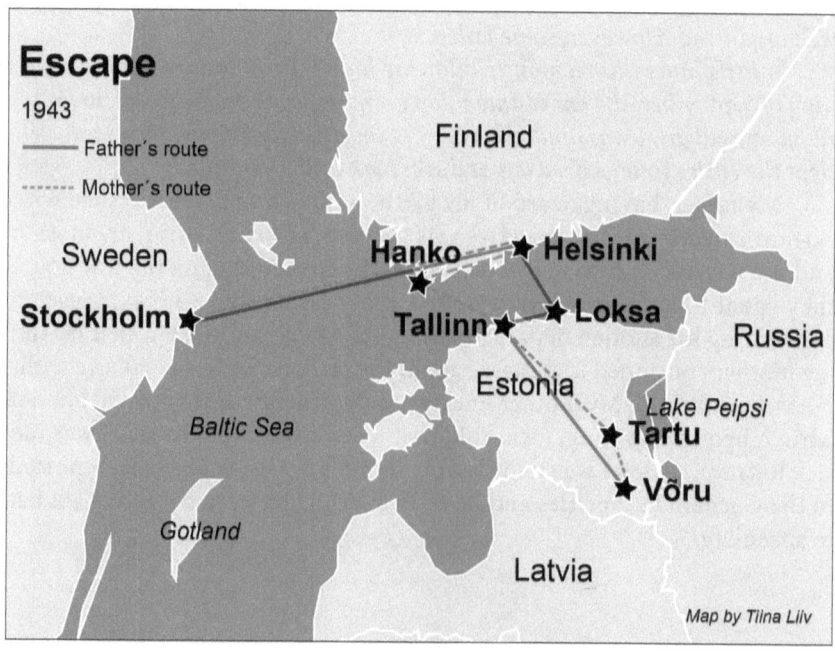

My parents' escape routes. Finland was the first stop for both on their way to Sweden (Map by Tiina Liiv).

9. Escape

and arrived in Helsinki, she would still have to survive air raids and wartime travel prohibitions before she undertook the final leg of her journey to Stockholm, once more risking the natural and man-made vagaries of the Baltic Sea.

Throughout the German occupation and later, throughout the Soviet occupation, Estonians were prohibited from crossing the Baltic Sea and escape routes were closely guarded. The 146,000 square miles of what the Estonians call the Western Sea and the Finns call the Eastern Sea was one of the most densely mined waters in the world. German naval vessels and Soviet torpedo bombers made any crossing perilous. For most of World War II the Baltic Sea was a virtual German lake, abetted by a reluctant Finland.

On the last day of November 1939, the Soviet Union had invaded Finland. The Winter War raged for three and a half months, longer than anyone except possibly the Finns expected. They put up a valiant fight, eliciting world-wide admiration and sympathy. Volunteers from a number of countries, including about a thousand Estonians, joined the Finnish forces to fight the overwhelmingly larger Soviet force. The Finns ultimately succumbed, signed a peace treaty which ceded a portion of their territory to the Soviet Union but maintained their independence.

When Operation Barbarossa began in June 1941 with Germany attacking its erstwhile Soviet ally, the Finns sought to regain the territory that had been taken from them. In order to increase its military strength Finland entered an alliance with Germany and, thus allied, Finland resumed its fight against the Soviet Union in what is referred to as the "Continuation War."

As part of the Continuation War alliance, the Finns and the Germans had erected an anti-submarine net across the Gulf of Finland. This net effectively blockaded most Soviet shipping and trapped Soviet naval vessels in the Leningrad (now St. Petersburg) docks.

Unable to use their naval ships the Soviets patrolled the Baltic Sea with their torpedo bombers. In 1943 from September through November the Soviets sunk seven ships cruising the Baltic and severely damaged at least six others. These were the waters my father had crossed three times. These were the waters my mother would have to cross in order to reach Finland and then Sweden.

During my mother's last two weeks in Võru, her 11-year-old half-sister Hilja lived with her. When I spoke with her, Hilja still remembered German soldiers hanging around, peering at my mother through a window. When my mother was ready to leave, necessity required that she travel light. I was bundled in a sheepskin sack. The hope was that once the war ended, she and my father would return.

Mother: *Once more, I face the unknown. Rumors circulate that the Germans have captured Alfred. My house is under surveillance. I must be careful about every step I take, where I go, what I do. I decide this could not go on. My final decision—I must flee, regardless of the risks.*

I became friends with a young nurse at the hospital. She gave me an authorization to take my baby to the hospital in Tartu. Instead, we went to Tallinn. I stayed with an older lady who had previously helped me and had offered me advice when I lived there. She resided on Roopa Avenue.

I had to find a way to get to Finland. I had to find it quickly. If I was absent from Võru for too long the authorities would begin to look for me. Secretly, with the help of people I trusted, I explored many possibilities. Two weeks went by and hope started to dim. I prayed for God's help every night as I put Jaak to sleep. And help did come, giving me both courage and common sense. I met a crew member from a Finnish, coal-powered ship. He agreed to meet me at the entrance to the Port of Tallinn. He would escort me past the guards telling them that I worked in his ship's dining room.

A light rain drizzled. The roads were muddy. It was the night of October 20, 1943. My baby and I arrived at the port. A guard house was located on each side of the entrance gate. Inside each was a single guard, sheltered from the rain. The sailor who was supposed to walk me past these guards was nowhere to be seen. What to do?

"Courage Valli. Courage!" I smiled at the two young guards. They smiled back. I strode through the gate with outward assurance. Walking through the various docks I eventually found the small, coal powered ship I was looking for. The sailor who was supposed to escort me inside the port and take me to his captain was standing on deck, smoking. He was so shocked to see me, he was speechless.

I asked him to take me to the captain. He did. The captain was a bulky man with a benevolent appearance. He told me he had taken men across, but a woman, and a woman with child no less.... I told the captain I would accept any type of accommodation. He finally agreed. My baby and I were stowed in the coal bunker.

The ship was due to leave in the morning. I heard the sound of guard dogs and officers speaking on deck. My baby began to cry. I was afraid he would be heard. I tried to quiet him by bouncing him up and down, rocking, kissing, praying. He stopped crying. The on-deck voices dimmed and the boat began to move. I breathed easier—one more step toward freedom. Jaak was black from the coal dust as though I had birthed a black baby.

As we moved away from shore, the weather turned more inclement, the gusts of wind became a storm and the ocean's swell rose higher and higher. The boat was supposed to go to Helsinki. Instead, the storm blew us

9. Escape

80 miles off course. Our battered boat finally reached land at Hanko on the tip of the southern coast of Finland. It stayed there for repairs.

In the mid–1950s, about a dozen years after my mother fled Estonia, my father wrote his understanding of how my mother's escape took place. What he wrote conforms with my mother's description but adds the not-so-minor detail that the storm caused what was normally a one day crossing to take three days. Today the trip by ferry takes 2½ hours; by plane, less than half an hour.

Father: *On October 20, 1943, mother bundled Jaak in her arms as her only treasure. Under cover of darkness, she slipped past German guards and entered the restricted Tallinn port. She came to a small, coal powered Finnish boat loading coal for its trip to Finland. A friendly Finnish captain greeted them and hid them on his boat.*

Every ship leaving the port was searched by the German guards. The next morning the guards came to search the Finnish ship before its departure. For whatever reason, Jaak began to scream as loudly as he could, as babies sometimes do. Mother hugged him, kissed him and prayed. At the very last, critical moment he became quiet. The guards passed by without seeing them. The trip across the Gulf of Finland usually took one day. Because of an extraordinary storm their trip took three days.

Mother: *I went to the Hanko police station and told the officer on duty that I was a ship's dining room attendant, that my ship was docked for repairs and I wanted to go to Helsinki to meet my husband, who was serving in the Finnish army and was there on leave. Right away, I was given a pass to travel by train to Helsinki.*

I arrived at the Helsinki train station in the middle of the night. I stood in the depot whispering to Jaak and murmuring an Estonian song. Suddenly a young man stepped next to me. He spoke to me in Estonian. "Where are you going?" I told him I planned to find the Estonian Aid Center in the morning. I hoped they would help me make contact with my husband, who was in Sweden.

The young man told me that I couldn't stay in the train station all night with a baby. He took me to his apartment. It consisted of one room at a Finnish home. My baby began to cry. The landlady came. She exclaimed angrily, "You are bringing strangers to your apartment!" The young man explained who I was and why I was there. The explanation made no impact. The landlady ordered me to leave. My first impression of Finns was not very nice.

At four o'clock in the morning the young man called a taxi and we started to look for a hotel. At that hour the trainloads of soldiers had not yet arrived and there was a greater chance of finding a vacant room. We visited many hotels, without success.

Finally, at the Young Women's Christian Association the desk clerk listened to me as I told her that I was a refugee and that my husband was in Sweden. She gave me a room. Later I found out that her two sons were in Sweden. More than likely that contributed to her favorable decision. I could finally wash my baby and myself.

For years I have been embarrassed that I can't remember the names of the young man or the YWCA's desk clerk. These helpful people acted out of human kindness. I am very grateful to them.

The next day I went to the Estonian Aid Center, leaving my three-months-old baby in my room. At the aid center I related my story and asked that Alfred be notified of my arrival in Finland. Vilja Uustalu worked there and promised to help. I returned to my hotel feeling happy. I entered my room. Jaak was not there. I panicked. While I was gone there had been an air raid. Jaak had been taken to the cellar. My heart and hand trembled when I got my child back.

A message that his wife and son had arrived in Finland reached my father. On November 20, 1943, a month after my mother fled Estonia, he replied:

> Dear Wife!
>
> Today, in the late evening, I received the joyous news that you have, together with Jaak, arrived in Finland. Congratulations on the occasion of your happy arrival.
>
> I did not dare to truly hope that you would undertake that difficult journey. You have been sturdier than I dared hope.
>
> The first thing you must do is to apply for a visa at the Swedish Embassy in Helsinki. By that time everything will have been done from this end to make sure you won't receive a negative response. At the same time, you need to ask the Finns for an exit permit.
>
> I am sending you another letter, which will arrive early next week. It would be good if you would not leave Helsinki before receiving this letter.
>
> I know nothing about your arrival other than that you have arrived in Finland with Jaak. I hope however, that everything goes well.
>
> With heartfelt greetings,
> Alfred

Mother: *With Vilja Uustalu's help I soon had the papers I needed to travel to Sweden. I left Finland on December 8, 1943. As I was ready to board my ship a Finnish border guard checked my purse and found some Finnish money. It could not have been much. The border guard got mad. I'm not sure what he wanted to do to me but it wasn't anything nice. Next to me stood an Estonian, Mr. Laur. He spoke Finnish. Laur was able to resolve the situation. I was able to board the ship. This was my second discomforting incident in Finland. I thought of the Estonian young men who were helping defend Finland. Estonians have only had warm feelings toward Finland. I don't know. Were these feelings and actions reciprocal?*

9. Escape

Ernst Laur was well suited to speak with the Finnish border guard on my mother's behalf. During the Winter War he had joined the Finnish army. He parachuted behind Soviet lines and engaged in guerrilla warfare. When he returned to Estonia the Germans conscripted Laur. Instead of serving in the German army he fled to Finland and then Sweden. After six months he returned to Estonia to bring his pregnant wife to Sweden. Eventually Laur came to Los Angeles. In one of life's serendipitous quirks, he would be my predecessor as Estonia's Honorary Consul in Los Angeles.

My mother ruminates about whether the good feelings Estonians have for Finns are reciprocated. She references her two "discomforting" incidents—the Finnish landlady who denied her and her baby shelter in the middle of the night and the Finnish border guard who questioned her possession of a small amount of Finnish currency. She does not consider the Finnish sea captain who took her from Tallinn to Finland (apparently for free), the Hanko policeman who immediately gave her a pass to travel to Helsinki and the Finn working at the YWCA who gave her a room. Given the ordeal my mother had just completed and the uncertainties waiting for her, her reactions are perhaps understandable even if unfair.

10

A New Life: Joys and Worries

*"Freedom is priceless. Living under dictatorial
power destroys a person's life."*

The day after my mother arrived in Sweden, her father died. She would not know about Samuel's death for the next 45 years. Neither would she know anything about other members of her family. While some refugees tried to maintain contact with friends and relatives, my parents did not.

All letters to or from Estonia were routed through Moscow, to be read by censors. Given the well-known history of the NKVD's and its successor KGB's long tentacles and given their witnessing the horrors of the Soviet occupation, my parents did not want to become a blip on the Soviet authorities' radar. They also knew that for those living in Estonia serious penalties, ranging from loss of a job to imprisonment, were sometimes assessed against those who had any connection with the West. They did not want to jeopardize their relatives' lives by sending them letters.

My mother was now in Sweden—a refugee. A baby in her arms, the joys of Ravila a memory, she and countless others tried to adapt and survive. Her narrative offers vignettes of my parents' early life in Sweden including descriptions of various jobs she held and a serendipitous job exchange.

Mother: *I arrived in Sweden on December 8, 1943. After many months, Alfred and I were reunited when he met me as my ship docked in Stockholm harbor.*

People ask, "Why did you leave Estonia?" The will to live; the right to live a complete life! A person must be able to think freely, to criticize, to express oneself! And, no life can be complete if a person is not permitted to live according to her own beliefs, if a person is unable to develop one's abilities. Freedom is priceless. Living under dictatorial power destroys a person's life. For those and other reasons I and many others left.

Stockholm, Surbrunnsgatan. Alfred had rented a room and a crib.

10. A New Life: Joys and Worries

The room contained a sofa, a small table and one chair. The sofa was also our bed. We shared the kitchen with our landlady. She was generous and understanding. In addition to holding a job, Alfred was active in politics. When he wasn't at work he was at meetings, conferring with people or helping newly arrived refugees. I only saw him late at night.

Sunday. We visited our friends Arvo and Maarja Horm. They had a daughter, Anne-Mari, who was a year older than Jaak. We talked about this and that. Who had been able to get out of Estonia? How to help them? What will happen going forward? Living conditions were another typical topic of conversation. Arvo knew of some five-story apartment buildings that were being built in Hägersten, on the edge of Stockholm. He promised to get information about the possibility of renting and what it would cost.

Christmas Eve. We placed our treasure—our son—into his carriage and strolled through the city. Even though Sweden was a neutral country, Christmas lighting throughout Stockholm was modest. In case it was attacked, Stockholm did not want to be highly visible. Even so, store windows were decorated for Christmas. There were beautiful clothes and other temptations.

Regardless of my parents' work hours, I did not lack for love, or toys. My mother kept the teddy bear in the picture, taken circa 1944, well into the 21st century. She finally, reluctantly, disposed of it, after asking my permission, when she discovered moths had mutilated it beyond any reasonable hope of remediation (Treiman family archive).

When we returned to our apartment, we saw that Arvo and Maarja had dropped by. They had left us a Christmas present, two chocolate candies. I will remember and treasure that gift as long as I live. They could easily have enjoyed the candy themselves. Christmas was over.

Stockholm, January 21, 1944, my 26th birthday. I received a little notebook from my dearest. Alfred gave it to me saying that I should use it as a diary. Joys and worries. Today wasn't really a happy day. I was sick and I felt tired. My thoughts were confused. I wished I could turn my gypsy home into a real home. I wanted to go outside and to socialize—to see people, to speak with them. I burst into tears. Alfred comforted me. It was enough that he caressed my hair. The confusion and doubts passed.

Alfred was at work. My little boy and I were home alone. He was a good boy. He went to sleep after getting his bath. I darned Alfred's socks and waited for him to come home.

Days passed into weeks, weeks into months. Spring was at hand. Then June and the start of summer. I didn't want to stay in the center of town with a small child for the entire summer. I looked for work outside of the city. I found it, working for a family that had three children.

I worked hard from morning to night. It wasn't until late at night that I could finally look after my own child. I earned 60 kronor a month. My little boy is the joy of my life. He will grow up to be a good man in a free world.

Summer is past. We returned to the city, to Surbrunnsgatan. Arvo had good news about the Hägersten apartments. One more week and we could move in. The buildings were on a hillside. Arvo and Maarja's apartment was on the third floor of the building that was on top of the hill. Our apartment was on the fourth floor of the fourth building from the top of the hill. Each apartment had a balcony. We were able to signal each other if the need arose. Our apartment had two rooms, a kitchen, bathroom and a small entryway.

We subleased the small room. The large room was for us. That room was our living room, visitor's room, bedroom and frequently a reception room for newly arrived refugees and a place for them to sleep. Our apartment was always full of people, endless conversation and cigarette smoke. The worst thing was that our child had to breathe in the smoky air. I opened the balcony door so he could breathe fresh air but I couldn't keep it open for very long. The constant, loud conversations coming from our apartment bothered the people living below us.

Almost every building in Hägersten had some Estonians. Milvi Laid, the well-known Estonian actress, lived on the lower level of our building. Across the street was a grocery store. Every time I shopped there, I heard Estonian spoken. It gave me a homey feeling.

My parents were among the first wave of refugees to flee Estonia. This

10. A New Life: Joys and Worries

Not all people are willing to disrupt their lives and travel into the unknown, regardless of how dire their circumstances. The certainty of familiar surroundings, the presence of family and friends (and even enemies), the closeness of objects that trigger memories, all serve as anchors to movement. Uprooted people are disconnected. As they search for new certainties in uncertain surroundings, they try to move forward, sometimes in a daze, toward a hazy future. Back row, second from the right: My father. Front row: Maarja Horm and Arvo Horm. The names of the other three men are unknown (Treiman family archive).

Stockholm was the new home for many Estonian refugees. One who lived with us for a time was the well-known artist Eduard Ole. Born in 1898, he was one of the founders of a modern and experimental style that was adopted by artists who collectively became known as the "Group of Estonian Artists." Ole was noted for his broad range of style, palette and subject matter. A number of Ole's works are on display at the Kumu Art Museum in Tallinn. Pictured is a self-portrait (photograph by Margus Välja, Treiman family collection).

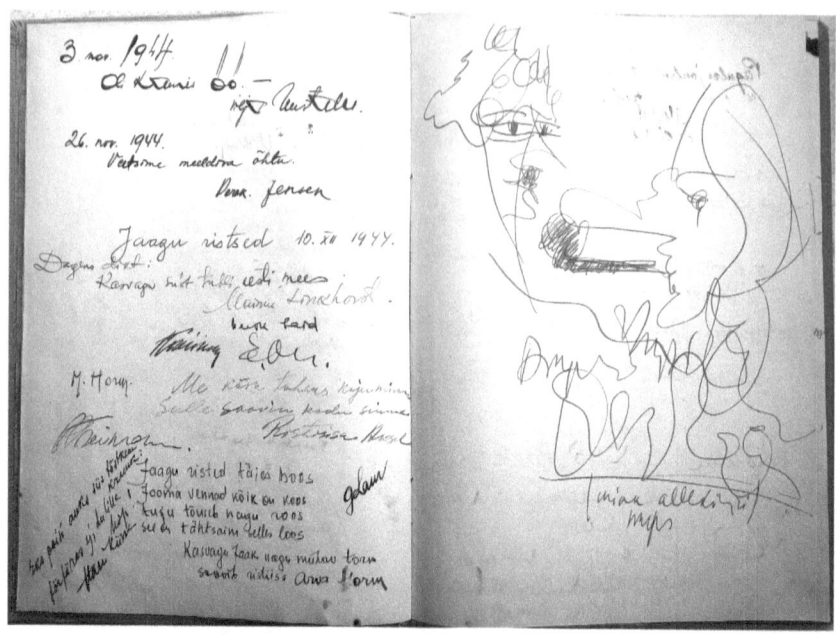

Our family guest book was a wedding gift to my parents on January 9, 1943, the date of their church wedding. They used the guest book frequently while we lived in Sweden. In Australia they used it for major occasions and only sporadically after we arrived in the United States. When I got married, the guest book was passed on to me. I used it regularly for our guests in the late 1980s but only sporadically since then. Regardless, it is an old-fashioned time-machine that contains interesting names and notes, and includes several of Ole's sketches (photograph by Margus Välja, Treiman family archive).

was in 1943, during the German occupation. The secret protocols of the Molotov-Ribbentrop Pact, the agreement between Hitler and Stalin that Germany would not attack the Soviet Union and the Soviet Union would not attack Germany, had earmarked Estonia, Latvia, Lithuania and Finland to the Soviet "sphere of influence." Most of Poland had been assigned to the German sphere.

Molotov-Ribbentrop was signed on August 23, 1939. Nine days later Germany invaded Poland. World War II became reality. Three months later, the Soviet Union attacked Finland. In June 1940 the Soviet Union occupied Estonia, installed a puppet government and then in August, annexed Estonia, claiming it as one of the republics of the Union of Soviet Socialist Republics.

On June 22, 1941, the Molotov-Ribbentrop Pact disintegrated when Germany attacked the Soviet Union. German forces moved toward Russia, replacing the retreating Soviet troops in Estonia with German occupation troops. The Germans laid siege to Leningrad, less than 80 miles from the

10. A New Life: Joys and Worries

Estonian border. After 900 days and 800,000 civilian casualties the Germans withdrew. The unsuccessful siege ended in early February 1944.

By the beginning of summer, 1944 Soviet troops were poised to re-enter Estonia. A contingent did so in August. Then, on September 14, 1944, a mass influx of 1.4 million Soviet troops invaded the Baltic States. The first order of business for the Soviet secret police, the NKVD, was to stop anyone from fleeing Estonia, Latvia or Lithuania. The largest outflow of persons seeking to escape the Soviet onslaught was during a few weeks in September. After that the incoming troops consolidated their positions and the flood of refugees exiting Estonia quickly dried up.

Mother: *September 1944. Alfred was at one of the Swedish landing points, making arrangements for the arrival of the last of the Estonian refugees. Responsibilities were divided. Bank director Klaus Scheel—directing operations and finances. Former ambassador August Rei—political leadership and communications with the relevant Swedish authorities. Arvo Horm—financing, contacts with Estonia regarding landing sites, lists of persons to be evacuated. Alfred Treiman—contact with the refugees, list of refugees who have arrived. Rudolf Schmuul—fuel, team supplies and reception. Aleksander Veske—recruiting boats and crew. Aksel Linkhorst—contact with Swedish officials.*

People who wanted to flee gathered at various places along the Estonian coast, hoping to board almost anything that floated. My father was one of the people in Sweden who arranged for boats to go to Estonia to pick up refugees. He would then help receive the boats as they arrived in Sweden, loaded with refugees. By September 27, as he waited on the island of Gotland, the second Soviet invasion of Estonia had already taken place and the number of boats arriving in Sweden was only a trickle (Treiman family archive).

A signboard at Puise Beach provides an overview of the 1944 mass exodus. It headlines the emotion felt by many refugees: "I don't want to leave but I can't stay" (author's photograph).

There was joy whenever a boat landed, sadness and tears for each boat that was lost. I received a letter from Alfred, dated September 27, 1944, sent from the Slitebaden Hotel on the island of Gotland, He described the hotel as one of the largest buildings in the area.

> My daily activity is intermittent. I talk about the weather with the boat people, I check out the boats, I listen to news about boats that have landed elsewhere. In good faith I receive addresses in Tallinn of people who wish to escape. I promise to do everything possible to save those people. All together we have sent out 12 boats. A few more are going to go. However, the odds of bringing people here based on the lists is small. Events in our homeland have moved too quickly. Now we must consider ourselves lucky to get whatever number we can out of there.... Therefore dearest, don't be angry that I am not yet home. Every little thing that isn't done to launch the boats may mean many people left in the hell over there. I must be here for a short time more and then we can be together again.

Mother: *We have an apartment. But our shelter is not free. Rent must be paid each month. Alfred has worked many different jobs but Horm and his friends have convinced him of the importance of politics. Most of the time was spent on politics. Paying jobs were undertaken sporadically. Our income was limited.*

10. A New Life: Joys and Worries

One day a person came to the door asking for our rent. I could give him nothing. I had always been self-sufficient, never being in debt to anyone. I always believed that borrowed money belongs to the lender, not the borrower. I was embarrassed and offended. When Alfred came home, I told him that both of us should work. He would work during the day and I at night. He agreed.

I secured a position at the Ericsson Telephone Factory. I worked there at night for six months. Then, by chance, I met a family whose grandmother told me that if I found a daytime job she would look after Jaak.

I did find daytime work, in a mink factory. When I was hired, I had no idea what I would have to do. The important thing was that I had a job. In the morning I took Jaak to the grandmother's apartment. From there I walked half a kilometer to ride the streetcar to the mink factory. The factory wasn't far from where I got off.

I learned how mink coats and stoles were made. The mink was killed, skinned and the pelt was tanned. The long mink hairs had to be pulled out using a special comb. Then, what was left was an even, shiny layer of mink fur. The long hairs that I pulled out stuck to my sweater. When I wore the sweater, I looked like a dead mink. I was sorry to have to throw away that sweater. I had knitted it myself.

Vilja Uustalu and I would meet and talk. She worked at the post office. Vilja suggested that I meet with her director. I did and I was hired. My work was clean and pleasant—adding numbers on a calculator. It was a refreshing change from the mink factory. I held that job for seven months. Then, the grandmother who baby sat Jaak became ill and I lost my babysitter. Instead of looking for more night work I looked for work that I could do at home.

I tried a succession of jobs. There was the job making shades for desk lamps. It paid poorly. Then I sewed baby clothes. I was a poor seamstress; I didn't like the work; and the pay was bad. While doing that I got to know a lady who worked for a company that made magic fans—three small, honeycombed paper balls attached to a stick that changed shape when you flicked your wrist. She didn't like her work anymore than I liked mine. We exchanged jobs. Our bosses didn't care as long as the work was done. Everyone was happy. I did not realize it at the time but this simple exchange was a defining moment in our lives.

The magic fan's paper balls were handmade by gluing sheets of colored tissue paper together using two wooden racks, alternately placed on a cloth covered with glue and then on a sheet of tissue paper. This was heavy labor but much better than combing dead minks or sewing baby clothes. The technique for making magic fans originated in China. When the glued tissue paper was folded open it looked like a honeycomb.

Tissue paper came in reams. One ream is 3 × 2 feet big and I believe 100 sheets. We brought reams of paper from the factory to our apartment by taxi. We then glued the sheets of tissue paper and hung the heavy, freshly glued packs to dry. We used every available place in our apartment to hang the packs, including a lead pipe that brought gas into our apartment. The kitchen was our workroom. In the morning Alfred would take the dried packs of glued paper to the factory. In the evening he would return with new reams of tissue paper.

Our subtenant left for work very early each morning. One morning when he awoke the apartment was filled with gas. He shouted for us to get up. He was afraid we were dead. The weight of the freshly glued packs of tissue paper caused the wire which we used for hanging to cut through the gas pipe. Our subtenant turned off the gas and opened all the windows. We were alive. From then on, we were careful.

Two people, unhappy with their jobs, decide to switch. I do not know what happened to the person who took over my mother's task of making baby clothes. I do know that the job exchange not only made my mother happier in the short term but in the long term ordained our family's future.

My parents appreciated their good fortune in the job switch, my mother perhaps sooner than my father. They learned to make magic fans and other honeycomb objects—objects that delighted the eye, were a bit mystifying and were used on celebratory occasions—work that wasn't politically or culturally contingent. They were able to take the skill they acquired in making these objects wherever life's opportunities took them. It enabled them to have some economic freedom, even if in a very small niche ... and even if risky. They did not have to depend on others but could rely on themselves ... success or failure would be in their own hands.

The knowledge and skills needed to make honeycomb decorations formed the foundation on which our family would operate for the next half century. It also formed one of the images of Sweden that I carry around to this day, that of reams of tissue paper on top of the kitchen table, being glued, sheet by sheet.

I also have other recollections of Sweden, at least I think they are recollections. Who knows when memory begins? I arrived in Sweden as a four months old baby. I left as a three and a half-year-old child. Perhaps some of my memories have been generated by overheard conversations. Other memories are possibly duplicate images my mind has created from old photographs. Still other memories may be products of my imagination, influenced by who knows what. Yet all have some connection, however colored, to events that actually took place around me. Whatever the source, to this day I carry assorted images of our life in Sweden. Some are more focused than others:

10. A New Life: Joys and Worries

The "magic fan" that my parents learned to make in Sweden provided the foundation for our lifelong family business. A sample of that original magic fan no longer exists. At some point, I don't know when, we stopped making magic fans and instead concentrated on making tissue balls, bells and such other honeycomb decorations. The magic fans shown here resemble our product but only as rough approximations. These are made in China. I found them on eBay, offered by a Florida seller (photograph by Margus Välja).

A blackout, when all curtains in our apartment had to be tightly shut and lights throughout the city were turned off.

An image, obviously based on photographs, conversations and the Treiman family guest book rather than actual memory, of my christening on a rooftop. Arvo Horm and Aksel Linkhorst were my joint godfathers and Vilja Uustalu was my godmother. Also present was the well-known artist Eduard "Ed" Ole, who lived with us for a time. These names would, over the years, come up in my parents' conversations over and over again.

My mother related, with a shudder how, immediately following the rooftop christening ceremony, I was held upside down over the side of the rooftop apparently either as a good luck charm or a joke.

I see my father and me walking in a tree-lined area near our apartment building, my father with a small axe in hand. We are looking for a Christmas tree. We find one. My father cuts it. As we drag it back toward our apartment a Swede comes out of his house, yelling. My father has cut down a tree from the Swede's front yard, thinking it was part of the forest and available to everyone. An often-told family story may well be the source of this memory.

I remember playing outside our apartment building, finding a brick, playing with the brick and then having it slip from my hands and gash my knee. With blood streaming down my leg, I run upstairs to our apartment where my mother patches my wound and soothes me. She then takes me to the store across the street and buys me candy. I still have a scar on my knee. I still like candy.

I recall playing on the side of the hill, near the building where the Horm's apartment was located. I was with my best friend forever, Anne-Mari. I slip and go into an uncontrolled, downhill slide. I feel as though I am falling into an abyss. I grab something and desperately hold on to whatever-it-was. Anne-Mari and I both scream. Help comes.

My best friend forever, Anne-Mari Horm, and me. "Forever" turned out to be finite. After we left Sweden, my parents stayed in touch with the Horms; Anne-Mari and I did not. We saw each other only once more, at the World-Wide Estonian Days celebrated in Stockholm in 1980 (Treiman family archive).

My mother and I often went to meet my father at the nearby bus or streetcar station when he returned from work. One time he came home early. I remember telling him in no uncertain terms that he had to go back to the station so we could go meet him.

I think I recall overhearing a discussion between my parents about how to get to Australia—whether to travel east or west. The eastern route would be on one of the world's last passenger sailing vessels, sailing around Africa's Cape Horn. Later I am told that the vessel had ship-wrecked off the coast of Africa. I haven't been able to confirm this memory. Nevertheless, it remains stored in my memory bank.

My mother, Maarja Horm, Anne-Mari and I are in a taxi on our way to the train station. There we will catch a train to Gothenburg and the ship that will take us to New York.

10. A New Life: Joys and Worries

Anne-Mari and I have a vehement argument about whether a building the taxi drove past was or was not a fire station. I said it was. She insisted it was not. Even today, I'm convinced I was right!

All these memories are blurred. They belong to a child barely old enough to have memories. Yet amongst these and other images, the image that repeats over-and-over again is one I see through the haze of Goethe's Faust at the Walpurgis Night celebration—an image of people whose faces I cannot make out, raucously circulating in smoke filled rooms with drinks in hand, engaged in unintelligible conversation. Uprooted people seeking certainty in uncertain surroundings.

11

Uncertainty

"...it is Sweden's wish that refugees return to their homes."

By the summer of 1945 the war in Europe was over. My parents and many other refugees had begun to adapt to life in Sweden. Normality seemed within grasp even as they continued to keep a wary eye on whose army had liberated what territories and an equally wary eye on the continuing meetings between America, the Soviet Union and Great Britain. Suddenly, their hopes for normality became fantasy.

> *His Royal Majesty has instructed the National Commission on Foreigners to announce that every Baltic refugee may return to his country at no cost. Soviet Russia has publicly declared that every returning refugee will be able to return home. Refugees can notify their nearest police authority or the corresponding Baltic refugee camp commander of their decision to repatriate. Following the notification, the refugee will be given further instructions. The Commission has also been instructed to emphasize that although there is no compulsion, it is Sweden's wish that refugees return to their homes.*
>
> *In addition, His Royal Majesty has ordered the National Commission on Foreigners, acting through camp commanders, through staff serving in the*

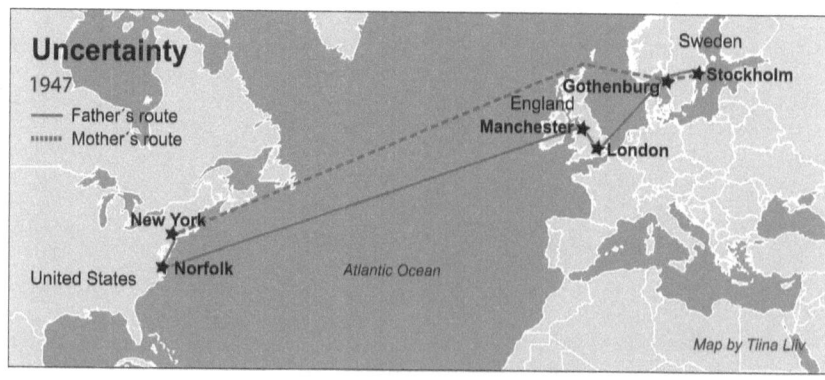

Departing separately from Sweden in 1947, the Treiman family reunited in New York (Map by Tiina Liiv).

11. Uncertainty

camps and through other persons working with refugees, to reiterate previously announced rules that under no circumstances are attempts to influence refugees not to return to their country permitted. Baltic refugees who are not within the jurisdiction of a refugee camp, are further notified that they are not permitted to engage in any political propaganda in Sweden.
National Commission on Foreigners

Mother: *This letter scared us. We received it twice, in June and again in July 1945. The first time it was written in Estonian; the second time in Swedish. All our friends received the same letter. Alfred and I decided that we had to find a new home, outside of Sweden, where the Soviet tentacles could not reach us.*

At the end of World War II, Soviet military controlled most of Eastern Europe and the Baltic States. The status of people who had fled from those areas was precarious. My parents and most other Baltic and East European refugees gave no credence to Soviet assurances that they could go home without risking their lives or freedom.

Estonians had lived within the Soviet police state. They had experienced the mass deportations of 1941. As my mother described earlier, "It was a terrible time. A person couldn't be real. One had to be either silent or lie. Who is or isn't your friend?" Few wanted to live lives bereft of freedom.

Starting with the early war years, Sweden's actions had dovetailed with Soviet policy. In the summer of 1940, the Swedish government acceded to Moscow's demand that the Estonian, Latvian and Lithuanian embassies in Stockholm be surrendered. This effectively affirmed the Soviet contention that Estonians, Latvians and Lithuanians had willingly chosen to have their countries become an integral part of the Soviet Union. It seemed to follow that not only in Soviet eyes but also in Swedish eyes, Baltic refugees were Soviet citizens.

Sweden was not an outlier. As part of the February 1945 Yalta Conference Roosevelt, Churchill and Stalin agreed, among other items, that all Soviet citizens would be returned to the Soviet Union. Their agreement included not only Soviet prisoners of war but all Soviet citizens, whether or not they wished to be returned. While not a party to the Yalta Agreement, Sweden was a fellow traveler.

On June 2, 1945, Moscow demanded that Sweden extradite all Soviet citizens who had fought with the Germans. According to Moscow's definition, based on its annexation of Estonia, all Estonians were Soviet citizens. Any Estonian who had fought against the Soviet occupation was, as far as Moscow was concerned, a traitor and subject to extradition. The Soviet Embassy in Stockholm broadened Moscow's demand to include all Estonian refugees regardless of military service. The Swedish Communist Party echoed the Soviet embassy's demand.

Shortly after those demands were made, the Swedish government sent their letter urging Baltic refugees to return to Estonia. Then, as if to prove the adage that actions speak louder than words, in January 1946 Sweden extradited, at gunpoint, 150 Latvians and Estonians to the Soviet Union. Estonian refugees were shaken by Sweden's willingness to accede to Soviet demands. Some, including my parents, decided it was best to leave Sweden.

My parents weighed their options. America was their preferred choice; they applied for permanent residency. But, the length of time before their application would be acted on and the limited number of refugees America was willing to admit, were major drawbacks. My mother and father considered and rejected a move to the Dominican Republic, which had issued them an entry visa.

My parents decided to move to Australia—a country distant from the Soviet Union where economic opportunities seemed to exist. Obtaining an entry visa to Australia was relatively fast. Australia's Labor government had begun to recognize the need to increase the country's postwar population. Australia's past practice of limiting immigration primarily to the British was no longer a viable option. "Populate or perish" was a common slogan. The government was ready to accept "…any white aliens who can be assimilated and contribute satisfactorily to economic development…."

My parents' decision was made before Australia began to accept displaced persons under the International Refugee Organization's resettlement program. My mother, father and I would immigrate to Australia as ordinary immigrants, not as DPs. My father had found an Estonian in Australia to act as our sponsor—Aleksander Selg.

My mother's narrative leaves the impression that the Swedish letter that urged their return to Estonia and our move to Australia followed each other in short order. In fact, there was more than a year and a half gap between the two events. I can only speculate as to the reasons. Certainly, the fact that the move required preparation was one reason. A new country willing to receive them had to be found, money had to be raised, documents obtained and passage booked. Personal belongings had to either be disposed of or packed and shipped.

My mother had no passport. The still functioning Estonian Embassy in London mailed her a temporary passport. When that passport expired on January 11, 1947, shortly before she and I were scheduled to leave, it was extended for a year in a handwritten note entered in the passport, and signed by their friend Heinrich Laretei, Estonia's ambassador to Sweden before Sweden shut the embassy. Laretei made the extension look official by placing the embassy seal next to his handwritten extension. The British Legation in Stockholm issued a "Landing Permit" for our family's entry into Australia and placed it inside the temporary passport.

11. Uncertainty

As my mother acquired the necessary documents, the Estonian Maritime Union office in Stockholm certified, probably with a wink, that my father was a qualified ship's steward second class. The certificate was authenticated by one of my godfathers, "A. Linkhorst Attaché at the former Estonian Legation in Stockholm."

Mother: *We submitted our application to come to America. Under the quota system* ["The Immigration Act of 1924 limited the number of immigrants allowed entry into the United States through a national origins quota. The quota provided immigration visas to two percent of the total number of people of each nationality in the United States as of the 1890 national census."—Office of the Historian, U.S. State Department.] *we would have had to wait many years. We didn't want to wait. We could go to Australia immediately. We seized the opportunity. We began to make plans. "How and when?" "By ship. Right away!"*

At the beginning of 1947 we booked passage for Australia on an old American warship, the Marine Phoenix. *She was scheduled to leave for Australia from San Francisco in the middle of May. We hoped to reach San Francisco by then. How to get there?*

Our route would take us from Stockholm to New York and then New York to San Francisco. We had enough money for Jaak and me to book passage on a ship to New York. Alfred was able to hire on as a steward on board a British ship scheduled to sail from Manchester, England, to Norfolk, Virginia. There, Alfred planned to jump ship hoping that by that time Jaak and I would have arrived in New York.

My father hired on as a ship's steward on board the *S.S. Nicaragua*, scheduled to sail to the United States from Manchester, England. Several of my father's letters suggest that the *Nicaragua* was originally scheduled to sail for New York.

> *They say that we will be on our way to New York in a couple of days.*
> *The ship was supposed to load with coal yesterday so it could immediately start for New York....*
> *We loaded coal all day and it is reasonable to believe that at the latest on Monday or Tuesday we will be on our way to New York.*

On the other hand, in her narrative my mother writes as though Norfolk, Virginia, was always the *Nicaragua's* destination. Regardless, after crossing the Atlantic, the *Nicaragua* docked in Norfolk, some 400 miles from New York, where my father was supposed to meet my mother and me.

Ill with a fever, my father had left Stockholm for Manchester, leaving my mother to take care of the final preparations. He carried a guilty conscience along with a suitcase packed by my mother—a suitcase that

Before leaving Sweden, my parents booked passage on a ship scheduled to sail from San Francisco to Sydney even though they didn't have sufficient funds to get from Stockholm to San Francisco. My father left Gothenburg for Manchester on the steamship *Britannia*, pictured here, to work his way to America as a ship's steward on the steamship *Nicaragua*. His sea contract with the *Nicaragua* required him to serve a full voyage: Manchester to America, America to Belgium and back to America. There was no certainty that he would be able to jump ship in America during the ship's first layover and join my mother and me in New York. Even if my father succeeded in leaving the *Nicaragua* and meeting us in New York, how we would get from New York to San Francisco was yet to be determined. Our life was a mixture of uncertainties and hope (Treiman family archive).

included food (bread and honey) and a delicacy my mother had sneaked into the suitcase—oranges. He traveled by train from Stockholm to Gothenburg. There he boarded the London-bound steamship *Britannia*. Built in 1929 the *Britannia* offered thrice weekly service from Gothenburg across the North Sea, to London.

From London my father went by train to Manchester, offering commentary along the way. Once in Manchester, he boarded the former troopship S.S. *Nicaragua* as a steward.

With time on his hands, my father contemplated, worried and wrote. His letters convey multiple personas. He was a reporter, describing London, the British countryside and his shipboard surroundings and official duties. He was a cheerleader, urging my mother to be strong even as he expressed regret over leaving her to fend for herself. He was the man in charge, telling my mother what to do and who to speak with. He was a man afraid. If he was unable to jump ship once it docked in America he would have to continue as a crew member to the ship's next destination, Belgium, even as my mother and I would presumably be traveling to Australia.

11. Uncertainty

On February 2, 1947, while crossing the North Sea toward London, my father composed a letter:

Dear Wife and Little Son Jaak,
For the past night, and half of the following day, the steamship Britannia *has been sailing the North Sea toward England. The waters have been stormy. High waves toss the ship up and down. Relatively few people were at the breakfast service. Most are probably seasick. My stomach is not queasy and the fever I had when I boarded is completely gone. Wise men say that a change of scenery will cure any Stockholm illness.*

I am alone in the ship's large dining hall as I write this letter. After mealtime the dining hall converts to a salon. My dear wife and son, I am thinking of you as I sit here. I so wish that I could be with you, helping with the preparations for your trip.

The train from Stockholm arrived in Gothenburg at 3:00pm. The shipping company's bus was waiting for us and took us to our ship. Another bus had already brought our luggage to customs and my luggage was waiting for me when my bus arrived. The first stop at the customs house is passport control. This only takes a few minutes. Next is luggage control. There the luggage must be opened but that is more of a formality. After that, the luggage is taken to your cabin. I boarded my ship a few minutes before five.

I have a pretty good cabin that I share with another man. It turns out that my ticket includes dining privileges. Dear wife, the food you packed for me is so bountiful. I am so sorry that you aren't here to share it. And, you tricked me with the oranges! Many thanks to you for all your troubles. Also, everything else packed in my suitcase has been packed so well and so handily that I lack nothing.

We will reach London tomorrow around 10:00am. I will post this letter then. From London there will be a 6 to 7-hour train ride to my ship. I hope your letter will be waiting for me when I arrive. That would be a great comfort to me, the person who once more left his dear wife and son alone to struggle with difficulties. Please forgive me. When I see you again, I want to hug both of you, kiss you and feel both your hands around my neck.

It is 9:00 o'clock already and I will soon go to sleep. I spent the day inside. I looked through the window at the sea covered with whitecaps. I had a series of thoughts about both of you—Jaak on the doorstep of our apartment; you, dear, on the station platform; both of you together, bustling around at home. Continue to be good, eat well and sleep properly. You will then be strong for your trip. If you have any spare time from all your hassles, write a few words to me every day. I don't yet know how quickly letters will arrive but when I do receive them, I will be very happy. I close, thinking of you and wishing you both a good night. Kisses, kisses and hugs to both of you.
Father

Two days later, February 4, 1947, having reached Manchester, my father continued to update his travel report. He digressed briefly for practical issues, referring to Johannes Kaiv, the Estonian Consul General in New York, and to Aleksander Selg, my parents' sponsor in Australia.

Hello Dear Wife and Little Jaak,
I am writing to you from Manchester. Perhaps you have received the letter I wrote from the North Sea?

I met a vacationing Estonian couple named Toomingas from Southwest Africa—an area that is experiencing a gold rush. The husband is a chemist. Every year they are given tickets to Europe and a three to four-month vacation. Without those benefits they would be unable to tolerate the conditions and the climate.

My first impression of London was wretched. Black and dirty, perpetual mud, poorly dressed people, bombed-out houses. Along the way, we stopped at a restaurant, where they fed us. The food was heavily peppered rabbit—yet I thought it was tasty.

At 3:00pm we returned to the train and continued our journey to Manchester. During the train ride I peered through the window to try and see what England looked like. Because of the fog and the falling blotches of snow, visibility was limited. From what I could see, the English countryside was pretty. The landscape reminded me a little of southern Estonia. The ground was covered with snow. I could see herds of animals, especially sheep. Endless rows of houses that looked like rabbit cages lined the roads. Coal dust was everywhere—I don't think I would like to live here.

We arrived in Manchester around 8:00pm. A bus took us to the ship, which was still docked. The ship's name is S.S. Nicaragua. It is pretty large—it takes some effort to walk from one end to the other. It has just been repainted but it is still dirty all over—there is a lot of clean-ups left to be done. Most of the men sleep at the rear of the ship, the officers in the front. I have a cabin all to myself at the middle of the ship.

I have yet to find out exactly what I will be doing. Today I helped set the table for the officers (five people) and performed housekeeping duties in the second mate's cabin. The ship has a fixed dining schedule: Coffee is at 6:30 in the morning, breakfast at 8:30, lunch at 12, coffee at 2:30 and dinner at 5:30. I assume I will be serving the gentlemen. We speak a mix of Swedish-English with the officers, who are all Norwegians.

Today the ship will leave the dock to load up with coal. I am told that in a couple of days we will be on our way to New York. That makes me very happy. I will arrive before you and perhaps I can actually meet you when you get there.

I wrote a letter to [the Estonian Consul General in New York] Kaiv. I explained our situation and asked him to assist you in America. For myself I sought advice and help in finding a place to stay. I also wrote to Aleksander Selg in Australia bringing him current on our current circumstances.

I would be happy about how things are progressing here if I only knew that everything was going well for you at home. You are a strong woman. You have overcome difficulties before. May you have strength and good spirits to overcome all obstacles.

I am now a Steward II—it doesn't look like the work will break my back. It's a different story for the sailors working on deck and in the engine room. I plan to study my English a little more. Jaak is probably getting ready for bed—perhaps sitting on the toilet, writing his father a letter. Good night to both of you.

> Good bye,
> Father
> Address: A.T. s.s. Nicaragua, c/o
> Lambert Bros, Cunard House, 88,
> Leadenhall Street, London EC3

In a postscript to his February 4 letter my father said he had found his address book and gave my mother contact information for Linkhorst, Veske, Laid and Laretei in Sweden and Aleksander Selg in Australia. He noted that packages to Australia should be addressed to "Valentine Treiman c/o Selg."

Dear Wife and Little Jaak,

Again, I have finished my day's work. I sit in my hut and think about the two of you. I am so sad—I have not yet received your letter. Not knowing what you are doing and how things are going is heart wrenching. Are you still well? Were you able to raise some money? I couldn't post my last letter until this evening and this also makes me sad. We are on the road that fate has given us. We will try to push on, you there and me here. The ship was supposed to load coal yesterday so it could get started for New York. That hasn't happened, even today. Now they are saying we will leave on Friday, but that's not certain either. I hope that at the very latest we leave on Monday. That way I will arrive a few days before you. It would be so nice to be able to meet you when your ship docks! Right now, I can't think of anything better.

My immediate supervisor is a 68 year old, very sympathetic Norwegian. Together we carry boxes of equipment here and there, we give bread, butter, sugar and milk to the men and food supplies to the cooks.

Little Jaak would have a lot to do here. He could climb high up on the masts or down the numerous stairs to where the machines are.

It would be very nice if your letter arrives tomorrow. I am so waiting for it. My health is very good. Don't worry about me. If there is time, I will visit the city tomorrow. I will then write both of you, telling you what I saw. Think good thoughts about your husband-father and cross your fingers that we will meet in New York and stay together from there.

Father

Dearest, when you write, tell me when you are scheduled to arrive in New York.

Another letter from Manchester followed, dated February 7, 1947:

Dear wife and dear son,

Today was a good day for your father. I received the letter you wrote on September 3 [?]. Reading each line of that letter gave me such warm feelings and made me feel so good. As you fight hardships and as you overcome each one that arises, I hope your joy of life and your love for me will continue on and on. I am always with you in my thoughts and ask only that everything goes well.

Today our ship moved away from the dock. We loaded coal all day and it is reasonable to believe that at the latest on Monday or Tuesday we will be on our way to New York. If only I could receive one more letter from you telling me that you have somehow succeeded, that there are no more obstacles to your travel, then I could be sincerely happy. I know that we will be re-united and we will then enjoy the sweetness of again being together.

Dear Jaak, continue to be a good boy to your mother and help when you can—you must now also stand in for your father. When we are together again then I will tell you everything that I did and saw on the ship.

I have very little writing paper. In fact, this is my only sheet. I can't buy any and borrowing is difficult. Because of that I can't send you a very long letter and I can't make drawings. All day I work on the ship and at night it is very dark and the stores are closed. Truthfully, here there aren't any stores because we are quite far from the city. Yesterday I wanted to go to the city but it was snowing. I therefore walked around the docks and thought of you and mother.

Dear wife, from here I can't give you any advice or help. I am mad at myself for not being able to arrange things differently. You were left there alone with all the difficulties. Please forgive me—I will never do that again.

Keep up your joy of life, even in the face of big difficulties. When you are finally on board your ship, then relax and eat. If you feel seasickness even then eat. You will feel a lot better.

Your loving father.

After my father left Stockholm, my mother had two weeks in which to close our life in Sweden and make final arrangements for the move to Australia. She tried, not very successfully, to raise money by selling a few personal belongings. She sought funding from some agencies. My parents had decided, at my mother's insistence, that once in Australia they would try to earn their livelihood by making honeycomb decorations. With that in mind, essential supplies such as tissue paper were shipped directly to Australia from Sweden—a gamble on their future.

Neither my mother's narrative nor her surviving letters dwell on the details of what she had to do to prepare for our voyage to New York. In her narrative she does mention the transfer of our apartment to Bishop Kõpp and his wife. I believe this took place before my father left.

Mother: *We gave our apartment to Bishop Johan Kõpp and his wife, Maria. Bishop Kõpp was head of the Estonian Evangelical Lutheran Church. They moved in right away but we continued to use one room until we left Sweden. Jaak and the Bishop had a good time together. Bishop Kõpp had an exceptionally loving personality. He understood people—children and adults. His wife was the personification of love and kindness.*

A brief summary of some of the difficulties she had to overcome is contained in my mother's February 13, 1947, letter to my father, written just hours before we left Stockholm.

Dear husband,

It is 2:00am at night, prior to the day of our departure. I am stumbling around like a ghost. Finally, I actually believe we will leave tomorrow. Everything should now be in order. Money was a very big problem. Luggage cost 380 kronor. The ticket to Australia required 200 kronor more. The ticket to America, 100 kronor.

Now they are all paid. I did not get the funding support from Flütningsnend. I will arrive in America with a couple of kronor in my packet.

These are all just headlines. When I see you, I will tell you the full story. As always, Jaak talks about you every day, misses you and pretends he is you.

Hopefully, I will be able to survive all this to the end.

All the best, kisses, hugs from both of us.

Good bye,
Mother

11. Uncertainty

Mother: *Jaak and I left Stockholm on February 14, 1947. The morning we were to leave I was out of bed before the alarm went off. I couldn't sleep. Jaak was also excited. Our ship sailed from Gothenburg. We would get there by train. Mrs. Kõpp had laid out a full breakfast table for us. I wasn't hungry. I just drank a cup of coffee.*

The Kõpps, Jaak and I bid an ardent farewell. Even the bishop's eyes were wet as he hugged Jaak. Auntie Kõpp came down to the street to see us off. A taxi was waiting to take us to the railroad station to board the train for Gothenburg. Our friends were already at the station, waiting to bid us farewell. Gathered were Ida Poom, the Muld family, Veske, Linkhorst, Roop, Liberik, Eerik Laid, Jaak's godmother Vilja Uustalu with her husband, Evald. All of us had tears in our eyes. We were refugees—one family. The train started to move. Our hands waved final goodbyes. Soon the people faded from sight.

I felt as though I was riding the wind, carrying us to unknown parts of the world. My heart ached. It felt as though someone with an iron hand had compressed my heart into a tiny fragment. The pain from my heart reached my throat which hurt so much that my face wrinkled with tears.

There were no tears when I left my homeland. There was only a wish to get far away from the terror, to get to the free world, to see my husband again. This time it was hard to leave, to leave friends and travel to an unknown land.

12

New York

"I will jump ship at the first opportunity."

Mother: *The ship left Gothenburg early in the morning. It was very cold. The ship plowed through banks of ice. My cabin was at the bottom of the ship. The way the ship rolled made me seasick. Four year old Jaak was good. He looked after me. I don't remember how long the trip took. It seemed as though forever.*

My mother and I were booked on the *Drottningholm*, a transatlantic ocean liner launched in 1904 as *RMS Virginian*. The *Drottningholm* and her sister ship were the first steam turbine liners on the North Atlantic. Because she tended to roll in the waves like a roller coaster, she had earned the nickname "Rollingholm" or "Rollinghome." In 1944 she was used by the Red Cross to transport prisoners of war and civilians being repatriated from Germany to the United Kingdom and Sweden.

My mother's description of our February 1947 departure and voyage to New York is short. Another *Drottningholm* passenger, Ruth L. Weiss Hohberg, sailed on the *Drottningholm* on the voyage that followed ours, less than a month later. In her book, *Getting Here: An Odyssey Through World War II*, she left a more detailed description of her experience.

> Tourist class turned out to be below the waterline, the tiny inside cabin accommodated four, and the bunk cots were narrow.
>
> My parents arranged train transportation to the port of Goteborg. We would board the ship before midnight on March 14th [1947]. In addition to mother and me, there were two other women in the tight little inside cabin that had lower and upper bunks on each side…. My most vivid memory of that voyage … remains the dreadful weather and the awful seasickness that afflicted me for nine consecutive days with varying degrees of severity.
>
> At night, when there was no passenger activity, outside sounds became enhanced. A major Atlantic winter storm was raging in our path. Riding it out during the night we could feel and hear every vibration and shudder of the engines in the icy water, the whack of the waves against the hull, the rolling of the ship in the endless, wildly churning expanse. When daylight came

12. New York

The *Drottningholm*, a ship that had once carried one of the great actresses of classic cinema, Greta Garbo, brought my mother and me from Sweden to New York. The waters of the North Atlantic were rough and our ship was infamous for riding waves like a roller coaster. My mother was seasick for most of the voyage (Treiman family archive).

the sky and the water were a steely gray with no hint of sunshine, the wind was still howling, and the waves were crashing high over the deck, inundating it in a freezing cold seawater that sloshed back and forth with the rolling of the ship. We were tossed way up in the air, and then plummeted down rapidly with the most ominous creaking sounds. The icy rain was lashing sideways. It felt as if our toy boat would break apart into splinters at any moment. The horizon bounced up and down, and so did my insides.

… I was much too seasick to appreciate anything.…

When mother coaxed me to come up to the deck for some fresh air, the horizon line was not where it should be; it kept changing its height relative to the ship's tilt. I couldn't get back to my bunk to lie down fast enough. I still feel that awful, queasy feeling in my stomach when I think of that crossing. I swore that I would never set foot on a ship again.

Late one night most of the dishes on the tables set for breakfast slid to the floor of the dining room with one prolonged loud crash. They were swept from their places by waves tossing the ship from side to side with abrupt lifts and falls that seemed endless. I lay in the upper bunk holding on to its edge tightly for fear of being tossed off in one of its heavings. I think my body was still moving upward when the abrupt downward motion began. Then suddenly the whirr of the engines stopped. All was quiet, but the motion of the ship hitting the waves continued, and it seemed the banging against the hull was even more violent. I thought for sure this was the end of our story. The following day we found out that the engines had been turned off as a safety precaution while we waited out the storm.

Carried by a Magic Fan

It was late February 1947 when the *Drottningholm* docked in New York. Though I have no memories of New York from that time, history books tell me that the port was unkempt, in need of refurbishment. The rest of the city was at the apex of its post–World War II prominence. It was one of the world's few metropolitan areas untouched by the War's devastation. The aurora of the "Wonder City," as it was then referred to, was palpable.

The Statue of Liberty offered hope to new arrivals, though I have no recollection of seeing it as we sailed into port. The Empire State Building was a world wonder. The gray, concrete and steel canyon known as Wall Street was renowned as an international finance center. America's print and media hub was headquartered in an expanding Rockefeller Center. New York's American Museum of Natural History, Harlem and Central Park were simultaneously real and mythical. Its subway system was still "spic and span." The Brooklyn Dodgers had a new rookie, Jackie Robinson.

Broadway's ticker tape parades were world famous, as was its annual Fifth Avenue Easter Parade. Bruno Walter conducted at Carnegie Hall;

Mother and I arrived in New York in February 1947. While I have flashes of memory about our *Drottningholm* voyage, except for visions generated by old photographs, I have no memories of our stay in New York as we waited for my father and hoped that he would be able to join us. Here, we are on a New York sidewalk, possibly around the area where we lodged, in Queens (Treiman family archive).

12. New York

Toscanini at Radio City. *A Streetcar Named Desire* would premiere on Broadway later that year. Arthur Miller's *All My Sons* had just opened. *Brigadoon* and *Finian's Rainbow* also premiered that year. *Oklahoma* continued to extend its record run.

The students in New York's public high schools included four future Nobel laureates. E.L. Doctorow and William Safire were also in attendance.

My mother and I stayed in Queens, waiting and hoping to reunite with my father. I don't know how much of New York's texture we experienced, but old photographs show us visiting the natural history museum and standing on a New York sidewalk. Perhaps we visited the Estonian Consulate General in Rockefeller Center.

Mother: *It was evening when we arrived in New York. We disembarked into a large, warehouse-size building filled with people and luggage. I stood there, holding Jaak's hand, not knowing what to do. Suddenly a young woman stood next to me and introduced herself. Her name was Leida. How on earth did she get here? How did she know I was coming? Dear Vilja Uustalu, Jaak's godmother, had arranged everything.*

Leida had found a place for us to stay. She took us to the home of an elderly bachelor. Now we could wash and eat and try to figure out how to contact father. Has his ship arrived in Norfolk? I did not know what had happened to him. I sent him a letter but I wasn't sure he would receive it. I contacted the Estonian Consulate in New York and told them where Jaak and I were staying. I knew that was the only way father could find us.

Shortly after our arrival in New York, we received a telegram from my father, in Norfolk trapped on board the *Nicaragua*. The same day, February 27, 1947, my mother wrote a short reply.

Dear husband,

The bearer of this letter is Captain Küün, He lived on the same street with us. He was with the first small boat on which you came. Perhaps you should speak with him about how to get off the ship. I have spoken with someone who thinks you can remain here and nothing will happen. Kaiv promised with great certainty that he can get you a transit document.

Jaak and I were very worried about you. Today we received your telegram and immediately our mood got better. There have been many difficulties. There is much to talk about. We wait for you with much longing. We are always thinking about you.

Your wife and little son with kisses and hugs until we meet.
1826 124 Street c/o Bock New York.

On March 3 my father wrote to Mother from Norfolk. He included a promise that combined irony, understatement and an Estonian sense

Someone, I don't know who, showed my mother and me around New York and took the pictures now stored in the family archives. Here, Mother and I visit New York's American Museum of Natural History (Treiman family archive).

of humor. He would "try whatever is possible to become rich"—in other words, to get the money needed to travel to New York.

> *Dear wife and little Jaak!*
>
> *My earlier letter has not been mailed because it was impossible to do so. Circumstances here are very confusing and difficult. In all probability the captain is suspicious of the Estonian crew members. He is afraid we will jump ship once the ship docks.*
>
> *Just now we sailed closer to the dock. Tomorrow we are supposed to begin loading coal. This will take 10 hours. Wages have not yet been paid. I hope we will be paid some time tomorrow morning. Then we can go ashore for a little while to make purchases. If loading the coal begins right away in the morning then we will finish sometime after*

12. New York

lunch. *Personally, I hope to receive a few dozen dollars and then go ashore. Anyway, the captain promised that I could go to use the telephone. I will then try whatever is possible to become rich.*

Dear, if my plan is unsuccessful, then I can probably only send you a few dozen meager dollars (probably 80) and pray that you will be able to make do alone. Dear, my heart aches constantly when I think of that possibility—I will do everything to make sure that does not happen. That should not, in the end, be harder than my return trip to Estonia and the risks aren't the same.

This will succeed, I am firmly convinced, if I get enough money together to even buy a part-way ticket. In that case I would travel to Baltimore and look to the chairman of the Estonian society there.

If my plan is not successful then please, I ask you dear and little Jaak, please continue to think well of your father. I will still reach you within a couple of months and I will then make it up as much as possible with hugs and tenderness.

Write to Aleksander Selg in Australia.

The ship's return cruise is to Belgium and then back to America.

If we are separated, I don't know how you will arrange your life in Australia. I will write to Selg and will send him my wages, which aren't much—only 20 pounds a month. But let us maintain our determination and peace of mind. We are comforted that we are at least still young enough not to be overwhelmed. If we could do it over, we would not repeat our mistakes and recklessness—but dear—we can't change what has been done.

No! I must get to you and I will do so.

I will mail this letter in the morning, as soon as I can and during the day, I will write a new letter. Believe me dear, everything will go well.

In my thoughts I hold both of you on my lap and hug and kiss you so hard, so hard. Both of you do the same.

Loving you both,
Father

Just as my mother had promised earlier, my father received a letter, dated March 4, 1947, from Captain Küün. The captain asked a series of questions.

Mr. Treiman,

I am in receipt of a letter from New York, written by your wife. She advised me that you will arrive in Norfolk around March 3. I was aware of your ship's arrival here but I was unable to send my letter earlier. Your wife explained your circumstances and asked if there was some way I could help you. I now have a few questions.

Do you have a transit visa? Did you hire on only for the voyage from Europe to the USA? Does the captain know you want to leave the ship?

Reply right away. Also, try to find out how long the ship will remain in Norfolk. Once I have received your letter, hopefully by March 6, I will try to travel to Norfolk and we can speak at length.

Respectfully,
A. Küün

I do not have a copy of my father's reply to Küün. Neither do I know what role, if any, Küün had in my father's departure from the *Nicaragua*.

Father's March 4 letter to my mother, written before he could have received Küün's letter, offers snippets of insight into what transpired.

> *Dear wife,*
>
> We have been anchored, in a queue, since Sunday night. We are waiting our turn to begin loading. Perhaps it will be another week before I am able to go ashore. No one knows the exact timing.
>
> Forgive me dear, that I have made you a part of so many difficulties. I know your situation is desperate. You are without money and in an inhospitable environment. Were it possible I would swim to shore, the sooner to be with you and little Jaak. I asked the captain if he would let me visit New York. He would not. Much less would he agree to me leaving the ship for good. Now, I will jump ship at the first opportunity. Dear, continue to exert yourself and hold fast. I will come as soon as I possibly can. And believe, everything will be alright.
>
> Be so good and talk to people in New York about our business plans. Initially, we could make at least 100,000 pieces per month. I don't know the cost of materials and labor in America but I think we could make them for 4–5 cents each. Whoever has any business sense should be able to grasp the concept.
>
> Dear, please write to me. My address is:
> Mr. A.T.
> S/S Nicaragua
> Smokeless Fuel Co
> Norfolk, Va
>
> Since I plan to leave the ship without permission, do not put your address on the letter. I will continue to write to Mr. Kaiv at the Estonian Consulate. As soon as I get ashore, I will try to telephone the consulate. While at sea I sent Mr. Kaiv a telegram. Unfortunately, I have not received a reply.
>
> Just before I jump ship I will write again. Let us comfort ourselves that sunny days follow cloudy days. I so long for you both. Wait for me. Hugs.
>
> > Hugging you and little Jaak
> > Father

I do not know how my father got off the ship. Neither do I know how he made it to New York or whether his arrival sometime during the week of March 16 was truly a complete surprise. What we have is my mother's narrative.

Mother: *A week passed; then another. One morning Alfred found us. Jaak had just woken up when father walked in the door. Jaak screamed, "Isa, terrrrre [tere]" [father, hello!]. Until that moment Jaak had been unable to make the sound of a drilled letter "r." Now he couldn't stop saying it. He had a lot to tell his father.*

13

America to Australia

"The passport control people even wished us a good trip."

Once our family reunited, our distressed financial condition became the next immediate concern. Except for the few kronor my mother brought with her from Sweden and whatever dollars my father may have had left after traveling from Norfolk to New York, they did not have the money to pay for travel to San Francisco. The narrative states the essence of their immediate problem:

Mother: *Now we began to plan our travel to San Francisco. Where can we get money to buy bus tickets? We learned of an organization that helps*

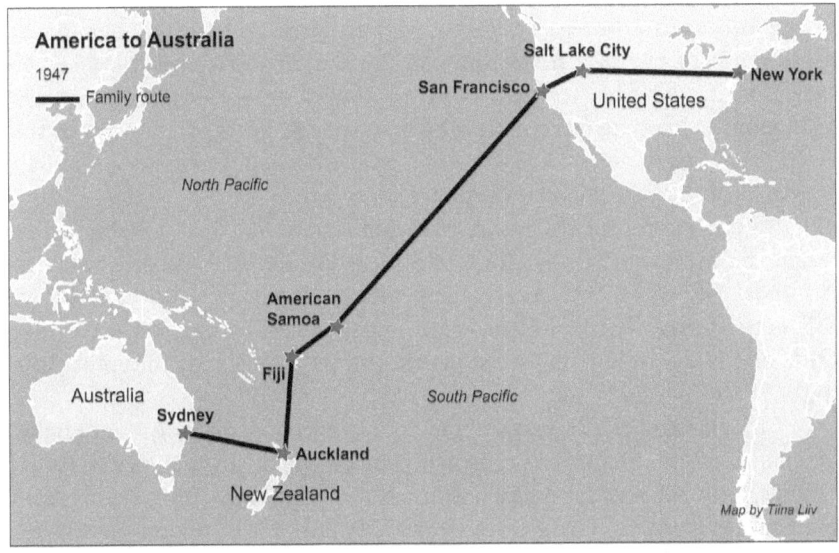

We continued our journey by crossing the North American continent and then sailing to Australia with stops at a few islands in the South Pacific (map by Tiina Liiv).

refugees—*Relief Committee. We turned to them and received two bus tickets for San Francisco. Jaak could travel for free.*

In a May 13, 1947, letter to Arvo Horm, my father described additional assistance they received:

> *I will address a question that you and many others are curious about—and about which not enough has been written. Namely, how did we subsist; how did we cover our travel expenses in America? Travel alone from San Francisco to Sydney cost us $1,000.*
>
> *In brief, we turned to a Baptist organization in New York that was recommended by a New York Estonian. In the morning we told people at the organization that I needed $50 for my travel to San Francisco. In the afternoon they called back. They had decided I should not travel apart from my family. They gave me the money our entire family needed for travel and maintenance all the way to Sydney. They also provided me with some useful contacts in San Francisco.*
>
> *As you know, we had to remain in San Francisco for nearly two months. Without me having to take one step, the Relief Committee and the Baptist organization did everything necessary to help us. Each was aware of what the other was doing.*
>
> *A little later we contacted the local San Francisco Estonians. We could not have asked for better hospitality.*

Sometime in the second half of March, funds in hand, we began our cross-country bus ride from New York to San Francisco. As opposed to Jack Kerouac who began the first of his storied cross-country road trips four months later, also from New York, ours was not a celebration of the freedom of the open road. Ours was a goal-oriented journey—get to San Francisco and catch the boat to Australia.

But, except for the difference in seasons, our two trips probably began much the same way, along the same route. As Kerouac describes in *On the Road*, "It was an ordinary bus trip with crying babies and … countryfolk getting on at one Penn town after another, still we got on the plain of Ohio and really rolled, up by Ashtabula and straight across Indiana in the night."

I recall little about our journey to San Francisco—only some hazy, black and white memories—a crowded bus; stretch stops at bus stations; being sleepy. My mother offers few details. Her narrative only devotes five brief sentences to our cross-country trip. My father fills in some gaps in his May 13 letter to Arvo Horm.

Mother: *We began our bus ride across America. The trip from New York to San Francisco took five days. The roads were snowy. The bus made many stops. Just before we reached San Francisco I became sick. When we arrived in San Francisco I was hospitalized. It was only a bad cold and fatigue.*

13. America to Australia

Father: *...we began our journey to San Francisco from New York, a journey that did not take place without some incidents. The kind passengers squeezed together so that Jaak could have two seats so he could lie down and sleep. However, the four days and nights trip were too much for mother. When we arrived in Salt Lake City, she became ill. With the help of fellow passengers, we were able to get a hotel room. A local doctor came to look after mother. He didn't charge for his services or for the medicines. A few days later we were able to continue our bus ride toward San Francisco. But when we arrived mother's health was so bad, she had to be hospitalized. Mother recovered but now we had to wait two months before we could leave for Australia. We survived those two months through the help and generosity of friends we met by chance.*

Mother understates the severity of her illness. I recall being at the hospital over a span of at least several days. I waited in a not unpleasant children's play area while Father visited my mother in her room. Why the hospitalization should have delayed our departure to Australia by two months, as my father says, I don't know. According to my mother's narrative our ship sailed on schedule. Both agree that we were well taken care of during our San Francisco stay.

My father makes a point of mentioning the free medical care my mother received in Salt Lake City. I don't know what, if anything, they were charged by the San Francisco hospital but whenever they spoke about the trip my parents never distinguished between the Salt Lake City medical care and the San Francisco hospital care. They always spoke as though both were free. They continued to be grateful throughout their lives.

I don't know how my father obtained the contact information, perhaps from one of the New York Estonians, but once in San Francisco my parents connected with the Tamberg family. They in turn introduced us to other members of the local Estonian community. In his May 13 letter to Arvo Horm, my father described them:

> There are about 1,500 Estonians living around the San Francisco area. Most of them arrived here during the Russian Revolution, coming through Manchuria and Japan. The older generation speak fluent Estonian and sympathize about their countrymen's situation. They try to help by sending packages, etc.

The Tamberg family and the San Francisco Estonians received us with warmth and hospitality. We were escorted around the San Francisco Bay area and introduced to what is today loosely referred to as "California living." I remember bits and pieces of those excursions, especially a visit to the Stanford University campus. My mother offers her recollections.

Mother: *I don't recall how Alfred found the Tamberg family. They had come to San Francisco from Manchuria in 1920. The Tambergs had three*

Mother became ill during our bus ride across America. When we arrived in San Francisco, she was admitted to a hospital. I wait with flowers at the hospital gate, hoping to see her (Treiman family archive).

13. America to Australia

sons. One, Dick Tamberg, played basketball at the University of California at Berkeley.

They found us shelter at the home of a bachelor who had a three-room house. We were given the use of one of the rooms. During the month or so we spent in San Francisco father found work washing pans in a bakery. I don't remember how much he was paid.

The Tambergs introduced us to the San Francisco Estonian community. We were treated as though we were royalty. Not only were we provided with all the essentials, we were pampered with all the comforts. The three of us were shown San Francisco and its neighboring areas. We experienced weekend and weekday California life; we were told about California history, art and social mores. We were treated as though we were very important people.

Our ship, **Marine Phoenix**, left on schedule. On May 10 the Tamberg family took us to the port. About twenty people had come to send us off. Through tears and with heartfelt, warm feelings, we bid them farewell and then boarded our ship.

Before boarding, each passenger had their papers examined. When it was Alfred's turn it was obvious that he was in the country illegally. He was asked how he got to America. He explained. Because he was leaving and

Our newly made San Francisco friends and benefactors came to the Port of San Francisco to bid us farewell on May 10, 1947, as our ship raised anchor for its voyage to Australia (Treiman family archive).

The Tamberg family gave us two of their shipping trunks. They had acquired them when they fled from Russia during the Russian Civil War. Their escape route took them through Manchuria and Vladivostok. Shipping trunks generally contained items that would not be needed during a voyage. The trunks would be stored in the cargo hold of the ship. We used the Tamberg trunks during our voyage from San Francisco to Sydney and later on our return trip from Australia to America (photograph by Margus Välja).

since he had family with him, no one made an issue of his status. The passport control people even wished us a good trip.

Our ship began to move. Our well-wishers became smaller and smaller until they disappeared from view.

The *Marine Phoenix* was launched in August 1945, too late to participate in World War II. For a short time, she had carried troops from Japan to Tacoma, Washington. In 1946 she was chartered to Matson Line and given an extensive refit, with accommodations for 520 tourist class passengers. The fare from San Francisco to Australia ranged from $225 to $370 per person. I assume my father's reference to $1,000 as the cost of our travel from San Francisco to Sydney included, in addition to our tickets, which had been purchased while we were still in Sweden, expenses related to our extended San Francisco stay plus other travel-related costs.

The *Marine Phoenix* took us from San Francisco to Auckland, New Zealand, and then to Sydney, Australia, with brief stops at two South Pacific islands. Despite improvements made to the vessel's original military accommodations, some travelers, such as Katie Hargreaves, also traveling in 1947, found the voyage to be less than enjoyable. She is quoted in Peter Plowman's *Across the Pacific: Pacific Liners from Australia and New Zealand to North America*:

> I embarked September 2, 1947 from San Francisco on the Marine Phoenix, operated by Matson Navigation Co and Oceanic Steamship Co in cabin #305 with 20 bunks, mostly occupied by Australian women and their babies. Men were mostly veterans. Altogether, there were about 200 passengers. It definitely was a troop ship! After stops at Pago Pago and Suva, my parents and I arrived in Auckland, NZ, September 18 and Sydney on September 22.

Another traveler, Kitty Emmanuel, also quoted in Plowman's book, had an even harsher view of the *Marine Phoenix's* accommodations. Traveling first class, she perhaps had higher expectations.

> At the beginning of August 1947 my husband Tony, baby Sally (10 months) and myself left Southampton on board a Holland America Line ship bound for New York, where we stayed for two or three nights. We then caught a train to San Francisco before embarking on the infamous "Marine Phoenix." I, with Sally, was allocated two bunks in a cabin housing 20 or more women. I had to raise Cain, as they say, to get a railing put up at the side of Sally's bunk; otherwise there was a very real danger she would fall out. Tony was given a berth with 11 other men, one of whom disappeared during the voyage. No one ever knew whether he was pushed overboard or just fell, nothing was done for at least a couple of days—far too late to ever find him!
>
> The dining facilities were laughable. Long trestle tables—no tablecloths or napkins, very primitive. The food wasn't much better. Other facilities too were very basic–4 loos for we women and lots being sick when the sea was rough. To bathe my baby I had to fill a tiny bath and carry it back to the cabin. Not easy with a rolling ship! Another difficulty was the rampant whooping cough that affected most of the children, but thankfully not Sally. Our first stop was an island where the locals came out to the ship in long boats and swarmed up the sides on rope ladders, and then tried to sell their beads and trinkets to the passengers. We would loved to have gone ashore but that apparently was not possible.
>
> On top of this most of the crew were drunk during the whole voyage! And all this for first-class fares!"

Technically, flying fish don't fly. They do take powerful leaps and then glide long distances above the water's surface. From time to time our ship would travel through schools of flying fish, some of which would land on our deck. Here, a crew member gives me a closer look (Treiman family archive).

My parents, who did not travel first class, had no complaints. For them, after three initial days of turbulence, the remaining 17 days of the cruise were more like a vacation, the world in abeyance while they delighted in the tropics of the South Pacific and were mesmerized by the occasional flying fish that landed on deck.

Mother: *As the San Francisco skyline dimmed into the distance, I gazed at the horizon and watched the waves glisten and change colors in the sunlight. Time passed. All of a sudden, it was time for dinner. The calm sea that greeted us on departure changed suddenly. During our first on board meal chairs, tables and anything else not battened down began to move. We could hear the clang of shattered dishes. The* Marine Phoenix *had entered a stretch of ocean known for its massive waves.*

Seasickness attacked me and many other passengers. For three days I was in pitiful shape. As the swell receded, I started to again feel like a human being. Even as I and most of the other passengers were debilitated by seasickness, Jaak played calmly with his ball. When his father told him to hold on to the wall's handrail, he asked, "Why?" and then unhurriedly continued to play.

Following our encounter with the high seas, the days warmed. People

13. America to Australia

My mother and I played shuffleboard on the *Marine Phoenix*. For my parents, even though they faced an unknown future, the opportunity to play games and do nothing must have been a welcome respite (Treiman family archive).

sunbathed on deck. Jaak found playmates who were almost his age. Alfred and I studied English. We looked at the endless sea, our line of vision broken only by some seagulls trailing a ship far from shore or an occasional flying fish, breaking the water's surface, soaring as though they were birds. In the evenings there were movies—initially in the social hall, later under the open, tropical skies.

Often, we sat on deck in the mild southern night and enjoyed its magic. Holding hands we reminisced and recalled the four or so years we had been together. We fashioned beautiful, optimistic plans for our future. We wondered about family in Estonia. We spoke about our compatriots in Sweden and the friends we had made in San Francisco, whose kindness we continued to appreciate.

On the morning of our tenth day, we arrived in the lagoon where the port of Pago Pago is located. Pago Pago is a settlement on one of the Samoan islands. A stretch of about one hundred fifty yards of the beach was settled. The rest of the landscape seemed to be nothing but a steep, thickly forested mountain side where human feet had never trod.

Greeting our ship were a small, lively, barefoot military band and the

The horizon and the wake of the *Marine Phoenix* behind us, my father and I are barely visible as we explore the stern of the ship (Treiman family archive).

13. America to Australia

For a four-year old, our ocean voyage was new, exciting and fun (Treiman family archive).

island's equally barefooted police chief. The port was filled with native merchants selling jewelry, baskets and rugs. When we disembarked for our brief stop, we were amazed at the quality of the workmanship.

Three more days past and we arrived in Suva, located on one of the Fiji group of islands. Suva resembled a civilized, world-class city. In San Francisco we had been told that an Estonian who went by the name "Smith" lived in Fiji. When we arrived, we asked about him from a car driver. It turned out everyone on the island knew Mr. Smith. He owned an electrical supply store. We found him and were his guests for four hours. He and his wife had come to Suva 15 years earlier.

Estonians like to brag that Hemingway said he could find an Estonian in every port in the world. My parents finding Mr. Smith in Fiji brings that claim to mind. However, for the sake of literary accuracy, what Hemingway actually wrote in his 1937 novel, *To Have and Have Not*, was not quite that encompassing.

> At pier four there is a 34-foot yawl-rigged yacht with two of the three hundred and twenty-four Esthonians who are sailing around in different parts of the world in boats between 28 and 36 feet long and sending back articles to the Esthonian newspapers. These articles are very popular in Esthonia and bring their authors between a dollar and a dollar and thirty cents a column. They take the place occupied by the baseball or football news in American

For a small country, Estonia has a surprisingly vast network of Estonians. Somewhere, most likely in San Francisco, my father heard that an Estonian lived on Fiji. When our ship stopped in Suva, he found "Mr. Smith," who invited us to join him and his wife for lunch at their home (Treiman family archive).

newspapers and are run under the heading of Sagas of Our Intrepid Voyagers. No well-run yacht basin in Southern waters is complete without at least two sunburned, salt bleached-headed Esthonians who are waiting for a check from their last article. When it comes they will sail to another yacht basin and write another saga. They are very happy too.

Mother: *Our next stop was in Auckland, New Zealand. Some new passengers boarded our ship. Alfred engaged one of them in conversation—a New Zealander. Father told him that in Europe, New Zealand is known as one of the world's best countries. The gentleman's friendly voice became sarcastic as he replied, "Oh sure. The climate here is very good but you know that we have a workers' government and our laws and regulations limit human initiative. Consequently, we are one of the most backward countries." Mr. Smith had expressed the same opinion about Australia and New Zealand.*

14

Australia—Getting Started

"We moved five times during our first year."

When my parents decided to leave Sweden, America was their preferred destination. But, emigrating to the United States in 1947 was problematic. Gaining legal entry was a slow and uncertain process.

Their second choice was Australia. While continuing to prefer immigrants from Great Britain, the "Island Continent" was beginning to open its border to other Europeans, especially if they were white and from northern Europe. For my mother and father, Australia seemed a decent substitute destination.

Our arrival in Sydney, at the beginning of the Southern Hemisphere's winter season, did not start well. From 90 or so miles away, *The Singleton Argus* for May 30, 1947, under the headline "Sydney in Wartime Austerity Garb," observed that:

> With cold and wet weather prevailing today, Sydney faced additional discomforts, when several suburbs were blacked out. Urgent radio appeals were made to housewives to restrict to an absolute minimum the use of power. Sydney today presented a picture of gloom unequalled in any large city in the Commonwealth. A succession of blackouts and brownouts in industrial and residential districts, combined with a darkened shopping area has given Sydney a wartime austerity appearance as depressing and uninviting as any time in the city's history.

My mother's first impressions of Sydney were no better.

Mother: *As we left Auckland the weather became cold and rainy. A few days later, on the morning of May 30, 1947, the Marine Phoenix arrived in Sydney harbor. Getting off the ship was fast and easy; customs was not. We spent all day and late into the night trying to retrieve our luggage. Finally, with the help of a bribe, we were able to retrieve the trunk that contained our clothing. We then found our way to the housing that Mr. Selg, our guarantor, had arranged for us.*

I do not know how Aleksander Selg came to be my parents' sponsor.

The November 19, 1953, issue of the Australian-Estonian newspaper *Meie Kodu—Our Home* carried a story about Selg's 70th birthday celebration. A well-known member of Sydney's Estonian community, Selg was in the same business that my parents planned to engage in—producing paper ornaments. He had a factory in the suburbs and was constructing a new building.

Selg was President of Sydney's *Eesti Maja—Estonian House*, a position he had held since 1943. *Estonia Houses* were located around the world, wherever groups of Estonians lived. Each was a place for people of Estonian heritage to socialize and eat. Each also served to promote Estonian culture, language and history.

Mother: *We paid Mr. Selg £7½ per week for our one-room apartment. Later I learned that a typical worker's pay was a little more than £7 a week. When I asked for a table lamp so I could write, Selg told me that a lamp was not included in our rent. We had to settle for the 25-watt overhead lamp in our cold, damp room. We thought back longingly to our comfortable San Francisco quarters.*

Our guarantor turned out to be a man who wanted to control our destiny. He saw us as his indentured servants. He had taken possession of our earlier arrived Stockholm shipment of tissue paper, gluing racks and dies that were essential to starting our business. But for the fact that we came to Australia at our own expense and were not obligated to him, he might have succeeded. As it was, he had little power over us.

At the end of our second week, we found a place to live and escaped what was now a £20 apartment debt to Mr. Selg. We were able to get a small loan so we could pay Mr. Selg his £20 plus an additional sum that had been agreed to in our earlier correspondence. That correspondence had been between Alfred and the local Estonian Relief Committee, of which Mr. Selg was the secretary.

The room we found belonged to an elderly lady. Rent was only £1½ a week. Our room had two beds—one for Jaak and one for Alfred and me. The lady had an additional building in which no one lived. We also rented a room in that building.

We planned to use the paper and tools we had shipped from Sweden to make and sell honeycomb toys. When our work space was ready, we hired two men who used our gluing racks to glue the tissue paper into honeycomb cells. We then cut the honeycomb paper into the appropriate designs using our dies. I added finishing touches before the items were ready for sale. Alfred was the salesperson.

There was a market for our items! We had work to do, so much in fact that finding adequate work space became a big problem. We moved five times during our first year. All the places were temporary. Our last rental was on a chicken farm. There was a room where chicks were brought after

14. Australia—Getting Started

they hatched. We were able to use that room as our factory space until the next group of chicks were brought in.

As my parents strove to start their business, 9,500 miles away, unknown to them, my mother's youngest brother and closest sibling, Aleksander, was arrested. Before the Soviet occupation Aleks had served as a guard with the Estonian border control. His family assumes this was the reason for his arrest. He was tried, in secret, on October 21, 1947, before a military tribunal. The formal charges against him were never revealed. He was sentenced to 20 years in Russia's far north, near Vladivostok. This "blemish" on the Uibo family would prevent my mother's half-sister Hilja from fulfilling her dream of becoming a teacher.

My parents established a routine. Mother stayed home and made the decorative toys. Father went on the road, selling. He would review the day's personal and business news in letters to my mother. A typical example was an excerpt from his February 29, 1949, letter: *"I was awake all the way to Melbourne. I stared out the window at the yellowish, brown countryside filled with sheep and a few settlements. I developed my strategy for acquainting buyers with my samples."*

The following day he followed up with a report on that day's activities.

When I arrived [in Melbourne], I met with our sales agent. We will try to sell our product for a couple of days—some places we will go to together. I also went to look at the agent's office. A buyer from Adelaide happened to be there and gave us around a £250 order.

I went to 4 or 5 department stores to see whether there were any items similar to ours for sale. Other than Cole's, there were not. Cole's was selling Selg's fans for six pence each. Tomorrow I will try to get together with Cole's commercial goods buyer.

I got the entire price list for the English products. I was also able to see their samples. We have better prices. However, they vastly surpass us in terms of quantity. They have many hanging items, such as we saw last year in Parramatta.

Many stores have already purchased the English items. Some had planned to also buy Thompson's goods but they changed their minds as soon as they compared price lists.

Manton is a growing firm in Melbourne. They promised to definitely place an order with us. Myer Emporium is richly stocked with English products. These are the goods that were ordered for the king's visit.

The drawing Jaak made for me gave me much joy. The proportions are much improved from earlier drawings and the Estonian flag complements everything very well. For his amusement I am sending Jaak a couple of pennies worth of stickers that depict the king's family—there is nothing else.

Another letter, this one written from Brisbane on April 19, 1949, offers his experience with non-business-related interactions with Australians.

My train ride happened to be pretty bad. The rail car was old and filthy. Besides that, my seat was directly over the wheels. This disturbed my sleeping and reading. Stars floated in front of my eyes. My mate in the compartment was a railway official. He was very talkative. He said he had met many Estonians and knew them to be good people. Later in our conversation it turned out the Estonians he had met were really Poles. He thought we were one and the same.

My parents overcame their initial obstacles. They established their business and it met with success. The magic fan, those three honeycomb balls on a stick that would change shape as the wrist was snapped, was their centerpiece. They marketed the magic fan as a toy rather than a decoration, hence the name of their business, "Toytex."

Australian business operated under the government's rigid, bureaucratic oversight. Australia's Labor Party had been in power during World War II and remained so until 1949. In his PhD dissertation at the University of Sydney, *The Career of Class: Intellectuals and the Labour Movement in Australia 1942-56*, Professor Sean Scalmer described Labor's economic policies. "By the end of the war [Australia] was heavily industrialised, directed towards maximum production, and characterized by a strong, even dominant Federal Government presence, which both employed a host of bureaucrats and factory workers, and which exerted substantial directive force over economy and society. This was a transformation which, it could be argued, would not have been possible without the Labor Party's commitment to socialism...."

Members of the Labor Party had an on-going infatuation with the Soviet Union and its conversion from a peasant to an industrial society. Some of Labor's policies tried to imitate their myopic understanding of the Soviet experience.

When the war ended Labor remained in power. Its leadership did not modify the party's wartime, government directed, economic interventionist policies. Interventions "included the prohibition of certain production, the control of new business, disemployment orders, control of building, and the fostering of the concentration of industry." Luxury goods were targeted as frivolous and affirmatively discouraged. Five months after we arrived in Australia, the Labor government nationalized all banks.

The Communist Party was another force in Australian politics. The Party's membership had peaked during World War II but when the *Marine Phoenix* docked, its later decline had not yet started. Communists held leadership positions in some of Australia's key labor unions.

Although it impacted both their personal lives and their business, my mother does not mention Australian politics in her narrative, except for referencing Mr. Smith's comments in Suva and my father's shipboard conversation with a passenger from New Zealand. My father's letters display no such hesitation.

14. Australia—Getting Started

On April 21, 1948, my father wrote a lengthy letter to my parents' San Francisco mentors, the Tambergs. The letter summarized our first 10 months in Australia. Along with tidbits of family news and a description of the success of their business, perhaps mildly exaggerated, my father shared his blunt opinions about Australians and Australian politics:

Without wasting any time, we began to manufacture our honeycomb toys. Our items aroused great interest in the local markets and were received warmly. Today in Australia there are hardly any large stores that don't have our goods for sale. Currently we have around 25 steady employees. Financially we are not doing badly.

We aren't dissatisfied with life here but neither are we satisfied. Our achievements over the past 10 months have taken a lot of hard work, especially considering our poor language skills, our initial ignorance of the economy, our "dear" countrymen and on-going obstacles that we have had to overcome. The energy we have put into our business would have brought us better results in any other country I know of. There are many reasons for this.

First of all, our socialist boss, the government, rolls out countless, hundreds of years old English laws that are outdated, time-consuming stumbling blocks to operating a business.

Let's take, for example, the local masonry unions. While an average bricklayer can easily lay 600–800 bricks in a day, the union does not allow him to lay more than 300 bricks each day. One may assume that under such a system the worker becomes slothful and home construction becomes expensive.

Small producers are disparagingly referred to as the "backyard industry." By law, their activities are very restricted. Their emergence and development are not considered desirable even though I am sure that most large-scale industries in the world have developed from such backyards.

If someone wants to start a two or three employee factory the first thing is to find a building in a good location. The country here is divided into zones. The criterion is whether a particular endeavor disturbs the neighbors and the surroundings. One cannot work in a residential zone. Neither can one live in a work zone. A person starting a business must therefore have enough capital to acquire two properties. Of course, rules are circumvented but there are rabid nationalist Australians ready to poke every foreigner in the eye. If they see anything at all wrong, they will, in the spirit of "good neighborliness," complain to the authorities.

Another painful question is the cost of products. The government sets the sales price for each individual item. It takes weeks before you are told what price an item can be sold for. No sales can be made until the price has been determined. The basic pricing formula for our products is that the sales price of each item is the sum of multiplying the cost of materials by two. In other words, the sales price can be 100 percent of the cost of materials. However, for us, materials are cheap and labor is expensive. Of course, there is gamesmanship when it comes to the formulas.

The Australian business world resembles "holy" Stalinist Russia, where wages are established with the understanding that every employee will steal from the company. The entirety of the business world here seems to be based on cheating the government. If one doesn't do that then enterprise becomes impossible.

A third issue is the progressive income tax system. The tax on £1,000 pounds is £200 pounds. On £2,000 pounds it is £800 pounds. In the end it turns out that a company generating tens of thousands of pounds of sales earns as much as one small producer generating only a few hundred pounds of sales. The state earns the rest. Recently I have read why many Americans who were enticed to come to Australia return to America. One of the most common reasons is the high tax rate.

Jaak is reaching school age. We have looked for schools. They are poorly built, lack adequate furnishings and equipment and from what we have heard, have poor instructors. Instruction concentrates on English history, the lineage of the Royal family, the British Empire and the uniqueness of Australia. Teaching aids are poor, even if compared to what we had in Estonia. In higher schools there are widespread, well placed centers for communist propaganda.

On board ship, on our way to Australia, I read an American grammar school text book which began, "America is made up of many nationalities. Each nationality has brought something special to America. Because of that America is what it is." Such a textbook would be unimaginable here. A foreigner has less credibility in court than a native.

The climate, with its large temperature fluctuations, is something we are not used to. Central heating is not common here—after all, that would not be in line with English tradition.

Australia's living standard lags far behind America. A worker can't hope for much purchasing power from his wages. A person is considered rich if he owns a shack for a home and has a 1928 automobile. (An automobile would be essential for our business. I have been waiting for months for the government to give me a permit to buy a car. I continue to wait.)

All these difficulties make life unpleasant, futile and insecure. That is why I resubmitted my earlier Swedish era paperwork to emigrate to the United States. This time I submitted the papers to the American Embassy in Australia. We have no doubt that we will also succeed in America and we will feel much more at home there than here.

My father's disgust at having escaped one "socialist paradise" only to find himself subject to a government of fellow travelers was palpable. Less than a year after arriving in Australia he resubmitted the paperwork he had prepared in Sweden, seeking to emigrate to America.

Life did not stop after my parents submitted their application to the American Embassy in Canberra. Time passed, they heard nothing and eventually little further thought was given to moving to America. Through long hours of joint, hard work and some luck, "Toytex" became successful at what in retrospect seems like lightning speed.

15

Australia—Settling In

"More Estonians are coming to Australia."

Because of a business that was doing well, a friendly banker and perhaps even some of the Labor Party's policies, our sixth home in Australia was one that my parents were able to buy rather than rent. The purchase took place a little more than a year after our arrival. The house was in Cabramatta, about 19 miles west of Sydney's central district.

Mother: *We found that it was possible to receive a bank loan for up to 90 percent of the purchase price of a house. We began our hunt, looking through for-sale advertisements. When the price fit, the house did not. When the house and neighborhood was to our liking then the price was too high.*

One day our real estate agent told us about a house whose price matched our budget. We went to look at it. The area, Cabramatta, was beautiful. On one side the property bordered on a river. The lot contained two houses. They were old but livable. The house next to the river had tenants. The yard contained lemon, apple, plum and fig trees. The yard and the houses exuded charm. Ten chickens and a rooster also came with the house.

The bank gave us a loan. We bought the property. We paid on the loan each month to clear our debt. Our rent from the other house was £1 each week. The property also had a garage that we used for our factory.

We cleaned, painted and wallpapered the house. It looked quite nice. My first gardening project was to prepare an area of the yard for strawberries. I planted multiple rows. That turned out to be wasted effort. The birds ate all the strawberries. I also planted spinach, peas, carrots, potatoes, onions and rhubarb. The birds left that portion of my garden alone. It was very dry. I had to water every evening. After a while we still had six chickens and a rooster.

The milkman came by once a week and filled the milk container for those who wanted milk. Those who were late putting out their container had to wait another week before getting their milk. The local grocery store carried lamb and chicken—beef and pork were not to be found.

One Saturday my husband suggested I go to the city—perhaps I wanted to buy something. I took his suggestion to heart and soon found myself at the train station, which was only a ten-minute walk from our house. I barely noticed that the railway car was nearly empty. Cheerfully I made plans about the essentials I would buy. I arrived downtown and marveled at how the streets were bereft of people. I found a large department store—the doors were shut. I couldn't understand why. Unsuccessfully, I looked for a soft drink stand where I could quench my thirst. Disappointed, I returned home. I did not know that in Australia Saturday and Sunday were days of rest—no business was conducted.

While my parents worked, I adapted to country living. A month before our move to Cabramatta, while we still lived on a chicken farm with its flock of 5000 chickens, my father wrote to Mr. Tamberg, "*Jaak has grown. He does not feel lonely on the farm. He describes to me in the minutest detail everything about raising chickens, knows the size of all the nearby chicken farms and knows all the neighborhood dogs by name.*"

My first, enduring recollections of Australia date from our time in Cabramatta—the sounds of laughing kookaburra birds marking their territory; the endless flow of the Cabramatta River that was our back boundary; an old fig tree that I climbed so I could daydream from within its branches; a small brood of hens that mesmerized me as they pecked in our yard.

During our first year in Australia, we lived in five different places, usually in the countryside. A local cow and I eye each other while a disinterested chicken ambles away (Treiman family archive).

15. Australia—Settling In

The Cabramatta River ran through the backyard of the first house either of my parents had ever owned. Continuing a tradition that emanates from both sides of my family tree, my father tried to teach me the tricks and techniques of fishing (Treiman family archive).

It was Cabramatta where my father took me to a local school, tried to enroll me, was told I was too young and walked me back home as I cried, heartbroken. It was also here, one Christmas Eve day, that not only did I meet Santa Claus walking to our house from the direction of our backyard river but to this day I know that I not only saw Santa but also his elves, in cone shaped hats, sitting in his boat waiting for him to return.

Our river was where my father introduced me to fishing although I don't recall either of us ever catching a fish. The river was where we threw a small, stone weighted sack containing all the bad words my father sometimes used.

I remember a bathroom that my father converted into a darkroom so he could develop his own photographs—if Toytex didn't succeed his Plan B was to earn a living as a professional photographer. I recall watching him develop film, the room lit with a macabre reddish glow, pans filled with different chemicals and the magical tools that produced images on paper of what his camera had seen.

Time has perhaps modified what I actually saw and felt yet all these images of Cabramatta are still as real to me as though I witnessed them this morning.

Bishop Kõpp and his wife continued to live in our former Stockholm apartment. In a letter to Mrs. Kõpp dated August 2, 1948, Mother updated our lives.

> *We attend events at the Sydney Estonian House. We have gotten to know Estonians who have lived here for years. One of them is a married couple, the Petersons. They have accepted us as though we were family. The Jaansons, Dr. Ruut and Dr. Tohver arrived here a year before us. I had worked with Dr. Tohver at the Tallinn children's clinic. We visit each other often. At times we talk about the night shifts we worked and recall some of our frightening experiences.*
>
> *Dr. Ruut's son is a year younger than Jaak. On some Sundays we play tennis with the Ruuts. Roland Sarv and his family live in Astra. They had arrived in Fiji a month after we stopped there. They lived there for a year but they could not get used to the tropical climate and the isolation. They left Fiji and arrived in Sydney about a year after we did. Their son is a year older than Jaak but the two became immediate playmates. Sarv has started a successful plastics factory.*
>
> *Touring Estonian visitors from Germany have refreshed our lives. A 20-member men's chorus gave two concerts. The master pianist, Mrs. Teder, has performed several times. They have rejuvenated our spirits.*
>
> *More Estonians are coming to Australia. Our numbers steadily increase. It is said that around 700 people have arrived. Those who know English are more or less able to find work in their own occupations. However, it is difficult for doctors. They must retrain if they do not want to work illegally, which is a fallback, emergency measure.*
>
> *According to the newspapers, a young Estonian doctor, Dr. Vahtrik, who worked in a hospital, killed himself last week. However, acquaintances say the communists killed him. He had found himself in a nest of people belonging to the Communist Party, including his only relative. He was stabbed in the neck with scissors.*
>
> *A number of people have arrived from Sweden, although no acquaintances. We have met Mr. Perti, who came from Sweden with a supply of wall paper that he had originally brought with him from Estonia. The Maasep family is living with relatives. Mr. Mihkelson has a chicken farm. Estonians are scattered throughout the Sydney area, each living in their own section of town. Visiting takes at least a couple of hours."*

In January 1949, as my father crisscrossed Australia by rail selling Toytex products, the Soviet Council of Ministers issued a secret decree "on the expulsion and deportation" from the Baltic states of "all kulaks and their families, the families of bandits and nationalists" and others. The decree was soon implemented. During a three-day period in March over 20,000 Estonians were marshalled into cattle cars and deported to Siberian gulags. Of these, 6,000 were children under the age of 16.

Mother: *We began to look for a bigger house with an adjoining room located in a place with a good school for Jaak. This time our search for a house was easier. We had accumulated enough money for a down payment.*

15. Australia—Settling In

Our last home in Australia was in the Sydney suburb of Punchbowl. We lived on the second floor. The Toytex factory was on the ground floor. Here, a piece of heavy equipment, possibly a punch press, is being delivered. In my father's 1948 letter to the Tambergs he complained that "The country here is divided into zones. The criterion is whether a particular endeavor disturbs the neighbors and the surroundings. One cannot work in a residential zone. Neither can one live in a work zone...." I have no idea how or if we circumvented the local zoning laws (Treiman family archive).

We found a two-story house that was a couple of years old located in the small town of Punchbowl. The building was ideal. The top floor was for living. The bottom floor had one room that was a good fit for an office. The rest of the bottom floor was a large space that was ideal for setting up a small factory. So, again we moved.

The living area had two bedrooms, a living room, a bathroom and a kitchen. The top floor also had a large open-air area with laundry space and a large kettle and stove. I could boil the dirty clothes before washing. Clothes lines were strung above the open area. I could easily hang clothes to dry. Normality entered our life.

I don't know how my parents learned English. We always spoke Estonian at home. My father could communicate in English. His language skills were obviously good enough for sales work. However, he never lost his strong accent. When he was angry, such as at a customer who had a past due account, his English became close to unintelligible (but sometimes effective—his bad debt ratio was, and continued to always be, minuscule).

My parents wanted to improve their English. They hired an English teacher to come to our home in Punchbowl. The teacher insisted that we speak English at home. He was not asked to return. We continued to speak Estonian.

I don't recall my mother's level of English proficiency when we lived in Australia—in America her proficiency was good, albeit with an accent and grammatical mistakes. Notwithstanding the lack of formal instruction, she worked to improve her English throughout her life, even into her 90s. After her death I found numerous reminder-notes she had written to herself consisting of definitions of English language words she had come across.

As children seem to do with languages, I just picked up English. I would sit on my father's knee and read comic books—Donald Duck and Uncle Scrooge were two of the earliest, followed by dozens and dozens of others of every variety. I was a voracious reader, not just of comics but books that my parents gave me. *The Story of Robin Hood and His Merry Men* and *The Life and Adventures of Robinson Crusoe* were two of my favorites. Around my eighth birthday my parents gave me a 10-volume set of the *Children's Encyclopaedia* and another multi-volume set of classic children's stories. I devoured both sets.

I recall a time when a man tried to break into our house in Punchbowl. My father caught him in the act and called the police. The police came and nearly jailed my father. I don't think anything was done to the would-be-burglar. At least a portion of the local citizenry did not care for neighbors who spoke broken English.

I began school after we moved to Punchbowl. Until I read my mother's narrative, I did not realize it was a Catholic school. Punchbowl is where I attended kindergarten through second grade. I recall shooting marbles and playing cowboys and Indians during recesses.

My parents worked hard. From my bedroom on the second floor of our Punchbowl house I could hear them working downstairs until late at night. Sometimes my father would supplement the hard work with a little white lie. When a prospective customer visited Toytex he would be seated in the front office. Depending on the visitor my father would sometimes, before his arrival, turn on all the machines in the factory area to leave the impression that Toytex was even larger and busier than we were.

Mother: *We explored. We visited Melbourne, Brisbane, Adelaide, Katoomb and the Jenolan Caves. Australia was and is, an interesting country. There was much to see and much to get used to.*

Jaak attended a Catholic school. It was the only school in the area. Jaak liked it very much.

We traveled—Brisbane where the houses were on stilts; Adelaide and its crabs on the beaches; Canberra, where at the time a person could see from one end of town to the other. In addition to Australia's cities, we went

15. Australia—Settling In

to the Blue Mountains, where my love of the outdoors began. We visited the Jenolan Caverns, one of the world's great, natural wonders. I also remember the thousands of dead rabbits on the highways and the sound of thump, thump, thump as our car hit them, one after the other, after the other.

Life settled into a routine. Along with long hours of hard work there was relaxation. My parents never used a babysitter. I therefore went with

While Father usually travelled by train on his sales trips, as the Toytex business grew, he would sometimes fly. Here, I stand with him, a plane from the sometimes crash-prone Australian National Airways fleet in the background (Treiman family archive).

As our business grew, Father bought our first automobile, a Singer convertible. In addition to using it for some of his business trips, we would use it for family outings. I recall a kangaroo jumping over the hood as we drove along a narrow mountain road in Australia's rugged Blue Mountains (Treiman family archive).

them to all events—movies, live theater, tennis matches (my father played) and visits with other Estonians. Over time, my father's opinion of Australia improved, no doubt partly because the Labor Party lost the 1949 elections and the Communist Party's influence diminished.

Mother: *Our business grew. There was plenty of work. By early 1951 the work space on the first floor of our Punchbowl home had become too small. Our bank manager told us about a nice parcel of land and suggested we buy it. We did. We began plans to build a factory on the site.*

16

Leaving Australia

"Go? Of course! America."

Mother: *In 1951 a letter arrived from the American Embassy in Canberra. We were told that our 1947 application to emigrate to the United States had been approved. We had nearly forgotten about it. The letter queried, "When do you want to leave?" Our plans for an Australian life imploded. "What should we do?" Our bank manager advised against a move. Our friends wanted us to stay. Our decision, "Go? Of course! America!"*

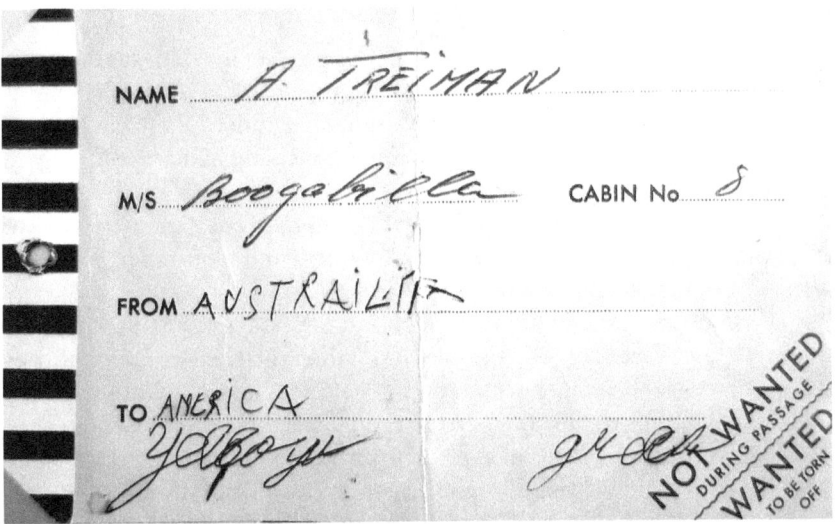

An ocean voyage for the purpose of moving one's residence from Point A to Point B is very different from a vacation cruise. When moving by ship, essential items are kept in the cabin, the rest stored in the ship's hold. This is a label from one of our shipping trunks, indicating the trunk was traveling with us from Australia to America and access to the trunk would not be required during the voyage. The label's top two lines are in my father's handwriting. The "from" and "to" lines are possibly my handwriting.(Treiman family archive).

Much needed to be done, quickly, to make our move a reality. Our house had to be sold; Toytex had to be liquidated; travel arrangements had to be made. Obviously, we would travel by ship. Commercial plane service between Australia and California did not exist. The former American warship Boogabilla *was scheduled to leave for America from Brisbane during the first week of November, only a month away. We booked passage.*

We sold our home. The lot on which we had planned to build our factory remained unsold. We gave our bank manager a power of attorney to handle all our financial matters.

Toytex's machinery and our personal belongings had to be shipped to Brisbane so they would be dockside for loading a few weeks before departure. We purchased plane tickets to Brisbane. We got everything done.

In a period of one month, my parents gave away my dog, liquidated a successful business, sold their home, said goodbye to friends, packed their goods, booked passage and appointed a banker to wrap up what they could not wrap up. What drew them into this frenetic flurry of activity? All we have are my mother's words, "Go? Of course! America!"

"Of course!"? Why was the decision to move so self-evident? My parents owned a successful business in which they had invested time, money and sweat. They had warm friendships. The home we lived in was ours, not rented. The Labor Party had lost the last general election. Australia's political and business environment was becoming friendlier. What was it about America that spurred my parents to abort what they had and once again face the unknown?

My parents were never explicit about what motivated them to move to America. For them the reasons were self-evident and required no explanation. Given their silence, I will suggest a few reasons.

Perhaps the most obvious, though not necessarily the most important reason, was security. My mother and father and their contemporaries were scarred by the Soviet occupation of Estonia. They had witnessed the mass deportations of 1941 that snared family, neighbors and friends. They had lived amidst the random arrests, intimidations and terror that came with the occupation. Even though my parents now lived in Australia, distant from the Soviet Union's borders, they still did not feel total personal security.

Most of World War II's refugees saw the postwar Soviet Union as a continuing threat to peace and stability. They read news reports and heard rumors of assassinations by the Soviet secret police, the seemingly ubiquitous NKVD. My parents and many other refugees believed that Stalin and his successors were driven by ideology and that the Soviet Union sought to actively advance Marx's proletarian revolution. America offered more security than any other country in the world. America was seen as the guardian of democracy and the resistor against totalitarianism and authoritarian rulers.

Beyond security, the scepter of opportunity invited my parents to move to America. From his letters, it is apparent that my father saw America as "the land of opportunity"—a phrase that was already a cliché but held real meaning for my parents and many others. A person could arrive with nothing and through perseverance and hard work any dream, except becoming president, was attainable.

A person was not limited by social class or lack of family wealth. Horatio Alger's stories mirrored what many refugees believed. Reality was rarely examined or when it was, deviations from earlier formed expectations were dismissed as outliers. Plenty of refugee success stories buttressed the image of opportunities that awaited immigrants in America.

Perhaps the most powerful magnet that drew my parents and other refugees to America was what today may seem to be a mystical American Dream. America as a conglomeration of ideas and principles—a mixture of freedom and opportunity premised on a foundation of moral fortitude protected by the principles contained in the Declaration of Independence and the Bill of Rights.

While the application of the ideas and principles that made up the American Dream was imperfect, the dream itself contained its own undefinable reality. As Justice Potter Stewart said in a different context, "I shall not today attempt further to define the kinds of material I understand to be embraced within that shorthand description, and perhaps I could never succeed in intelligibly doing so. But I know it when I see it...."

But, just as Justice Stewart and his colleagues continued to grapple with definitions in the context of cases before them, many others have, in a broader context, tried to define the mystique of America. In *Democracy in America*, Alexis de Tocqueville alluded to it and then proceeded to write two volumes trying to explain it.

> There is a country in the world where the great revolution which I am speaking of seems nearly to have reached its natural limits; it has been effected with ease and simplicity, say rather that this country has attained the consequences of the democratic revolution which we are undergoing without having experienced the revolution itself. The emigrants who fixed themselves on the shores of America in the beginning of the seventeenth century severed the democratic principle from all the principles which repressed it in the old communities of Europe, and transplanted it unalloyed to the New World. It has there been allowed to spread in perfect freedom, and to put forth its consequences in the laws by influencing the manners of the country.

Many others have also tried to define the essence of America. In doing so, some have boosted the idea of an American mystique; contrarians have pointed out the mystique's fallacies and inconsistencies. Pessimists question whether today, the mystique even exists.

Barack Obama and Ronald Reagan, each with a gift for words, speaking years after my parents' decision, compared America to a shining city on a hill. Not everyone has shared the same vision. Contrast Irving Berlin's *God Bless America* with Janelle Monáe's *Americans*; Walt Whitman's *Leaves of Grass* with W.E.B. Du Bois' *The Souls of Black Folk*; the Mormon Tabernacle Choir with Jimi Hendrix; *Mr. Smith Goes to Washington* with *Dr. Strangelove*. Whether their vision is critical or friendly, joyful or sad, each constitutes a part of the American mystique. My parents saw the parts of the mystique they wanted, perhaps needed, to see and followed that vision to America.

Mother: *The* Boogabilla *was like the former military troopship,* Marine Phoenix, *on which we came to Australia. Women and children were quartered in one section of the ship, men in another section. The ship had a large deck that contained a makeshift swimming pool.*

Once underway, the ship moved quietly through the Pacific, surrounded by a boundless ocean of blue. I sat on a deck chair and observed my fellow passengers. I saw different emotions—some people happy and smiling, some worried, others with tears in their eyes. There were the business people. There were the migrants. Then there were the disillusioned. Those who had come to Australia full of hope and excitement but were now leaving, unhappy and disenchanted.

Traveling to Australia, some had not known what awaited them. Young women in love coming to meet their beloved. Soon they discovered that life here was not for them. The man they thought they loved was no longer a fairy tale prince but a mortal toiling in an outback, nether region of the world.

We had a calm voyage. I did not even get seasick. In a makeshift swimming pool, the captain taught our nine-year-old how to swim. Jaak was not bored. Besides swimming there were all sorts of games.

One of the beauties, and occasional frustrations, of being human is that a common experience doesn't generate identical memories. My recollection of our voyage to America differs in a few respects from that of my mother. Based on memory and a bit of research, it turns out that notwithstanding its Australian name, the M/S *Boogabilla* was actually a Swedish, commercial cargo ship, built in 1945. In addition to cargo, it was equipped to carry 12 passengers. We were three of the 12.

Opposite: The cargo ship *Boogabilla* was equipped to carry 12 passengers in addition to its load of cargo. An old postcard highlights the passenger areas. As far as I can remember, except for one dinner when horse meat was on the menu, I had no complaints about the ship. I don't believe anyone else did either (Treiman family archive).

16. Leaving Australia

M/s "BOOGABILLA

My mother's description of the passengers and their reasons for being on board was, I suspect, an amalgamation of general feelings and observations, perhaps of some of the passengers on board the *Boogabilla* but more likely other immigrants she had observed during the four and a half years we lived in Australia.

As for the actual voyage, for a nine-year-old boy our trip was a joy and an adventure. I was the only child on board and thus the center of attention. I recall the captain walking me down into the engine room and later, up to the bridge where he let me take the helm and steer the ship. As my mother mentions, I learned to swim in the ship's "makeshift swimming pool," which was actually a large cargo crate lined with tarp and pumped full of seawater. The *Boogabilla* was also where my father tried, with only mild success, to teach me the basics of chess. I tasted my first Coca-Cola on the voyage.

17

Establishing New Roots

"We arrived in Los Angeles on ... Thanksgiving Day."

Mother: *We arrived in Los Angeles on Thursday, November 22, 1951—Thanksgiving Day. We had booked passage to San Francisco but somewhere in the middle of the Pacific our ship received orders to first stop in Los Angeles. San Francisco was where our thoughts and plans were centered.*

We were told the ship would remain in Los Angeles for a month before continuing its journey. We used part of that time to acquaint ourselves with the city. During this interruption we also visited our friends in New York. They urged us to settle near them. We decided to remain in Los Angeles.

It was late spring when the *Boogabilla* put to sea and my parents and I left the Southern Hemisphere. We were used to the springtime comfort of Sydney's balmy, mid–70s temperatures. Our friends told us that sun-drenched California was even warmer. We shouldn't bother with cold weather clothing. We paid heed.

Two and a half weeks later we were in the Northern Hemisphere. Now it was late fall and cold. When we set foot in the Port of Los Angeles in San Pedro, everyone, natives and visitors, yearned for warm temperatures.

As we walked down the *Boogabilla's* gangplank, no one waited for us. When we arrived in Stockholm, New York, San Francisco, even Sydney to a degree, there had been at least one Estonian waiting, ready to help. Los Angeles was different. There were Estonians in Los Angeles who predated my parents' arrival but as far as I know, my parents did not make contact with them until later.

Los Angeles was, and continues to be, a city with many distinct areas, each with its own name and character. Metropolitan Los Angeles covers more land area than 66 of the world's countries and is larger than either

New Jersey or Delaware. Tallinn, Estonia's largest city, occupies 77 times less space than Los Angeles. I do not know how, after only a month in the city, my parents were able to decide not only that we would settle in the City of Angels but the part of the city we would settle in, namely the eastern portion of Los Angeles's San Fernando Valley.

I recall our taxi ride from San Pedro to downtown and the Biltmore Hotel—a ride of about 20 miles. Built as a luxury hotel in 1923, the Biltmore continued to be a luxury hotel in 1951, as it still purports to be now, nearly 100 years later. I don't know how or why my parents selected the Biltmore as our initial abode. Perhaps our room charges were paid for by the *Boogabilla* as compensation for the unscheduled layover? Unlikely. In any case, we did not stay there for long.

Across the street from the Biltmore was Pershing Square, a park that dated from the 1850s. It was the size of one square block and was in the center of the Los Angeles business district. It was being revamped in one of its periodic makeovers. Apropos of the Cold War, the park's newly constructed underground parking levels were designed to withstand an atomic bomb blast.

During our stay at the Biltmore, I recall the unsettling, disruptive layer of smog that enveloped Los Angeles, smog so thick that visibility dwindled to almost nothing. Our throats constricted. We could hardly breathe. Our eyes stung and streamed water. As my mother and I explored downtown, again and again we had to step into nearby stores, not to shop but to breathe.

From the Biltmore we moved about two miles northwest to a partially furnished apartment in the Westlake district of Los Angeles, not far from MacArthur Park and its large, natural spring fed lake. I remember the apartment only in black and white. I don't recall how long we stayed there although I know that is where we spent our first Christmas in America. My present was a small, horseshoe-shaped magnet.

While living in Westlake, my parents considered whether we should stay in Los Angeles. I had always offered a simple explanation of why we didn't wait for the *Boogabilla* to continue its voyage to San Francisco—my father was impatient. When told of the layover, rather than wait, he just took himself and his family off the ship and we settled in Los Angeles.

While there is truth in my explanation—my father could be very impatient—I now see that my response needs to be more nuanced. Mother's narrative discloses that my parents did explore options. We flew to New York to visit Oskar Poom. Oskar and his family were old friends who had sponsored our entry into the United States, guaranteeing that we would be self-sufficient and not become charges on the welfare system. Oskar was also my father's EÜS Põhjala fraternity brother. Notwithstanding the

17. Establishing New Roots

Pooms urging us to settle in New York and even though my parents had some familiarity with and friends in San Francisco, they opted for Los Angeles.

Once their decision was made, they acted quickly. Given the vastness of the city I continue to marvel at how they were able to make such fast decisions.

Mother: *With the help of an agent, we looked for factory space. We found a new, long, one-story rectangular building divided into 14 separate units in a Los Angeles suburb, Burbank. The building was on a street named Hollywood Way, even though the street had nothing to do with Hollywood. One of the building's units fit our needs. We bought it. Now we were able to take all our belongings off the ship.*

We found a nearby home in another, adjoining Los Angeles suburb, Sun Valley. The house was only a ten-minute drive from our Hollywood

My parents bought the property where we first operated our factory in Los Angeles in early 1952. It was across the street from the Lockheed airport and facilities. This picture, with my father standing in front, was taken some time after 1971, after my parents had sold the property to Buccaneer Enterprises and moved Metex to the Canoga Park area of Los Angeles. Except for the tree, the raised guard rails, and the big sign identifying the company, the building looked the same as when we occupied it (Treiman family archive).

My parents and I are sitting at our dining table in our home in Sun Valley, perhaps in 1953. Given the flowers on the table, we must have been celebrating a special event—maybe my parents' anniversary. *Pirukas* are on the table—high quality ground beef wrapped in dough and baked—a frequent food at our family table. My mother's favorite cookbook, which she may have brought with her from Estonia and at the very least dates from our time in Sweden, identifies the ingredients for *meat pirukas* as 2 eggs, 400 grams cooked, ground meat, a pinch of salt and pepper, 1 onion (which my mother may have skipped), 25 grams of butter and milk. The directions take for granted that flour will also be required in order to make the dough (Treiman family archive).

Way factory. A grammar school, Glenwood Elementary, was close—about half a mile away. Jaak could walk there. His friends all lived within walking distance of our corner house.

Jaak was active with the nearby Lutheran church and with the Boy Scouts. He earned Scouting's highest badge as well as a service badge for his church activities. Jaak was in good surroundings. We didn't have any worries about him. I felt bad that I didn't have enough time to spend with my only child. We wanted to give him a decent life and education.

As soon as we moved into our Sun Valley home, I entered Glenwood Elementary School as a fourth grader. Except for pained, vehement complaints to my mother about initially being sent to school wearing shorts, as was the custom in Australia, my transition to America was anything but traumatic. This was especially so after mother added jeans to my wardrobe. I felt welcomed and accepted. I still recall a substitute teacher calling

17. Establishing New Roots

me "Jack" and the entire class responding spontaneously, "His name is Jaak." [Yaak]

I don't know if my parents' transition to life in America was also seamless. I never really thought about it. If I had, I would have said it was. But as I write this, I recall my mother warning me after our arrival that we had to be alert so we would not be taken advantage of. People could tell from our speech that we were foreigners. That meant we had to be careful. How much should I now read into that warning? Were there similar caveats that I no longer remember?

Even with their strenuous work schedule my parents became part of a growing Los Angeles Estonian community. They supported the work of Estonian and other Baltic organizations that sought the restoration of Estonian, Latvian and Lithuanian independence. They supported the Republican Party, seen as the anti-Communist Party.

During our early days in Sun Valley my godfather Arvo Horm, who still lived in Sweden, passed through Los Angeles. He was accompanied by August Rei, one of pre-war Estonia's most prominent statesmen. Rei had been Estonia's ambassador to the Soviet Union from 1938 to 1940. He was one of the few Estonian government officials who escaped capture and death. Horm and Rei stayed with us on their way to an anti-Communist conference in Taipei. I still regret not appreciating who Rei was. The questions that, at least with hindsight, I wish I had asked!

Occasionally my father took time off from work to accompany me, my friends and other fathers

I was active with the Boy Scouts. Here, I am wearing a sash with my merit badges, and demonstrating how to roll up a sleeping bag at a Scoutcraft Fair around 1955 (Treiman family archive).

At age 14, I continued my scouting adventures into Scouting's Explorers program. In July 1960 I attended a national Scout Jamboree in Colorado Springs. I recall seeing President Eisenhower drive past our camp area (Treiman family archive).

on monthly Boy Scout weekend camping trips in the local hills that surround Los Angeles. One summer he took us to a more distant camping location. He drove my Scout patrol, the *Flaming Arrows*, consisting of me and four or five of my friends, to Sequoia and Kings Canyon National Parks.

I was a member of the John H. Francis Polytechnic High School basketball team. My parents would occasionally come to watch the games. Had I not spent most of my basketball career sitting on the bench, I am sure they would have found time to attend more games. They did come to our last game, when we won the Los Angeles City high school basketball championship.

Today, when someone asks where I grew up, my short answer is always, "Sun Valley." Located in Los Angeles's San Fernando Valley, our home was at the base of the Verdugo Mountains in a solidly blue-collar neighborhood. That is where I spent all my American grammar school years, all my junior high school and most of my high school years. My friends lived in Sun Valley or nearby North Hollywood. Our house was on a corner lot, making it a natural place for my friends to hang out and play.

17. Establishing New Roots

Our neighbors, Ervin and Doris Brown became friends who patiently instructed my parents about American customs and idiosyncrasies. For years and years after we ceased to be neighbors Doris would call my mother on the day daylight savings time began and on the day it ended to remind her to turn her clocks ahead or back. This was one of the many Americanisms my parents weren't aware of when we arrived in the United States and moved to Sun Valley.

Sun Valley is also where we lived when our daily routine was interrupted. My mother and father received a series of letters from East Germany telling them how good life was in Estonia and urging them to return. The letters scared them. After living at multiple addresses in multiple countries, how did the Soviet octopus know where they were? After all the years that had passed, why did the Soviet *apparatchik* still care? My parents turned the letters over to the FBI.

18

Restarting Our Business

"Father had put the fingertip in his pocket ..."

Mother: In America "*Metex*" would become the name of our family business. Christmas bells, wedding bells, balls and a variety of other decorations and ornaments made of tissue paper glued together to form a honeycomb pattern when folded open, were very popular. We worked out an efficient system for making these decorations. There were three basic stages to the production process.

Using racks, sheets of colored tissue paper were glued to each other so that when the sheets were stretched open, they formed a cellular, honeycomb pattern. We hired a man to do the gluing. There were different glue racks for different items and different sizes. Each rack had its own unique spacing between the glue lines.

After the glue in each packet of tissue paper had dried, the packets would be cut into rectangular pieces. I would then paste light-weight cardboard on each side of each rectangular piece. After that Alfred would, while sitting on his stool at the punch press, stamp out the desired shapes—shapes that would fold open into bells, balls, turkeys, Easter rabbits, etc.

Once the desired shapes had been stamped out, I would take the nearly completed decoration and finish the process by stapling, attaching metal clips and checking for flaws. I had help. After our business was established, we had up to nine or ten people working for us. Three were with us for many years.

The finished items would be stored as inventory on shelves in cardboard boxes. Alfred would use the inventory to pack and ship as orders came in. He also prepared the invoices, kept the books and spoke with the customers.

We arrived in America during the Korean War and in the midst of the Cold War. Our factory was directly across the street from a large airport and aviation facility. Unbeknownst to us, located within that facility was the site of Lockheed company's famous Skunk Works—a secret, high security area where advanced aviation technologies such as the U-2 spy plane were developed.

18. Restarting Our Business

A page from the Metex catalogue. This is from our later years. It lacks the extensive product descriptions found in our earlier catalogs. Weddings were always a primary source of business, as was Easter and Halloween. Our selection of Christmas items was limited. It was never one of our major sales seasons (Treiman family archive).

I recall lengthy family discussions about naming our family business. My father didn't want to use our Australian business name, "Toytex" because of the political climate of the time.

There was speculation that the fighting in Korea might expand into

My father was always secretive about permitting anyone, even friends, from seeing any part of the factory except our office space. This picture shows the part of the factory where the blocks of glued tissue paper were cut into the desired shapes. There are several punch presses and a guillotine. Glued paper stacks are in the background. When all three punch presses operated at once, it was rather noisy. When I opened my first law office in one of the office spaces at the front of the new Metex factory, I could hear punch presses at work as I spoke with clients (Treiman family archive).

This is the area of the factory where finishing work was done, including quality control. As opposed to the punch press and gluing side of the factory, this area was my mother's domain (Treiman family archive).

18. Restarting Our Business

full scale war between America and the Soviet Union. In order to efficiently allocate war-time resources, Congress passed the Defense Production Act of 1950, a law that authorized the president to require businesses to convert their peace-time production facilities to support the war effort.

Hypothetically, the President had the right to order my parents' business to stop using punch presses to make paper decorations and instead produce tin plates for soldiers. My father was concerned that a company with the name "Toytex" would be more likely to be required to convert its production facilities to support the Korean War effort or the speculated-about war with the Soviet Union.

I suspect that another reason for no longer using the name Toytex was that my father remembered the Australian Labor Party's antipathy towards "luxury" goods. He was afraid that the American Congress might legislate similar attitudes into law. Depending on the definition, our honeycomb decorations could be classified as "luxury" items, or if not "luxury," at least "nonessential." President Truman's attempt to nationalize the American steel industry in April 1952, gave credence to the willingness of the government, even in America, to control if not take-over, businesses.

Whether or not realistic, my father felt his concerns were fact-based possibilities. We discarded the name "Toytex" and settled on the neutral sounding "Metex." Later, as fears of war receded, we added "Partyline."

After my parents bought a home and factory space, they spent the bulk of their time in the factory producing honeycomb decorations. Their normal work hours were from 6:30 in the morning until around 5:00 p.m. They would come home and mother would make dinner. After dinner father would often return to the factory to continue working until 10:00 or 11:00 p.m.

In the mornings, before Mother learned to drive, she would leave for work with my father. I would eat the breakfast she left for me and then walk to school. After Mother learned to drive (my father was the instructor—a painful experience for all concerned), in the mornings she would feed me breakfast and then go to work. Since school started later than Metex's work hours, I would leave for school a little later, walking and later cycling, the half-mile or so. On weekends my mother sometimes took Sunday off to clean the parts of the house she had not cleaned during weekday evenings. Occasionally, with their seven-day workweek, they would rest at home on weekend evenings.

In Australia my parents' business took off at a lightning pace. There had been little competition and access to capital was easy. In America, there was more competition; money was tighter.

Metex's primary competitors were two companies, one based in Pennsylvania, the other in Denmark. Both had sold honeycomb decorations in

America long before we arrived in California. Hallmark Greeting Cards was also a competitor but they entered the field after us. In addition, some honeycomb products were made in Japan and a few other Asian countries. While they undercut our prices, their quality was trashy and they posed little competitive danger.

Starting around eighth or ninth grade, in addition to occasionally operating our Heidelberg printing press, the punch press and performing any number of other necessary tasks at Metex, I was assigned the responsibility of handling all correspondence. This ranged from composing collection letters to answering questions about our product line. I was also tasked with writing the product descriptions for our sales catalogs.

Our efforts to produce quality decorations and to maintain customer satisfaction were reflected in the slogans Metex used: "First in quality, fairest in price, fastest in service" and "A satisfied customer is our first consideration." I'm pretty sure I came up with both while I was in high school.

In Australia my parents had a friendly, supportive banker. Obtaining loans does not appear to have been a problem. This was not true in California. Even in his 90s my father was still bitter that, shortly after our arrival, he had gone to a bank, applied for a $500 loan and been turned down.

Ultimately Metex succeeded, but not with Toytex speed. There were times when bills weren't paid on time. On one occasion the gas at home was turned off because of nonpayment. We had no hot water, although my recollection is that this lasted no longer than a day or two.

Another time, when I was 13 or 14, I was at Metex discharging my front desk, secretarial duties. The phone rang. I answered. It was a bill collector from American Express. Never have I listened to as vicious a stream of invective as gushed into my ears from that man's mouth, telling me over and over what a deadbeat, worthless person my father was.

We sold to retail stores and to wholesalers. My father worked in the factory but also continued a modified, less strenuous version of his Australian practice of making sales calls. The appearance of the mailman (twice a day in those early days—morning and afternoon and always a man), was cause for my mother, father and me to pause whatever we were doing and congregate at the front office desk to peruse the newly arrived mail. We would immediately open the envelopes that looked like they contained a new order or a check. Our practice became so ingrained that to this day I am alert for my mail carrier, even though I know little more than advertising will be left in my mailbox.

As far as my father was concerned, certain jobs at Metex, such as quality control, were women's work. Once, when we needed an additional person for quality control my father drafted a large sign that he placed on the front office window, readily visible from Hollywood Way. The sign announced, "WOMEN WANTED." English grammar and the finer nuances of the English language were not one of my parents' strong points. I convinced him to change the sign to "Help Wanted."

Mother: *One morning I was late getting to work. When I arrived at our Hollywood Way home-away-from-home, I was told Alfred had gone to the hospital. While stamping out decorations on the punch press, he had been slow to remove one of his hands from the anvil before the ram with the attached die came down. The die had sliced off one of his fingertips. Father had put the fingertip in his pocket and had driven to a nearby emergency facility. The doctors could not reattach his fingertip. It had been contaminated while in his pocket and in any case, too much time had passed.*

We hired someone to work on the punch press. We also attached some protective guards that slowed work but minimized the chances of a similar occurrence. In later years, punch presses came with fail-safe buttons that had to be pushed with both hands before the die would come down.

After Jaak started college, during breaks between school years he would sell our line of decorations. He was a Metex salesman.

Notwithstanding some business ups and downs, by 1971 sales were so strong that we needed a new, larger facility. My parents purchased a new industrial building in a different Los Angeles suburb, Canoga Park.

While I was in college and law school, I would sometimes supplement the small Metex sales force by making sales calls. I spent a portion of one summer on the road, selling honeycomb decorations throughout California's Central Valley, then moving on to Oregon, all the way to the state of Washington.

However, though I continued to take care of any required correspondence and any catalog updates, my mother exaggerates the amount of sales work I did for Metex. In fact, most of my school breaks after beginning university were spent working for our local East Valley Family YMCA as a camp counselor, bus driver and later as a camp and caravan director.

19

Bridging Generations and History

*"Even if you don't see my parents' actual
words, they are still present."*

My mother began writing her narrative soon after she turned 93. She made her last revisions when she was 94, just before her final trip to Estonia. She died two months after our return, only seven weeks short of her 95th birthday.

In the coming pages, my mother's narrative describes in some detail her return to Estonia after an absence of 46 years. She also relished talking about the visit to California by her nephew Mati and his wife Ilme. Except for those two events, her narrative becomes abbreviated, consisting of brief sketches or passing references. This contrasts with her earlier detailed descriptions of life in Estonia, her escape to and life in Sweden, our journey to Australia and life there and our arrival in America.

When I commented on her brevity about the Baltic related political activities that took place in America and about my work as honorary consul, she looked at me and said, with a smile, "You know the details of the American part of our story as well as I do, if not better." She was tired of jogging her memory with old photographs, looking for time-worn letters—she was tired of writing her narrative.

In the following chapters, I try to enlarge on my mother's brief sketches and passing references. Where she mentions a happening, I quote her narrative and then expand on her references based on my recollections. In a few instances where her narrative was silent concerning significant events that had been part of my parents' lives, I bring those events into our story. I bridge the work and life my parents led with the activities of the 1980s that helped Estonia regain independence.

As I grew older, my parents followed my activities, offering suggestions, encouragement and financial help when needed. Notwithstanding the brevity and, in some cases silence, in my mother's narrative, both my parents were active participants in meetings, demonstrations and letter writing campaigns designed to help the Baltic States reacquire their independence.

A paucity of references to my mother's narrative in the text that follows does not mean my parents were absent from the events I describe. As you read the following chapters, even if you don't see my parents' actual words, they are still present—an integral part of every word you read.

20

Lessons Learned—University

"Don't believe what we say in public."

Even though Metex was an integral part of my life I did not want to take over our family business. In high school, possibly earlier, when someone asked what I wanted to be, I replied, "a lawyer." So, in 1964, after I received my undergraduate degree at the University of Southern California no one was surprised that I continued my studies at the U.S.C. law school. The next eight years, beginning with my three years of law school, were formative. Not because I learned rules of law but because my classmates and I learned how to identify issues and, once an issue was identified, how to delve for solutions. The broader the scope of our knowledge, the more creative and effective we could be in our search for answers. We learned that to practice law effectively required more than an ability to recite rules.

George Lefcoe, our real property instructor, applied this philosophy in his class. He expected us to read not only our casebook but a potpourri of other readings. *The Death and Life of Great American Cities* by Jane Jacobs, the two-volume treatise *Feudal Society* by Marc Bloch, *Lord of the Flies* by William Golding and countless articles written by authors ranging from Milton Friedman to James Galbraith and John Maynard Keynes were all part of our curriculum. And, although I don't specifically recall, Marx and Hegel may well also have been part of our mix.

During law school my interest gravitated to public international law. That is why, after receiving my law degree in 1967 I applied to the University of Chicago's Committee on International Relations. I thought a firmer understanding of international relations would strengthen my understanding of international law. I was accepted. In late August, immediately after I took the California bar examination, I left Los Angeles for Chicago.

Home of Chicago Blues and Chicago Jazz, prominent in Upton Sinclair's *The Jungle*, used as the setting for Lorraine Hansberry's *A Raisin in the Sun*, celebrated by Jim Croce as the "baddest part of town," the South

20. Lessons Learned—University

Side of Chicago was also the site of the University of Chicago, a place where Nobel laureates congregated and the Atomic Age was born.

The university is in an area of the South Side known as Hyde Park. Shortly after I arrived, I sat at the counter of a Hyde Park coffee shop. On my left was a professor discussing his latest book. On my right, a personable, persistent panhandler trying to sell stolen Martin Luther King, Jr., records. It was an appropriate introduction to my new environment.

While I was at the university, Jeremy Azrael re-kindled my interest in Estonia and the Soviet Union. Mr. Azrael (at the University of Chicago even the Nobel laureates are, or at least were, referred to as "Mister" rather than "Doctor" or "Professor") was an expert on the Soviet Union. His research focused on the political challenges Soviet leaders faced, especially their problem of managing the Soviet Union's many, disparate nationalities. He argued that these nationalities posed a fundamental challenge to the Soviet state.

Mr. Azrael would sometimes bring a guest to class. One such guest was an Estonian who was a member of the Estonian SSR government, a façade of democracy created by the Soviets. One of the comments this guest made to our small group was, "Don't believe what we say in public."

While classroom lessons were important, what made my time in Chicago formative was exposure to both the non-university life that surrounded the campus and seeing some of the extraordinary events connected with the 1968 Democratic National Convention.

I lived in a second-floor room rented from a retired University of Chicago physics professor and his family. Their home was on South Kimbark Avenue, close to the university. Sometimes when I got tired of studying, I would exit my cocoon and explore the surroundings beyond the campus. Except during the winter, the South Side was an open-air living room. Everyone was outside.

I drove past low rise, dilapidated slum housing pockmarked by massive apartment towers, towers once touted as the largest, most modern public housing in the world, now figurative prisons, isolating the poor and making gang fiefdoms virtually impenetrable to the police. I saw people playing, talking, mixing. I was an interloper. On one occasion small stones were thrown at my moving car, not with a force designed to injure but with enough energy to let me know I did not belong. Insults followed the stones.

During one of my explorations, I walked to a political street rally where the world-renowned gospel singer Mahalia Jackson made an appearance. I was one of the few white faces in the crowd. Another time, I had to cross the Midway so I could return to the main campus from a visit to the law school library. The Midway consisted of four roads, each separated by a broad, park-like greenspace. Hundreds of Blackstone Rangers, the gang that ruled the South Side, were gathered along and in the Midway. I walked through the conclave, with trepidation but no incident.

Martin Luther King was shot in the early evening of April 4, 1968. The next day Chicago's political leaders asked people to turn on their automobile headlights as a sign of respect and remembrance. That afternoon I had to go downtown. I drove north on Lake Shore Drive. On the other side of the highway, headlights of southbound traffic turned on as cars neared the South Side. On my return a few hours later, I watched headlights being turned off as northbound traffic left the South Side. Fear, hypocrisy or a bit of both?

My extended University of Chicago neighborhood consisted of diverse self-interests and life styles, imposed and self-imposed. I observed the fragile coexistence between a multitude of different worlds. I was introduced to an America very different from my parents' American dream.

In early August 1968 the Republican Party nominated Richard Nixon for President. In late August I witnessed the convulsions that accompanied the Democratic Party's National Convention. It was a time of protests against the Vietnam War. It was a time of protest against the political system. It was a time of reaction to protest. Four groups, four different goals. One stage.

President Johnson had announced he would not seek reelection. For the Democrats, Eugene McCarthy was the peace candidate, Hubert Humphrey the establishment candidate. Delegates to the national convention would select between the two. The National Mobilization Committee to End the War in Vietnam sought to influence whom the Democratic Party nominated.

The Chicago Seven, Abbie Hoffman, Jerry Rubin, Tom Hayden, et al.—the Yippies—became household names. They sought to revolutionize the political system, regardless of who the candidate was.

Mayor Richard J. Daley's imprint was everywhere, often distributed through the Chicago police. He sought to maintain his power and his ego by confronting the disrupters. One night during the convention a friend and I roamed, on foot and by car, the streets of downtown Chicago. As we moved from storm center to storm center, from Michigan Avenue and the Hilton Hotel to Grant Park and confrontation points in between, we watched and listened to the protesters and to the forces opposed to them.

Anti-war protesters chanted, "kill, kill, kill," many waving scrawled peace signs. Yippies thronged the streets, seeking confrontations. Troops with fixed bayonets stood at set intervals along Chicago's Michigan Avenue; a machine gun was towed back and forth. More National Guardsmen were packed sardine-like in military trucks parked on side streets close to Michigan Avenue. They held their weapons and waited for orders to disembark and reinforce the troops already on the streets.

The police were on extended duty. My friend and I watched as two Chicago policemen who were crossing an empty side street spotted a solitary, long haired, filthy hippie, walking silently the other way. The policemen made a U-turn, strode to the hippie, then without saying a word, knocked him down, kicked and clubbed the prone, curled-up body, and resumed crossing the street.

Only one week earlier, Czechoslovakia's Prague Spring had been crushed. I had stayed up all night listening to real time descriptions on shortwave radio as Soviet tanks invaded the streets of Prague, intimidating and killing as they rolled in, destroying the country's nascent movement toward democracy. Was I in Prague or in Chicago?

The horror of hearing "kill, kill, kill" echo through American streets—chanted by people opposed to war, the shock of seeing American soldiers prepared to bayonet their fellow citizens, the unreality of witnessing a machine gun being towed back and forth on an American thoroughfare, all the emotions engendered by those events linger to this day.

My mother said she fled Estonia because she wanted "the right to live a complete life. A person must be able to think freely, to criticize, to express oneself. And, no life can be complete if a person is not permitted to live according to her own beliefs, if a person is unable to develop one's abilities. Freedom is priceless."

America's mystique—of freedom, democracy and opportunity, the mystique that pulled my parents to America—presented a different face in the streets of Chicago. I never told them about my Chicago excursions, neither my explorations of the South Side nor my downtown Chicago observations during the Democratic Convention. I'm not sure what their response would have been to all that I had seen.

21

In the Army

"An education in the logic of the illogical"

As then legally required of all American males, in 1961 when I turned 18, I registered for the draft. As I began my studies at U.S.C. my 2-S student deferment was virtually automatic. Few people, if any, were concerned about the draft and possible mandatory military service.

Outside a few political science professors, most people paid little attention to the worsening conditions in South Vietnam. Disquietude that existed after Vietnam's 1954 division into North and South steadily grew as political instability increased with each passing year, exacerbated by propaganda and violence emanating from North Vietnam and the Vietcong. As conditions in the South deteriorated American military involvement increased, first with military advisors, then with combat troops.

In 1964, as I was about to begin law school, the American naval ship USS *Maddox* may or may not have been attacked by North Vietnamese patrol torpedo boats in the Gulf of Tonkin. Alleging the attacks, President Johnson asked for and received Congressional approval for direct U.S. involvement in Vietnam. Shortly after that, the first American combat troops landed on the beaches near Da Nang, South Vietnam, replacing the already present military advisors.

In 1965, I was studying constitutional law, civil procedure, unfair competition and such other subjects while American troops fought their first large scale battle against the North Vietnamese Army. Around the same time, in an apparently unconnected happening, my student deferment was changed to 1-A, available for military service. The rumor was that my local draft board had lost many files and reclassified everyone as available for military service on the assumption that if anyone's classification was wrong, the aggrieved party would appeal. I appealed. My student deferment was restored.

By the time I completed law school in 1967, mass anti-war protests were common. The draft was now on everyone's mind, especially men ages

21. In the Army

18 through 25. Deferments for whatever reason were highly sought. When I began my studies at the University of Chicago I was classified as 2-S. That lasted until the summer of 1968 at which time my student deferment expired.

I wrote my draft board and asked that it continue my deferment long enough for me to finish my master's thesis. I estimated this would be no later than January. Twenty-six was the age when men were no longer draft eligible. I reminded the draft board that I would not turn 26 until the following July. There was time enough to draft me if it so desired.

I heard nothing back. I was in the unique and somewhat uncomfortable position of having no draft classification. I did not have a student deferment. Neither was I reclassified as available for military service. In retrospect, I assume someone read my letter, sympathized with my situation, held on to my papers until January and then put my file back into the system as 1-A. From that point on, the government moved quickly.

Within two months of my graduation, I received a notice to report for my pre-induction physical. Shortly after taking my physical an official letter arrived in my mailbox. "Greeting. You are hereby ordered for induction into the Armed Forces of the United States...."

On May 13, 1969, I reported to the Los Angeles induction center. Except for two men who refused, all present took an oath to support and defend the Constitution and to obey any orders of the President and any officers as required by the Uniform Code of Military Justice. Following the administration of the oath, everyone was bused 300 miles north, past Monterey, for Basic Training at Fort Ord.

I was drafted into the United States Army in 1969, during the Viet Nam War. I completed Basic Training at Fort Ord, California, and spent several additional months there as a "hold-over" while the Army tried to determine if I was a security risk because of my Estonian birth. Ultimately, I was assigned to Fort Belvoir, Virginia, to serve as a legal clerk. At the end of my two-year tour of duty I had reached the rank of Specialist 5, equivalent to the lowest rank of sergeant (United States Army).

Within a day of our arrival, after being uniformed and receiving two-minute buzz haircuts, we were marched into a large auditorium for a non-denominational chapel service led by a chaplain, an Airborne Ranger who in an earlier life had possibly trained as a used car salesman.

He gave a pep talk. We were urged to extend our mandatory two-year tour of duty to three or four years. Doing so would give us a qualified right to pick our military occupation and to be trained in that occupation. The pep talk completed, the chaplain delivered a short sermon—in battle everyone believes in God. A prayer followed. The service climaxed with the chaplain leading us in ever-louder chants of, "kill, kill, kill." I felt a disconnect.

After Basic Training I received my MOS—Military Occupational Specialty, as a legal clerk. I was ordered to report to the then home of the Army Corps of Engineers at Fort Belvoir, Virginia. Fort Belvoir was located about twenty miles south of Washington, D.C., not far from Mount Vernon. When I arrived, people were still talking about a recently discovered phantom company. For years the army had delivered supplies to a nonexistent Fort Belvoir unit. The supplies had been intercepted and sold in the private market by senior noncommissioned officers.

My time in the military was an education in the logic of the illogical, illuminated by Joseph Heller as "Catch-22."

> There was only one catch and that was Catch-22, which specified that a concern for one's own safety in the face of dangers that were real and immediate was the process of a rational mind. Orr was crazy and could be grounded. All he had to do was ask; and as soon as he did, he would no longer be crazy and would have to fly more missions. Orr would be crazy to fly more missions and sane if he didn't, but if he was sane, he had to fly them. If he flew them, he was crazy and didn't have to; but if he didn't want to, he was sane and had to. Yossarian was moved very deeply by the absolute simplicity of this clause of Catch-22 and let out a respectful whistle.

Initially I worked in the Courts and Boards office. I helped process paperwork for administrative discharges—discharges that were less than honorable but better than dishonorable. Later, when an officer from the Post Commander's office dropped in and thought I had too much free time, I was moved to the Judge Advocate General's office—commonly referred to as JAG. This is where the army's lawyers worked. At JAG I had even more free time. In both the Courts and Boards office and at JAG, I usually completed my daily assignments in an hour or two and read books the rest of the day.

If I had been washing dishes, raking leaves or cleaning latrines I would have felt as though I were at least doing something that needed doing. Instead, I was simply a statistic, taking up space. My presence was not particularly helpful to the war effort.

21. In the Army

In the JAG office I would sometimes run errands for the officers, often to the nearest McDonald's to bring back lunches. Occasionally I would do something useful. One time an officer, a second lieutenant, came to the JAG office. He was on his way to a temporary duty assignment. He had an authorization form that had a slew of signatures but there was still one blank signature line. Without a signature on each signature line, he couldn't get necessary transportation.

He had been unable to find anyone at Fort Belvoir who knew what the blank signature line was for or who could provide the final signature. He hoped someone at JAG could either provide the needed signature or at least tell him what he should do. He circulated through the office, from captain to captain, all to no avail. I got tired of listening to the run-around. I also felt sorry for the lieutenant. I took his form and signed my name. Everyone was happy.

I became proficient at knowing who to see when something needed to be done. I knew that to resolve a problem at the stockade, the person to talk to was the corporal, a draftee, not the master sergeant who ostensibly ran the place. Similar rules of thumb applied to supplies, finance and other important areas.

Together with three of my friends, all draftees, graduates of the law schools at Harvard, Fordham and the University of Tennessee, all licensed to practice law, we volunteered to work in the post's legal aid office in the evenings and weekends, times when it would ordinarily be closed. Our offer was rejected. It would be too difficult to change the scheduling. Besides, we were enlisted men.

One weekend I was assigned duty at the Special Processing Detachment. This was a holding area where military personnel who had been apprehended in our district for being AWOL, absent without leave, waited for their cases to be disposed—often through an administrative discharge. The detachment consisted of several hundred men, all confined to their barracks. An officer and an enlisted man were required to be on duty at all times.

My assigned officer, one of the captains from the JAG office, made a perfunctory appearance and told me he planned to spend the weekend in his quarters. If there was any trouble, I should let him know. He gave me his service pistol.

In Basic Training I had qualified as an expert marksman with an M14 rifle. However, the weapon I was handed was something I was unfamiliar with. I looked at it with trepidation. I was pretty sure I could find the trigger but I had no idea where the safety was—if it even had a safety. Neither could I tell if it was loaded or unloaded. I assumed it was loaded. I locked it in my desk for the weekend.

Washington, D.C., was the site of many anti-war demonstrations. I observed several, including one of the largest, the November 15, 1969, mass protest by 250,000 people that enveloped the National Mall from the Washington Monument to the Lincoln Memorial.

At other times I saw any approach to the White House blocked by school busses, parked bumper to bumper, that encircled the White House. No one could pass between the bumpers. On several occasions, while walking downtown, I had to step inside a store to escape the acrid taste and smell of tear gas that floated in the air. Another time I watched the combat engineers from Fort Belvoir enter the Treasury Building basement in full combat gear, ready to exit and disperse crowds as needed.

Most draftees tried to do their job well. The prevalent attitude was to do our assigned tasks, such as they were, but ignore the rest of army life as much as possible. *M*A*S*H*'s Hawkeye Pierce and Trapper John would have understood.

I spent most of my off-duty time either watching movies in downtown D.C. or traveling. I once watched a twin bill of *Around the World in Eighty Days* and *Gone with the Wind* on a Saturday afternoon and then celebrated the evening watching another feature, the name of which I can't now recall. On weekends when I didn't have duty, I visited Boston, New York, Philadelphia, Baltimore, New Orleans and Atlanta. The military received significant discounts on airline tickets so long as we wore our uniform. I also explored places closer to Fort Belvoir in greater detail—Maryland, Washington, D.C., Virginia, West Virginia, and North Carolina. My reading was reserved for killing time while I was on the job.

The army experiences I have recited are, individually, inconsequential and not worth dwelling on. However, the cumulative effect of each inconsequential event was consequential. Living with the burlesque, inefficiencies and regimentation of army life led me to conclude that it wasn't just the army that suffered from these maladies. I felt they were endemic to any large organization, public or private. This conclusion eliminated my two likeliest prospective employers if I were to practice public international law, the government or a large corporation. I assumed that each would have an environment similar to what I experienced in the army. I discarded my plan to practice public international law.

Mother: *Time passed. Metex grew. Equipment became more modern. Our gluing system was slow, cumbersome and taxing. We needed to have a machine do the work. While Jaak was in the military, he was stationed near Washington, D.C. He was able to go to New York and find a company that built us a gluing machine. That was a significant forward step for our business.*

Perhaps my major accomplishment while in the army was to visit New York and inspect a gluing machine that was being built for Metex.

21. In the Army

This was a machine that would replace the slow, tedious job of a person standing hour after hour, planting alternate gluing racks on sheets of tissue paper. My father had found, how I don't know, a New York machine shop that promised to build a gluing machine to his specifications. I went to New York to check on the progress of the work and reported back to my parents.

Mother: *After eight years in Sun Valley, we had moved to a new home in a different part of Los Angeles's San Fernando Valley, Encino. However, our factory continued to be in Burbank. In early 1971 we began to look for a new location—a place that would have more space and be an easier commute. Stories about our company's need reached the ears of those selling factory buildings. It seemed as though every day brought us a new offer to sell an available building. We had a large selection to choose from.*

We found a brand-new building at the other end of the San Fernando Valley from Burbank. Located in Canoga Park, it had three front offices as well as its own parking area. We liked it a lot. We bought it. Now we had to figure out how to keep working while we moved our equipment. We had three salespeople who were actively sending in orders. Business was going well but we couldn't afford to stop fulfilling orders that arrived while we moved.

I completed my two-year army tour of duty on May 12, 1971. Metex started its move from Hollywood Way to Canoga Park on May 13, 1971. I have always been suspicious of how well the two dates coincided. Prior to my discharge I had floated the idea to my parents of returning to Los Angeles on a bicycle, cycling across country from Fort Belvoir to Los Angeles. I even had a couple of possible routes mapped out. My parents were not enthusiastic. The day after my discharge I was helping move Metex to the new, larger building in Canoga Park.

I established my own law practice, initially in one of the front office spaces in our new factory building. Clients could hear punch presses at work in the background but the rent was cheap.

As Metex became more firmly established, my parents began to take life a little easier. They found they could close the factory for a month each summer without losing customers. They used some of that newly available time to explore different parts of the world. They increased their participation in the life of the local, growing Estonian community. They continued and increased their support of political activities related to Estonia and the other Baltic states, especially their support of the Baltic American Freedom League, BAFL for short.

22

Baltic American Freedom League

"Unity brings strength."

Mother: We made time for political work. That was a very important part of our life. We had to let the world know about the injustice our country and people had suffered. Meetings on Saturday, demonstrations on Sunday, telephone calls during the week.

Nothing could stop our battle to regain independence for the Baltic States. A group of Estonian, Latvian and Lithuanian Americans formed the Baltic American Freedom League (BAFL). Unity brings strength. Joint demonstrations were organized. Conferences were held. Politicians were educated.

We called for freedom for Estonia, Latvia and Lithuania. We demanded that political prisoners be freed. We made contact with some of them. After his most recent release, we spoke with Mart Niklus who had spent nearly a third of his life in the gulags. We hosted Lagle Parek in Los Angeles. Each time Lagle was released from the gulags she resumed her campaign to return basic human rights to Estonians. She was a founder of the Estonian National Independence Party. Other freedom fighters also came to Los Angeles, among them Tunne Kelam, Trivimi Velliste and Tiit Madisson.

There was a gaping hole in the Communist wall—in the Iron Curtain. The workers at the Gdansk shipyards, the opening of the Berlin Wall, these events had produced a hole. We had to make that hole even bigger; so big that the entire wall would collapse.

The "political work" my mother refers to included demonstrations, conferences, receptions and letter writing campaigns. These were often planned and initiated by the Los Angeles–based Baltic American Freedom League, commonly referred to as BAFL.

Formed in 1981, during its first decade BAFL's projects were often innovative and its influence reached from Los Angeles to Washington, D.C. In 1982 it secured a first—a Congressional directive that the President issue a proclamation declaring June 14 "Baltic Freedom Day."

22. Baltic American Freedom League

The number of people willing to demonstrate in support of Baltic independence grew from half-dozens in the early 80s to 100s by the end of the 80s. The increase coincided with heightened dissident activity in the Baltic States. In addition to homemade placards, demonstrators carrying the national flags of Estonia, Latvia and Lithuania were a common sight (Treiman family archive).

Organizing human rights conferences with high profile participants, BAFL held awards banquets that publicized Baltic freedom fighters, initiated demonstrations, conversed with American political leaders, made donations of Baltic-related books to libraries, generated contacts with journalists and educated public media about the Baltic States. As a by-product of its activities, national ethnic organizations, thought by some people to be politically too timid, were invigorated.

The League was the inspiration of a Lithuanian refugee, Juozas Kojelis. During the day Juozas worked a blue-collar job at United Airlines. When not at work, he was a writer, an intellectual and an activist. As a young man during World War II, he had fought the Germans and the Soviets, had been tried in absentia by both and had been sentenced to death by both. During BAFL's 1994 Awards Banquet, Juozas spoke about the organization's genesis.

> I got the idea of Baltic American Freedom League as an organization indirectly from the different kind of "days" proclaimed by the U.S. Congress. I started to think: why not try to pass in Congress a "Baltic Day" resolution. After talking with Mrs. Leslie Dutton, who worked for the Hannaford Public Relations Company, we expanded the idea threefold:

Securing Baltic independence was not only a campaign to regain lost sovereignty. It was a movement to reestablish fundamental human rights for the people living in the Baltic States. Because human rights were a common denominator, following the 1989 Tiananmen Square massacre we held some joint demonstrations with the local Chinese community. Here Chinese demonstrators prepare to raise their "Goddess of Liberty" statue in front of the Federal Building in Los Angeles—at the time, the best place in Los Angeles to hold a demonstration (Treiman family archive).

(a) establish a Baltic organization,
(b) pass in the Congress an annual Baltic Freedom Day resolution, and
(c) engage the Hannaford Public Relations Company to help us in our endeavor.

The first exploratory meeting took place on February 21, 1981. Seven Lithuanians accepted this idea, pledged $4,000 to start this movement, and decided to explore this project with our Estonian and Latvian friends.

Not long after, we had a first meeting (if I remember correctly) with Avo and Viivi Piirisild, Dr. Ansis Blakis, Heino and Maie Nurmberg, Jonas Matulaitis, Danute Barauskaite, Tony Mazeika, Saulius Damusis and myself. This is how Baltic American Freedom League was born.

Hiring a public relations company was a first for Baltic activists, perhaps because no one had thought of doing so or perhaps because of the financial commitment it required.

The "Hannaford Public Relations Company" that Juozas refers to was a public relations firm started by Peter Hannaford, a political consultant to Ronald Reagan when Reagan was the Governor of California. Hannaford continued in that role when Reagan became President. Before his company would begin work, it required a guarantee that their monthly fee would be paid. The guarantee was given by an Estonian family, a Latvian family and a Lithuanian family. Each mortgaged their home as security for payment.

Valdis Pavlovskis, one of BAFL's founders although unavoidably absent from the inaugural meeting, was President of BAFL in 1982 when the Baltic Freedom Day Congressional resolution and the resulting Presidential Proclamation came to fruition. Valdis emailed me the following response when I asked him for the backstory:

> Baltic Freedom Day came sometime after we hired Hannaford. We had great difficulty in paying them $8,000 each month. We could not get enough contributions to cover their fees. We met with Peter Hannaford at his office. I told him about our financial problem.
>
> I suggested that we would receive more contributions if we could have a picture taken with the President. Only partly joking, I said we were ready to sit at the White, waiting for the President to walk by so if he did, we could jump up and snap a picture with him.
>
> Hannaford said what we needed was an event, a celebration or something of the kind. He wanted to know what were the important Baltic dates or occasions. June 14, Baltic Deportation Day, seemed to be the only date all three of the Baltic States had in common.
>
> We did not want to use June 14. We wanted to look forward, not backward. Mr. H. explained we could do both. We want freedom now even as we look back at the suffering we have sustained. He thought that approach might appeal to President Reagan. With that conversation, Baltic Freedom Day began to take life. We were promised that once the resolution passed the House and the Senate, the President would issue a proclamation at a signing ceremony that we would be invited to attend.
>
> Even with the President saying he was ready to sign our Proclamation, first we needed half plus one of the House of Representatives in support and 33 senators in support. It was not easy but we got them. In 1982 the Proclamation passed in the House and in the Senate and the President signed it. Because of the British war with the Argentinians in the Falkland Islands, the President did not want a public celebration.
>
> We wanted to make the Baltic Freedom Day Proclamation an annual event. The following year, we had dropped Mr. H., and we had to secure the necessary votes in the House and in the Senate by ourselves. And we did. The Falklands War was over. We had a public signing at the White House and BAFL gave the White House a list of 200 invitees. We invited JBANC [Joint Baltic American National Committee], both Lithuanian national organizations, the Estonian and Latvian national organizations. We included those who opposed BAFL. We did not exclude them. It made no difference. They still didn't like us. [Valdis alludes to the unfriendly response that the recently formed BAFL generated from some of the traditional Baltic organizations.—jt]

BAFL used Hannaford's services for about two years, trying to keep up with its monthly charges and learning the company's techniques. Valdis recalls that "During my term as BAFL President, Hannaford called

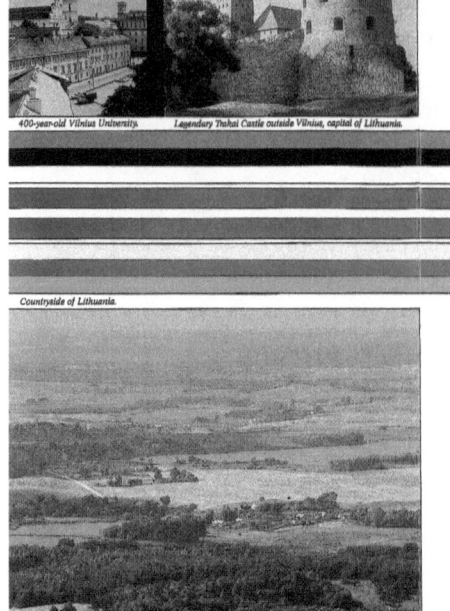

400-year-old Vilnius University. Legendary Trakai Castle outside Vilnius, capital of Lithuania.

Countryside of Lithuania.

Baltic Freedom Day, 1984

By the President of the United States of America

A Proclamation

It has been over 40 years since invading Soviet armies, in collusion with the Nazi regime, overran the three independent Baltic Republics of Estonia, Latvia, Lithuania and forceably incorporated them into Moscow's expanding empire. The new regime then ordered the illegal deportation, murder and imprisonment of tens of thousands of Baltic peoples whose only "crime" was to resist foreign tyranny and to defend their liberties and freedoms.

Oppression and persecution continue to this day but despite this long dark night of injustice, the brave men and women of Estonia, Latvia, and Lithuania have never abandoned the battle for their national independence and God-given rights. Although the full measure of their struggle and sacrifice is screened by the oppression and censorship under which they live, the friends and families of the Baltic peoples all over the world are aware of their heroic endeavors and aspirations.

Their peaceful demands for their rights command the admiration of everyone who loves and honors freedom. All the people of the United States of America share the just aspirations of the Baltic nations for national independence, and we uphold their right to determine their own national destiny free of foreign domination. The United States has never recognized the forceable incorporation of the Baltic States into the Soviet Union, and it will not do so in the future. The Congress of the United States, by Senate Joint Resolution 296, has authorized and requested the President to issue a proclamation for the observance of June 14, 1984, as "Baltic Freedom Day."

NOW THEREFORE, I, RONALD REAGAN, President of the United States of America, do hereby proclaim June 14, 1984, as Baltic Freedom Day I call upon the people of the United States to observe this day with appropriate remembrances and ceremonies and to reaffirm their commitment to the principles of liberty and freedom for all oppressed people.

IN WITNESS WHEREOF I have hereunto set my hand this fourteenth day of June, in the year of our Lord nineteen hundred and eighty-four and of the Independence of the United States of America the two hundred and eighth.

In 1982, with help from a public relations company it hired, the Baltic American Freedom League secured Congressional action and a Presidential signature for the first Baltic Freedom Day proclamation. Thereafter other Baltic organizations joined in what became an annual effort. A Presidential Proclamation was issued each year through 1991. Pictured is the 1984 Proclamation as incorporated into a BAFL brochure (Treiman family archive).

me on the first day of every month to remind me of our debt." At the time the relationship ended (amicably) the debt was $21,000+, still guaranteed by family homes.

Hannaford was, over time, paid in full. Continuing its work as a strictly volunteer organization, BAFL used techniques learned from Hannaford and relying on donations to cover their ongoing expenses. As before, Board members received no compensation for the work they performed. Most of its leadership came from a generation who had left the Baltic States as children but still had some memories of their respective home countries.

Another BAFL success occurred in 1983. At BAFL's initiative, President Reagan sent a letter to each member of the United Nations in which he explained why the United States did not recognize the Soviet Union's forced incorporation of the Baltic States. After reviewing how the Baltic States lost their independence, President Reagan's letter continued:

22. Baltic American Freedom League

Americans share the just aspirations of the people of the Baltic nations for national independence. We cannot remain silent in the face of the continued refusal of the government of the USSR to allow these people to be free. We uphold their right to determine their own national destiny, a right contained in the Helsinki Declaration which affirms that "all people always have the right, in full freedom, to determine, when and as they wish, their internal and external political status, without external interference and to pursue as they wish their political, economic, social, and cultural development."

For this reason, the government of the United States has never recognized the forced incorporation of the Baltic States into the Soviet Union and will not do so in the future.

The League wanted American government policy to mirror America's legal position concerning the non-recognition of the legality of the Soviet annexation of the Baltic States more accurately. As a result of BAFL's efforts, matched by the national ethnic organizations, in 1984 the American government transferred its Baltic languages radio programming from Radio Liberty, which targeted the Soviet Union, to Radio Free Europe, which targeted Soviet satellite countries. This was a strong, positive signal of support to Balts in America and the dissidents within the Baltic States.

From a BAFL brochure, left to right: Danute Mazeika, Tadas Dabsys, Valdis Pavlovskis, Jaak Treiman. The Baltic American Freedom League's Human Rights Conferences drew non–Baltic dignitaries in addition to Baltic activists. Valdis Pavlovskis, pictured above at the March 24, 1990, conference, later became independent Latvia's first Defense Minister (Treiman family archive).

The Baltic American Freedom League organized Human Rights Conferences, usually in Los Angeles, once as far away as Cleveland, Ohio. Well known politicians, statesmen, media representatives and academics appeared at these conferences as panelists or speakers. Among the participants were Eugene Pell, Director of Voice of America; Paul Kamenar, Washington Legal Foundation; Ambassador John D. Scanlan, ambassador to Yugoslavia; Ambassador Herbert S. Okun, ambassador to East Germany; R.L.J. Hawke, Prime Minister of Australia; and Professors Tõnu Parming, Rein Taagepera and Stanley Vardys.

On March 17, 1984, Assistant Secretary of State for Human Rights Elliott Abrams was the principal speaker at BAFL's Third Annual Human Rights Conference. He concluded his speech with a rousing endorsement of the right of the Baltic States to independence:

> I would like to take this opportunity to declare my solidarity, and the solidarity of the Reagan Administration, with the people of Lithuania, Latvia, and Estonia and to applaud you for your work on behalf of the Baltic peoples. Their cause is just; their courage is awesome, and their faith is inspiring. I am convinced that their struggle will be crowned with success.

Abrams' speech was politically significant because it was published as an official State Department document—public notice that America supported independence for Estonia, Latvia and Lithuania. German and British newspapers in particular took note and interpreted this speech and the fact it was officially published, as a signal that freedom for the Baltic States was an active part of American foreign policy.

Two BAFL events in particular stand out in my memory-bank. One was a Banquet where BAFL presented its Baltic Freedom Award to the Estonian former prisoner of conscience, Mart Niklus, via telephone. The other event was BAFL's August 1989 demand for Baltic independence that coincided with the Baltic Wave within the Baltic States.

In 1985, at my suggestion, the BAFL Board of Directors decided to present an annual "Freedom Award" that recognized individuals or organizations making significant contributions in support of the people of Estonia, Latvia and Lithuania regaining their freedom. When I told my mother about the Freedom Award, she was excited and suggested that the award be presented at a banquet. The BAFL Board thought that was a great idea. My mother volunteered to prepare the banquet meal.

My mother and one of her friends did the cooking and table service for that first banquet. Everyone grossly underestimated the number of people who would attend. In fact, my mother had to parcel out food in minuscule portions. Anyone who had ever eaten a meal at my mother's house, and experienced her insistence on second and third helpings,

22. Baltic American Freedom League

would know how painfully embarrassing this shortage of food was for her, even as she delighted in the large turn-out.

The first three Freedom Award recipients had been *The Chronicles of the Catholic Church in Lithuania* (1985), Bishop Julkionas Stepanovicius (1986) and Helsinki-86 (1987). *The Chronicles* were an underground Lithuanian publication, the bishop was the head of the archdiocese of Vilnius and had been designated a "secret Cardinal" by the Pope and the Latvian group Helsinki-86 was the first openly anti–Communist organization in the Soviet Union. Each presentation had been made to a stand-in representative, domiciled in the United States.

The 1988 recipient of the Freedom Award was to be the Estonian dissident Mart Niklus, recently released from a gulag. During his imprisonment, Amnesty International had identified Niklus as one of its "Prisoners of Conscience." President Reagan had advocated his release.

I suggested that the Freedom Award be presented directly to him via telephone. The Board liked the idea. However, a few hurdles had to be overcome. International calls required operator assistance and their exact timing could never be predicted. There was also a technical problem. Even if we succeeded in making telephone contact, how could the audience hear what was said? Conference calling and speaker phones were not an everyday item in 1988.

The banquet was to take place in the social hall of the Latvian Community Center in Los Angeles. I had a client in the telephone repair business who owed my firm money for past legal services. The two of us agreed that if he created a viable speaker system in the social hall, I would consider his debt paid. It took him a full half-day, but he did it. We were ready.

When the banquet began, I told the audience our plan. I tried calling Niklus from the head table early in the festivities. The circuits in New York were busy. This happened several more times. Doug Smith, a reporter for the *Los Angeles Times*, reported what happened next:

Then Treiman tried again. At 9:15, a loudspeaker attached to the phone sounded a ring and a distant "Hello."
"Mart Niklus?" Treiman said. "Jaak Treiman."
The conversation was long and sweet, the voice of Niklus, in English, barely audible over the speaker.
Treiman put on Vladas Shakalys, a friend of Niklus.' Shakalys recalled that they had spoken Russian together in prison.
"Yes," Niklus replied.
"That was enough," Shakalys said. "I learn English a little bit."
....
An old friend of Niklus' mother then stood to ask the final question. She wanted to know if the price for freedom had been too high.
"I don't regret anything that I have done," Niklus answered.

I presented Mart with the Baltic Freedom Award. He gave us fresh news, namely that Enn Tarto, another freedom fighter, had just been released from prison. Members of the audience, including Doug Smith, asked him questions. The call ended. Just as BAFL's then President, Avo Piirisild, finished closing the banquet, there was a giant roar from outside the social hall that matched and amplified the applause from inside.

The Los Angeles Dodgers baseball team, whose stadium is located about two miles from the Latvian center, had just scored a crucial run in a crucial, championship game. For baseball fans, Kirk Gibson had just hit his memorable, game winning, ninth-inning World Series home run. The timing was perfect! It felt as though the whole world supported us.

Another BAFL event, etched in my memory, took place on August 23, 1989. That is when about two million Estonians, Latvians and Lithuanians joined hands to protest the secret agreements between Moscow and Nazi Germany that allocated the Baltic States to the Soviet "sphere of influence" and resulted in their occupation by the Soviet Union. Michael Dobbs of the *Washington Post* offered his on-site description:

> Dubbed the "Baltic Way" by organizers, the human chain stretched from Tallinn, the Estonian capital, in the northeast through Latvia to Vilnius, the Lithuanian capital, in the southwest. Television pictures taken from helicopters showed an unbroken ribbon of people standing with linked arms along a route joining dozens of cities, towns and villages in the three republics. In Tallinn, many participants carried banners calling for an end to the Soviet "occupation" of the Baltic states and denouncing the 1939 Nazi-Soviet agreements that consigned their homelands to Soviet hegemony.

As the human chain stretched through the Baltic States, with many Estonians waiving the banned blue, black and white flag of independent Estonia with attached black ribbons to signify mourning, a BAFL Board member met with the German Consul General in Los Angeles while I flew to San Francisco to meet with the German Consul General there. We asked the Germans to publicly condemn the Molotov-Ribbentrop Pact.

After I finished my meeting with the German Consul General, I joined Bay Area Estonians, Latvians and Lithuanians for a demonstration in front of the Russian Consulate. They were there, ambulating back-and-forth along the sidewalk, waving handmade signs that demanded freedom for the Baltic States.

Following the demonstration, I flew back to Los Angeles and arrived at the Lithuanian church's social hall in time to participate in a massive rally. When the rally ended, everyone gathered across the street at the neighboring high school's football field. We formed our own human chain.

23

The 1984 Los Angeles Olympics

"A little too political."

Mother: *The Los Angeles Olympic Committee sent an invitation to our local Estonian, Latvian and Lithuanian folk-dance groups asking them to be part of the opening day ceremonies for the upcoming Olympic Games. Each dance group received their own invitation. A few days later each group was uninvited. They were told that Estonians, Latvians and Lithuanians were not permitted to participate. This caused a great deal of resentment. Even though we were living in a free country, the Soviet Communists still seemed to control our lives. The Baltic community was angry. Jaak was an energetic lawyer. He was asked to find a resolution. Ultimately, America did not want a confrontation with the Soviet Union so we were the losers.*

Estonians, Latvians and Lithuanians campaigned against the Soviet occupation of the Baltic States. In America the campaign took many different forms—speeches, demonstrations, articles and, not often but sometimes, lawsuits. *Spindulys, et al. v. Los Angeles Olympic Organizing Committee* was one such lawsuit.

Folk dance clubs from the Estonian, Latvian and Lithuanian communities in Los Angeles were excluded from the opening ceremonies of the 1984 Olympic Games. Almost all other ethnic groups were not. To understand the context in which this exclusion took place, we need to backtrack to December 1979.

That is when the Soviet Union overthrew Afghanistan's legitimate government, executed its President and replaced him with a puppet. At the same time, 100,000 Soviet soldiers were airlifted into Afghanistan and occupied the country. During the Soviet occupation an estimated one million civilians were killed. No one anticipated that three Los Angeles Baltic dance clubs would also become a casualty of that war.

The United States government protested the Soviet invasion and demanded restoration of Afghanistan's legitimate government. When the Soviet Union refused, President Carter announced that as one measure of protest, the United States would boycott the Olympic Games that were scheduled to begin in Moscow in July 1980.

He explained his rationale:

> ... there are times when our country must stand for principles and for what is right. The Olympic Games are supposed to enhance peace and brotherhood and friendship. When the Soviet Union just before the Olympic Games invades an innocent country and kills literally thousands of men, women, and children who had done them no harm and then professes with a great propaganda effort that they are the peace-loving nation on earth and that the Olympic Games were actually assigned to Moscow because their foreign policy and the principles were right, it's time for the nations to let them know that they cannot get away with that false claim and propaganda. [July 14, 1980 speech in Merced, California.]

The Moscow Olympics took place but 66 countries followed America's lead and joined the boycott. Would the Soviet Union and its vassal states retaliate by boycotting the next Olympics—scheduled for Los Angeles in 1984?

The 1984 Summer Olympics were to be a singular event for the Olympic movement. Instead of being organized by a governmental entity such as a country or city, they were organized by a private organization, the Los Angeles Olympic Organizing Committee (LAOOC), led by Peter Ueberroth. In a first, public money would not be used to subsidize the Games.

Ueberroth wanted the Soviet Union and the Eastern Bloc countries to participate. He had a number of reasons. As elucidated by Philip A. D'Agati in his book *The Cold War and the 1984 Olympic Games: A Soviet-American Surrogate War*, "Ueberroth ... calculated that a Cold War Games would boost the Olympic spectacle in four principal areas: spectatorship and viewership, the size of the events and the athletic contingents, the financial footprint of the Games and the levels of commercialism." For a privately-run enterprise, one committed to not operating at a deficit, Soviet attendance was an important goal.

The Los Angeles Games were planned as a Hollywood spectacular, one that would showcase L.A.'s distinctive features. One of those features was Southern California's cultural and ethnic diversity. This would be emphasized in the opening ceremonies by an International Parade. Parade participants, culled from the local ethnic communities, would enter the historic Los Angeles Memorial Coliseum immediately after the Parade of Athletes.

Virtually every ethnic organization in Los Angeles, including the local Baltic dance clubs, *Kivikasukas*, *Perkonitis* and *Spindulys*, were invited to apply to march in the International Parade. In early 1984 Yanis Braukis, Director of the Latvian dance club *Perkonitis*, was personally

23. The 1984 Los Angeles Olympics 157

asked to submit an application for his group. Yanis told the organizers about the Estonian and Lithuanian clubs, *Kivikasukas* and *Spindulys*. As a result, their participation was also solicited. Club members were excited. All three clubs applied.

Time passed. Not having heard from the LAOOC by the end of March, Yanis and Robert Anderson, a member of the Estonian dance club, enquired about the status of their applications. Each was told their application had been rejected. When they asked "Why?" Yanis and Robert were told their participation would be "a little too political." The Lithuanian group was rejected for the same reason.

Yanis and Robert came to see me. Following our conversation, I protested to the LAOOC on behalf of the dance groups. Correspondence was exchanged. I spoke with the Organizing Committee's representatives. No mention was made of the Baltic folk dancers' presence being "too

Pictured is a page from a BAFL brochure. The bottom picture is from a press conference BAFL held when the Los Angeles Olympic Organizing Committee refused to permit the local Estonian, Latvian and Lithuanian folk-dance groups to march in the International Parade portion of the opening ceremonies of the 1984 Olympics. Most other Los Angeles–area ethnic groups participated. From left: Jurate Venckus, Viivi Piirisild, Yanis Braukis, Valdis Pavlovskis, Anthony Mazeika, and Jaak Treiman (Treiman family archive).

political." Instead, I was told the Organizing Committee had no choice but to reject the Baltic folk dance clubs because neither Estonia, Latvia nor Lithuania was on the International Olympic Committee's (IOC's) list of countries accredited to have athletes participate in the Games. Accordingly, the local Baltic dance groups could not participate in the opening day parade.

I thought their logic was faulty—a *non sequitur*. The Baltic folk dancers were not asking to participate as athletes representing Estonia, Latvia and Lithuania. They were local, Los Angeles folk dance clubs whose members performed ethnic folk dances at community events and festivals. They were part of the multi-cultural fabric of Los Angeles.

I assumed that the LAOOC was using the IOC's list of eligible countries as a pretext to justify their decision. I suspected that by not having the names Estonia, Latvia and Lithuania appear anywhere in the Olympic program, they hoped to eliminate one potential excuse for Soviet non-participation, even after Moscow's May 8 announcement that they would not participate.

I spoke with BAFL's executive committee members. They were incensed. They were also energized. They saw the LAOOC refusal as a moral issue. At the same time, they felt the refusal was an opportunity to publicize the Soviet Union's unlawful occupation of the Baltic States.

My law firm was asked to represent Yanis Braukis and the dance clubs in a lawsuit against the Los Angeles Olympic Organizing Committee and BAFL agreed to fund the lawsuit. They would raise money from the Baltic community. My ever-patient law partner, Mark Schiffman, was delighted. For once, one of my Baltic digressions from the practice of law, often on firm time, might actually result in income, even if at a discounted rate. At the very least, it would not generate a loss.

Our lawsuit was premised on California's Unruh Civil Rights Act. We alleged that the LAOOC had discriminated against the local Estonian, Latvian and Lithuanian folk dancers because of their national origin.

Court calendars were congested. A trial of our discrimination claim could not take place until well after the Olympics. We therefore asked for temporary, immediate relief, namely that *Spindulys*, *Perkonitis* and *Kivikasukas* be allowed to either participate in the International Parade or, if they were not permitted to participate, that the LAOOC be prohibited from staging the parade. The judge would rule based on his evaluation of the probability of our success at trial.

A number of media representatives covered our hearing for temporary relief. Before our case was called, they waited in the hallway outside the courtroom. Among them was a Canadian-Estonian reporter for a local Los Angeles television station, Tiiu Leek. Before I entered the courtroom

23. The 1984 Los Angeles Olympics

we talked about the case, in Estonian, off camera. Her station, and others, covered the story in the evening news.

The court denied our bid for temporary relief. The International Parade would take place without the Baltic folk dancers. Our discrimination claim would be heard in due course, after the Olympics ended. We could still show, after-the-fact, that the LAOOC had discriminated against the dance clubs because of their members' heritage.

My father and I sat in the stands on July 28, when the Opening Ceremonies took place. He had won the right to buy two tickets through a lottery system that was used to allocate tickets among the hundreds of thousands who wanted them. I felt validated in our legal position as I watched Native Americans and other indigenous people, not recognized by the IOC for purposes of athletic competition, march past us as part of the International Parade.

The LAOOC was defended by one of the country's premier law firms. Their defense to our discrimination claim consisted of two basic arguments. One, there was no violation of the Unruh Act because the opening ceremonies were not a "public" event as defined in the law. Two, what I considered a more serious argument, that even if there was an Unruh Act violation, the court had no right to involve itself in our dispute because participation by the Baltic dance clubs raised a political issue that was beyond the court's power to decide.

The doctrine that courts should not involve themselves in "political issues" is an old but nebulous concept that tries to pay homage to the separation of powers between the legislative, judicial and executive branches of government. In theory, the doctrine is meant to keep courts out of controversies better handled by the legislative or executive branches of government. Historically it has been used most often when a court has faced issues relating to foreign affairs.

I anticipated that the LAOOC would support its position by citing a case that arose during the 1980 Winter Olympics, held in Lake Placid, New York. The Lake Placid Organizing Committee acting through the International Olympic Committee had faced a dispute concerning conflicting participation rights between athletes from Taiwan and athletes from Mainland China. The IOC made a decision the Taiwanese athletes did not like. They took the IOC to court.

The State Department intervened in the case by filing a position paper with the court. Its "Statement of Interest" said that the American government deferred to the IOC's determination as to which athletes could participate and asked the court to stay out of the dispute.

> The United States believes that judicial intervention in the IOC's management of the games is inconsistent with the United States' commitment to observe the

rules established by the IOC and calls into question the ability of the United States to host other international sporting events in a manner consistent with the decisions of international bodies.

I wanted to rebut the potential effect of the Lake Placid case by asking the State Department for a Statement of Non-interest—a statement that it had no interest as to who marched or did not march in the International Parade. With such a statement there would be no political issue. The court would be free to rule on the merits of our Unruh Act claim.

I contacted Linas Kojelis, son of BAFL founder Juozas Kojelis. Linas worked in the White House as Special Assistant to the President. I explained our situation. He gave me a contact in the State Department. From that point, I spoke with no less than half a dozen State Department officials. Some were very sympathetic. A few volunteered useful legal authorities, although they did so unofficially. No one offered to provide me with the Statement of Non-interest that I sought.

While the State Department failed to tender any official help, during the course of our lawsuit I received numerous expressions of support from other organizations and individuals, including a letter from a member of the United States Commission on Civil Rights. Such philosophically disparate organizations as the American Civil Liberties Union and the Washington Legal Foundation were aware of our case and followed it from the sidelines.

The media published stories about the litigation. When they did, they related the history and status of the Baltic States. The *Los Angeles Herald Examiner* published an editorial that began, "It is ironic that in the same week President Reagan commemorated the plight of peoples in communist captivity, a dispute arose over the L.A. Olympic Committee's refusal to let several such ethnic groups take part in the Games' opening ceremonies."

America's largest circulation Spanish language newspaper of the time, *La Opinion*, carried a sympathetic front-page story about our case. The *Los Angeles Daily Journal*, L.A.'s principal newspaper for lawyers and judges, devoted space to our lawsuit.

Also, I received a series of telephone calls from Japanese newspapers in Japan asking for updates on our case. During the third such call I told the reporter that my clients and I appreciated their attention. But, I asked, "Why are you interested?" The reporter told me that the Japanese saw similarities between the occupation of the Baltic States and the Soviet occupation of the Kuril Islands at the very end of World War II, hence their interest.

After the court denied our request for preliminary relief, the LAOOC asked the court to dismiss our lawsuit based on the pleadings and without a trial. They argued that the undisputed facts entitled them to a favorable

23. The 1984 Los Angeles Olympics

Civil No.
B009941

IN THE COURT OF APPEAL OF THE STATE OF

CALIFORNIA

SECOND APPELLATE DISTRICT

SPINDULYS, an unincorporated association, PERKONITIS, an unincorporated association, KIVIKASUKAS, an unincorporated association, and YANIS BRAUKIS,

    Plaintiffs and Appellants,

vs.

LOS ANGELES OLYMPIC ORGANIZING COMMITTEE,

    Defendant and Respondent.

2 CIVIL B009941

Los Angeles Superior Court No. C 504 847

APPELLANTS' OPENING BRIEF

On Appeal from the Judgment of the Superior Court of
California
Los Angeles County
The Honorable Robert B. Lopez, Judge

TREIMAN & SCHIFFMAN
By Jaak Treiman
21515 Vanowen Street, Suite 211
Canoga Park, CA 91303
Telephone: (818) 884-5850
Attorneys for Appellants

Supported by the Baltic American Freedom League, the local Los Angeles Estonian, Latvian and Lithuanian folk-dance clubs filed a lawsuit when they were refused the right to participate in the opening ceremonies of the 1984 Olympics in Los Angeles. They were deemed "too political." The dance groups lost at the trial court and appealed to the California court of appeals. Although unsuccessful, the lawsuit gained favorable editorials and brought renewed attention to the Baltic States (the brief is a matter of public record. A copy is in the Treiman family archive).

judgment. Their primary argument, citing the Lake Placid case, was that our case raised political questions which the court did not have the authority to decide.

The court listened to our respective arguments and ruled against us, finding that a political issue existed. Because of that finding it did not have to address our discrimination allegations. We appealed the dismissal to California's 2nd District Court of Appeal.

A panel of three judges heard our appeal in November 1985. Less than a month later they unanimously ruled against us. Their written, published opinion in *Spindulys, et al. v. Los Angeles Olympic Organizing Committee* did not address the civil rights allegations. Instead, the court held that our issues were "unquestionably a matter of political nature beyond the province of our courts of law" and therefore not subject to the court's jurisdiction.

We considered appealing to the California Supreme Court. Instead, we accepted a proposal by the Olympic Organizing Committee to settle the lawsuit. We dismissed our case. A joint statement was issued that said in part:

> While it regrets the dance groups' decision to file suit, the LAOOC compliments Spindulys, Perkonitis and Kivikasukas for the pride they display in their heritage and for the contributions made to American life by persons of Latvian, Estonian and Lithuanian heritage. The Baltic American dancers compliment the LAOOC on its organizational aptitude in producing and conducting the Olympic Games. Each party joins with the other in the wish that the Olympic movement shall henceforth be governed by a spirit of universal brotherhood and sportsmanship.

The 1984 Olympic Games were an athletic, artistic and financial success. It "has been heralded as an overwhelming, transformative success, ushering the Olympic movement into the modern commercial age." Relying primarily on private corporate funding and even without Soviet participation, this was the first financially successful modern Olympics.

Almost everybody associated with the lawsuit could claim an element of victory. The LAOOC won the lawsuit. Sympathy and favorable news stories were generated for the Baltic States and BAFL continued its crusade to secure independence for Estonia, Latvia and Lithuania. The only people who lost were the local Estonian, Latvian and Lithuanian-American dancers. They were deprived of a once-in-a-lifetime opportunity to parade in front of 92,000 people plus a world-wide television audience estimated at 2.5 billion, even as the President of the United States watched and opened the Games.

24

America's Nonrecognition Policy

> *"The people of the United States are opposed to predatory activities..."*

The United States maintains that no country has the right to forcibly take-over another country's territory. If it does, the seizure will be considered illegal. It will not be legally recognized. Had America not followed this rule of international law when the Soviet Union annexed Estonia, my life would have been different. I do not know what this other life would have been but I know it would not have been the life I now have.

References to this rule, sometimes as the "nonrecognition policy" or "nonrecognition principle," are woven throughout the following chapters. A short digression may clarify those references and why the rule was of crucial importance to Baltic activists outside of the Baltic States and to the dissidents within the Baltic States.

What happened in Estonia can be analogized to a familiar, domestic crime—burglary. Criminal law generally defines burglary as "the entry into a building with intent to commit a crime, especially theft." In Estonia, Soviet troops penetrated the Estonian/Russian border, much as a burglar breaks a door or window. Then, as burglars do, the Soviet Union took its booty. Farms and businesses were confiscated from their owners and nationalized. Items of value needed by Moscow were shipped to Moscow. Unlike burglars, the Soviet troops stayed.

Rigged Parliamentary elections followed with a Soviet front organization "winning" a huge majority. During the subsequent legislative vote, even given a marionette assembly, Soviet tanks surrounded the Estonian Parliament building, their turrets pointed toward the assembled, hand-picked puppets in a non-subtle reminder of how they were to vote. Soviet soldiers stood in the Parliament's chamber, their rifles at the ready, as the vote took place.

The newly populated legislature immediately asked that Estonia "rejoin" the U.S.S.R.—a choreographed request that was promptly accepted by the Soviet Union's Supreme Soviet.

Unlike Hungary, Bulgaria, Poland, Romania and the other countries of Eastern Europe that retained their sovereign identity even though their respective governments were populated by Moscow's minions, as far as the Soviet Union was concerned Estonia no longer existed. It had been annexed. It had become one of the republics of the Union of Soviet Socialist Republics; its inhabitants were deemed Soviet citizens. A similar sequence of events took place in Latvia and Lithuania.

Some countries, such as Sweden, accepted the Soviet annexations. They considered the Soviet conquest to be legal. They accepted the right of the Soviet Union to treat whatever happened in Estonia as a domestic Soviet issue. Sweden turned the Estonian Embassy over to the Soviet Union. Estonians were asked, sometimes forced, to return to their homes.

Many other countries, led by the United States, considered the Soviet annexations of the Baltic States to be illegal. They took the position that the Soviet Union had no right to be there. Estonian assets were not to be turned over to the Soviets. That position was first applied to the Baltic States on July 23, 1940, by Acting Secretary of State Sumner Welles. Applying the nonrecognition principle, he announced America's refusal to recognize the legality of the Soviet annexations. The Welles' statement set out the moral premise underlying America's position:

> The people of the United States are opposed to predatory activities no matter whether they are carried on by the use of force or the threat of force. They are likewise opposed to any form of intervention on the part of one state, no matter how powerful, in the domestic concerns of any other sovereign state, however weak.

Many other countries, including Great Britain, Canada, West Germany, Switzerland and at times, even the People's Republic of China, followed the American position.

One of the consequences of the nonrecognition policy impacted Estonia's diplomatic corps. World War II and the Soviet occupation had decimated but not destroyed the ranks of Estonia's ambassadors and consuls. Countries that followed the nonrecognition policy continued to accept the credentials and authority of pre-annexation Baltic diplomats, career and honorary.

The Estonian government had been in the process of establishing an embassy in the United States but the Soviet invasion made it impossible for Estonia's Ambassador-Designate to come and assume his duties. Estonia had established a Consulate General in America, located in New York's Rockefeller Center office complex. It was headed by Consul General Johannes Kaiv. After the Soviet occupation the consulate continued to function as a representative of the Estonian state and it continued to assist Estonian citizens.

24. America's Nonrecognition Policy

The State Department, recognizing the reasons Estonia could not establish an embassy and applying logic consistent with the nonrecognition policy, extended Johannes Kaiv the designation "in Charge of Legation." This meant that Kaiv was accorded all ambassadorial powers and courtesies.

Another career Estonian diplomat in the New York office at the time of the Soviet takeover was Ernst Jaakson, the person who would become my mentor. When Kaiv died in 1965 the State Department, again following the logic of its nonrecognition policy, extended to Jaakson the same ambassadorial privileges that had been accorded Kaiv.

The nonrecognition policy also impacted Baltic honorary consuls in America. Honorary consuls are not career diplomats but they are part of a country's foreign service. They provide representation in areas of a country where it isn't feasible, either financially or for some other reason, to post a career foreign service official. Most honorary consuls, including Estonia's, receive no pay and are expected to bear their own expenses. They are residents of the geographic area they service.

In ordinary times most honorary consuls expedite trade and commerce between the country they represent and the country where they live. They also offer assistance to citizens of the country they represent. Their duties may include some functions performed by career consuls but, depending on the country they represent, they are generally not permitted to perform certain other career consular functions.

When the Soviet Union annexed the Baltic States, Estonia had honorary consuls in America—in Chicago, New Orleans and San Francisco, as well as honorary vice consuls in Chicago and Los Angeles. As with ambassadors and career consuls, each honorary consul and vice consul who held office at the time of the Soviet annexation had been accredited by the U.S. State Department as representing the Republic of Estonia.

The State Department's continued recognition of Estonia's honorary consuls was confirmation that the United States rejected the Soviet Union's right to claim sovereignty over Estonia. However, American policy had some zigs and zags.

On July 22, 1940, the same day the sham Estonian parliament passed a resolution asking the Supreme Soviet of the U.S.S.R. to receive Estonia as a member republic of the Soviet Union, the Chicago Honorary Consul and Vice Consul resigned in protest—a move that at the time must have seemed appropriate and honorable but in retrospect, not so much.

The Honorary Consul in New Orleans continued in office but died two years later, in December 1942. Kaiv's April 1943 request to appoint a replacement for him was rejected by the State Department. "It is not the present practice of this Government to recognize new honorary consuls of countries which are at present without Governments."

San Francisco's honorary consulate, which had opened in 1926, also became vacant during World War II. The person holding the post was on active duty in the United States Navy. Kaiv tried to fill the San Francisco vacancy at the same time he sought accreditation for his New Orleans nominee.

The State Department repeated its position, that "It is not the present practice of this Government to recognize new honorary consuls of countries which are at present without Governments." Carried to its logical conclusion this practice would have vitiated America's non-recognition policy once current Estonian diplomats died or left office.

The San Francisco and New Orleans refusals by the State Department were matters of concern to Kaiv and to the Estonian community. They raised not only the question of how the Welles' statement would be applied but also the fundamental question of whether the State Department's rejection of Kaiv's nominees for honorary consul meant that America was preparing to abandon its policy of not recognizing the Soviet Union's claim to sovereignty over Estonia, Latvia and Lithuania.

Mother: *In 1985, through death, we lost Ernst Laur, our honorary consul in Los Angeles. There were two candidates to replace him, Mrs. Shore and Jaak Treiman. Ernst Jaakson named Jaak.*

25

Appointment as Honorary Consul

"I Can Always Quit."

My mother offers a concise, matter-of-fact statement that, "Through death we lost Ernst Laur." In fact, Laur's death on June 21, 1985, transcended the Los Angeles Estonian community. Word circulated among most Estonians scattered around the world. He had been one of Estonia's last remaining accredited diplomats.

Before World War II the San Francisco Honorary Consulate had expanded its physical presence to Los Angeles when, on February 23, 1934, an Honorary Vice Consulate was opened.

Reginald B. Olds, the owner of a factory that made and sold a popular line of brass instruments, including trombones, trumpets and cornets, was accredited by the State Department as Honorary Vice Consul. Even though the San Francisco Honorary Consulate disappeared during World War II, the Los Angeles Honorary Vice Consulate continued to be recognized and continued to function.

A number of Estonians worked at Olds' factory, including his Estonian secretary, Marta Janson. Olds did not speak Estonian. Whenever the need arose, he used Janson as his translator. In 1955 Ernst Laur, the man who 12 years earlier had helped my mother as she was leaving Finland for Sweden, arrived in Los Angeles. For a time, he worked in the Olds factory. While there he assumed Janson's translator duties.

Later Laur was named the Honorary Vice Consulate's Information Officer. In February 1970 the State Department elevated the Los Angeles Honorary Vice Consulate to an Honorary Consulate. Concurrently, Olds's title became Honorary Consul and Laur was accredited as Honorary Vice Consul. Following Olds's death in July 1970 Laur was named as his successor.

At the time of Laur's death, Estonia's only active diplomatic posts anywhere in the world were in New York, Toronto and Los Angeles. All three were Jaakson's responsibility. Assisting Jaakson in New York was Aarand

```
         EESTI VABARIIGI
   PEAKONSULAAT NEW YORGIS
      18 WEST 94TH STREET, NEW YORK
                                              7.märtsil 1934 a.
         Nr 2510.
                                        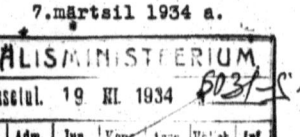

                  Välisministeerium,
                  Administratiiv osakond,
                  Tallinn.
                       Los-Angeles'i asekonsulaadi avamisest.
                       Saime täna hra Reginald B.Olds'ilt teate,
                  et tema on oma tegevuse Eesti asekonsulina Los
                  Angeles'is alustanud 23.veebruaril s.a. Konsulaadi
                  aadress on, nagu juba varem teatatud: 1914 Raymond
                  Ave., Los Angeles, California.
```

A note dated March 7, 1934, from the Estonian Consulate General in New York informing the Foreign Ministry in Tallinn that Mr. Reginald Olds has advised them that he has assumed his duties as vice consul as of February 23, 1934, at 1914 Raymond Avenue, Los Angeles (Estonia Ministry of Foreign Affairs, Archives).

Roos who served as consul. Ilmar Heinsoo occupied the post of Honorary Consul General in Toronto. Ernst Laur was the Honorary Consul in Los Angeles. Jaakson, Roos, Heinsoo and Laur were physical manifestations of America's nonrecognition policy. Estonia had not disappeared; the struggle to regain independence continued.

Laur's death meant that the State Department would again be asked to affirm America's nonrecognition policy when Jaakson nominated Laur's successor. Who would replace him? Would the State Department approve his successor? Most people assumed his successor would be accredited, yet an element of uncertainty remained.

In 1985 Ronald Reagan had begun his second term as President. I was preoccupied with my law practice and various Baltic American Freedom League projects. I rarely participated in the Estonian community's social activities. I gave little thought to who would be Laur's successor. This changed when two BAFL activists interceded.

Valdis Pavlovskis, past BAFL President and past President of the American Latvian Association, who would later become Latvia's first Defense Minister, suggested to BAFL's then president, the Estonian Avo

25. Appointment as Honorary Consul

Piirisild, that Avo urge me to apply for the vacant Honorary Consul position.

Avo did speak with me. He aroused my interest but not my acquiescence. While I still had doubts and many questions, Avo nevertheless went ahead and recommended me to Ernst Jaakson, who was now Estonia's Consul General in Charge of Legation in New York.

As gossip about the vacancy percolated through the Los Angeles Estonian community, my Mexican brother-in-law, Pepe Oseguera, and his family arrived in Los Angeles for their annual summer vacation. Soon after their arrival Pepe and I drove Barbie, the oldest of his three daughters, to her job as a summer camp counselor at a church in Pacific Palisades, not far from the ocean.

A shield given to each honorary consul to display outside their residence or office (photograph by Margus Välja).

After dropping Barbie off, Pepe and I decided to avoid the freeways and return home by a scenic route. We drove north along Pacific Coast Highway enjoying views of the sparkling surf as it crashed endlessly along the coastline. We talked as I drove. We weighed the advantages and disadvantages of applying for the honorary consul position.

At some point before we completed the 20-mile drive to my house Pepe and I concluded that I should apply. I remember telling Pepe, "Why not? If I'm selected and it doesn't work out, I can always quit." But I still wanted answers to some questions, the most elemental being, "What does an honorary consul do?" On a lark, I re-read Graham Greene's *The Honorary Consul*. Not unexpectedly, the story failed to provide any clues as to what I should expect if appointed. I spoke with my parents. Neither they nor any other member of the Estonian community I spoke with could answer my questions.

The archives of the Estonian Foreign Ministry contain a letter that I sent to Jaakson, who I had never met. I asked for details about an Honorary Consul's responsibilities and whether any conflict-of-interest issues might arise because of my work as an attorney. I asked the following series of questions:

1. Given current circumstances, what are the duties of an honorary consul?
2. Are there possible conflict of interests with my law firm? For example, is there a problem with my firm representing our local Baltic folk dancers in a law suit against the Los Angeles Olympic Organizing Committee? Or, is there a problem with my firm representing the American Latvian Association in a dispute with the National Broadcasting Company (NBC) in their false and misleading depiction of Latvians as war criminals?
3. Would being an honorary consul mean that I could not belong to certain organizations?
4. Are an honorary consul's out of pocket expenses reimbursed?
5. What is the legal basis on which an honorary consul operates?
6. Who is the honorary consul responsible to?
7. What are the qualifications to be an honorary consul?

The Foreign Ministry's archives also contain Jaakson's reply to my enquiry. He responded point by point. First, he told me that while under normal circumstances an Estonian Honorary Consul's responsibilities were much broader, given current circumstances the primary responsibility was to disseminate information about Estonia as widely as possible.

Jaakson went on to say that he saw no conflict of interest with respect to cases my law firm handled. There were no restrictions on my belonging to any organization so long as they weren't against Estonia's interests. Expenses would not be reimbursed. The honorary consul in Los Angeles reported to the Estonian Consulate General in New York. The honorary consul position was subject to and governed by international conventions and treaties between Estonia and the United States.

In his response Jaakson also said that he wanted someone who possessed a knowledge of Estonia, who had the support of the local Estonian community and who was financially able to maintain his own office.

I remember speaking with Jaakson on the telephone. I assume this conversation was after I received his letter. It may be that during this conversation I told him that I wished to be considered a candidate and asked for some further clarifications. Jaakson suggested that since Los Angeles had both an Honorary Lithuanian and an Honorary Latvian Consul, I should ask them for an overview of expected day-to-day activities.

During the years of Soviet occupation, Los Angeles was the only city in the world where all three Baltic countries had consular representation. I tried to contact the Latvian and Lithuanian Honorary Consuls. The Latvian, Leo Anderson, had served since 1932. By the mid-1980s he had become less active and, unbeknownst to me, was about to retire. I was unable to reach him.

25. Appointment as Honorary Consul

The Lithuanian, Vytautas Cekanauskas, had assumed his position in 1977. I called him several times, leaving messages, but my calls were never returned. Years later he explained that because of the bitter fight within the Estonian community concerning who should receive the appointment he thought it best to stay removed.

One other person in the Estonian community had publicly declared her candidacy—Astra Shore, a popular, active member of the Estonian community and an accomplished actress in Los Angeles Estonian theater productions. Some years later Jaakson told me that two other people had privately indicated a willingness to serve but preferred their interest not be made public.

As Jaakson solicited candidates, Laur's wife lobbied vigorously for the appointment of her son-in-law to be her late husband's successor—a position the son-in-law told me during an unexpected, unsolicited telephone call that he was not interested in.

The Capulets and Montagues would have understood the vehemence of the internecine hostilities that broke out among members of the Los Angeles Estonian community. I did not. As Astra Shore and I watched, combatants over whom we had little or no control displayed venomous hostility toward each other and toward the candidate they opposed.

Jaakson, standing slightly taller than my 6 feet 2 inches, maintained his usual unruffled, dignified demeanor and flew into the Los Angeles maelstrom in late September. He came to meet and interview the candidates. I remember nothing about my interview. I do recall that my parents held an afternoon reception for Jaakson at their home and that I drove him back to his hotel following the reception. I don't remember if Astra Shore and her supporters had a similar reception for Jaakson. I know nothing about Astra's meeting with Jaakson.

On November 7, 1985, Jaakson submitted my name to the State Department as his selection for the honorary consul position. According to his handwritten notation on that same letter, he advised me of his decision by telephone on November 12. On March 26, 1986, the State Department allayed any fears that may have existed about the United States deviating from its nonrecognition policy. A letter to Jaakson, signed on behalf of the Secretary of State, was to the point:

> I acknowledge the receipt of your note NO. 533, dated January 24, 1986, regarding the appointment of Mr. Jaak Treiman as Honorary Consul of Estonia at Los Angeles, California, with jurisdiction for the State of California, and stating that maintaining the consular establishment there would be in the national interest of Estonia.
>
> The Department is pleased to inform the Legation that there is no objection to the continuance of the honorary consulate at Los Angeles. In compliance with the request contained in your note, recognition is accorded to Mr. Treiman as Honorary Consul of Estonia at Los Angeles, California.

Jaakson issued a press release that was reprinted on the front page of possibly every Estonian newspaper outside of Estonia. Some émigré Latvian and Lithuanian papers also carried the story.

Even the Soviet propaganda mouthpiece *Kodumaa—Homeland*, published in Tallinn by *VEKSA–The Society for the Development of Cultural Ties with Estonians Abroad*, and sent to Estonians abroad, carried a brief story, buried on an inside page. The first paragraph was a short summary of Jaakson's press release. A second paragraph consisted of sarcastic commentary, "It is easy enough to see the purpose and idea of such news items: look how busily emigrant governments, ministers and consuls are engaged in diplomatic activity. The titles alone fill you with respect towards those who are entitled to bear them."

Between the time Ernst Laur died and the date I was accredited (June 21, 1985–March 26, 1986), Baltic émigrés had escalated their efforts to publicize the Soviet occupation of the Baltic States. Changes were also taking place within the Soviet Union—real or cosmetic was yet to be determined.

Hundreds of people demonstrated outside the Soviet Embassy in Copenhagen protesting the Soviet annexations of Estonia, Latvia and Lithuania. The demonstration took place as the Baltic World Conference, a Washington-based émigré group, opened a two-day meeting in Denmark in July 1985. They conducted a "Baltic Tribunal Against the Soviet Union" designed to draw attention to the Soviet Union's illegal occupation of Estonia, Latvia and Lithuania.

Around the same time Otto von Habsburg, a member of the European Parliament, a consistent advocate of a united Europe and a vocal friend of the Baltic States, insisted that "The Baltic Nations are a part of Europe and we have an obligation towards them."

Fifty-five hundred miles to the west, the *Los Angeles Times* ran a story on "Flying the Flag," a story about the Baltic States that featured the retirement of Latvia's Honorary Consul, Leo Anderson, after 53 years of service. The occupation of the Baltic States was garnering visibility even as concurrent, possible change was taking place within the Soviet Union.

Mikhail Gorbachev had become General Secretary of the Soviet Communist Party in March 1985. Only days before my State Department accreditation he addressed a party congress and used *"perestroika"* and *"glasnost"* for the first time. Most of us took notice but were skeptical about whether such restructuring and openness would happen.

The serendipitous timing of my appointment gave me a unique vantage point from which to view, and in a small way participate in, the changes that were about to take place in Estonia during Gorbachev's tenure as General Secretary.

26

Flying the Flag

"Subtlety was not his strong suit."

Those who had supported my appointment as honorary consul congratulated me; those who had been opposed grumbled but gave me space. I began to discover the particulars of my new job. As Jaakson had told me, the thrust of my job was to remind everyone that Estonia continued to exist, that the Soviet occupation was illegal and not permanent. The title "Honorary Consul" opened an array of opportunities for conveying this message, opportunities to fly the Estonian flag. How I used those opportunities was limited only by my imagination—and on one occasion, by my mentor Ernst Jaakson.

Answering Questions

As with any job, there was a daily routine, part of which was to answer questions: face-to-face at social and political events, in letters, on the telephone. I responded to questions from people I had never met and most likely, would never meet again. But even the routine can sometimes transform into the unusual.

Within weeks of assuming my post, I received a telephone call from a person who said he was a Finnish businessman, visiting California. He needed to get in touch with all Estonian language newspapers published in California. Could I give him contact information? I told him there were no Estonian newspapers in California but there were some in New York and Canada. I offered to put him in touch with those papers. I assured him they were widely read by California's Estonian community. Perhaps not understanding my response, the caller continued to ask about California-based Estonian newspapers. I asked for his address and offered to mail him contact information for the New York and Canadian publications. He ignored my offer. Our conversation ended.

Three or four days later the same person called again. He was now in New York. He repeated his earlier request. I repeated my response and renewed my offer. Again, no reaction. Our conversation ended. A week later I was, once more, on the telephone with the same Finnish businessman. This time he spoke as though we were old friends. He said he was calling from Helsinki. He was about to leave on a business trip to Estonia. Some of the border guards were his friends. They would let him take gifts into Estonia. Did I have anything I would like him to take to my relatives? I said I had nothing.

He became more insistent, repeating his offer twice more. I grew more and more impatient. Then he blurted, "Who are your relatives? Where do they live?" Exacerbated, I retorted, "I don't have any relatives," and hung up. As I did, I realized the caller must have been a KGB operative, trying to find out more about me and my family. Subtlety was not his strong suit.

Not all telephone calls were from KGB operatives. Some calls were from long-silent Estonians who, over the years, had blended into the general population. News reports had rekindled their interest in Estonia. They wanted to know what was happening. Other calls included journalists pursuing news stories and students working on term papers.

Still other telephone calls were totally unexpected. One time I thought Sheila, my assistant, was having some fun when she told me that California's Secretary of State was on hold, waiting for me. I picked up the phone wondering what the joke's punchline would be. The Secretary of State, March Fong Eu, was on the line. She was about to visit Estonia and wanted to know the protocol to follow.

On occasion I would be asked if I was part of the Estonian Government-in-Exile. My response was always an unembellished, "No." Formed in 1944, the Estonian Government-in-Exile had symbolic value but was not recognized by any government and was legally impotent. In some ways, its existence was a problem. As explained in the Lithuanian context by James T. McHugh and James S. Pacy in *Diplomats Without a Country: Baltic Diplomacy, International Law, and the Cold War*:

> The [Lithuanian] legation had received its credentials from the Lithuanian government that was illegally overthrown during World War II, so it was crucial to assert its continued legitimacy in order to support the theoretical legitimacy of these Lithuanian diplomats and their respective missions. Should "new" Lithuanian governments emerge, they could undermine this unique diplomatic situation, which, arguably, was more effective in promoting the cause of Baltic freedom (since it invoked formal recognition among those Western powers that allowed these missions to be maintained) than the claims of a non-elected government-in-exile.

I still recall one occasion when Ernst Jaakson mentioned the Estonian Government-in-Exile and sighed with mild exasperation as he did so. He was concerned that the Government-in-Exile would undermine the position of Estonia's diplomatic missions.

Social Functions

I grew more accustomed to my role and gained a better understanding of the very broad parameters Jaakson gave me to work within. I became acquainted with other members of the Los Angeles Consular Corps, one of the largest in the world. I developed a better understanding of the tools I had for flying the flag. Social events were important.

During the last half of the 1980s one of the Consular Corps' most memorable annual social events was a "Protocol Ball" held by Los Angeles County's southern neighbor, Orange County.

The Protocol Ball was a black-tie affair in honor of the members of the consular corps. It was, literally and figuratively, perfect for "flying the flag." Every year the banquet began with Orange County's political and cultural elite seated in a lavishly decorated banquet hall. Then, lights were dimmed. Each consul and their spouse would enter the room as a spotlight centered on them. They were formally announced and then escorted to their table by a Marine Corps color guard carrying the consul's country's flag. Each consul was seated at a table sponsored by one of the elites. One time we were seated with President Franklin Roosevelt's son, James Roosevelt. A decorated veteran of World War II, a former congressman, political activist and businessman, he was still engaging. He was also curious about Estonia.

Each year, as the Baltic States generated more and more headlines, my Latvian and Lithuanian colleagues and I received loud ovations as we were escorted to our tables. In 1988, following Estonia's declaration of sovereignty ["The Parliament of the Soviet Baltic republic of Estonia voted Wednesday to proclaim Estonian 'sovereignty' within the Soviet Union and to give itself the right to veto national legislation before it goes into effect in the republic."—*Los Angeles Times* November 17, 1988], I received an especially powerful, standing salute from the attendees.

In 1989 I sat at a table occupied by the editorial staff of the Orange County edition of the *Los Angeles Times*. They had asked that I be seated with them. Estonia was in the news and as Estonia's Honorary Consul, I was of interest to them. Of course, the interest was mutual. Sometime later, when I needed advice about publishing an article, they were very helpful.

A "what might have been" social moment took place in 1987. In late August a San Francisco postmarked invitation arrived at my office, addressed to "Jaak Treiman, Honorary Consul, Estonia." It was from "The

> *The Consul General*
> *of the Union of Soviet Socialist Republics*
> *and*
> *Mrs. Valentin M. Kamenev*
>
> *Invite you and your guest*
> *To attend the opening night performance of*
> *One of the World's Greatest Choirs*
>
> *The State Choir of Armenia*
>
> *September 17, 1987 at 8:00 p.m.*
> *at the*
> *Scottish Rite Auditorium*
> *#857 Wilshire Boulevard*
> *Los Angeles*
>
> *Reception immediately following the concert.*
>
> *R.S.V.P.*   *Attire: Black Tie*

Top and opposite: Given the Soviet position that Estonia no longer existed, this invitation was an obvious, embarrassing mistake. The Soviet Consulate General in San Francisco invited me, as the Honorary Consul for Estonia, to attend the performance of the State Choir of Armenia and the black-tie reception that would follow (Treiman family archive, now deposited with the Estonian Foreign Ministry Archives.).

26. Flying the Flag

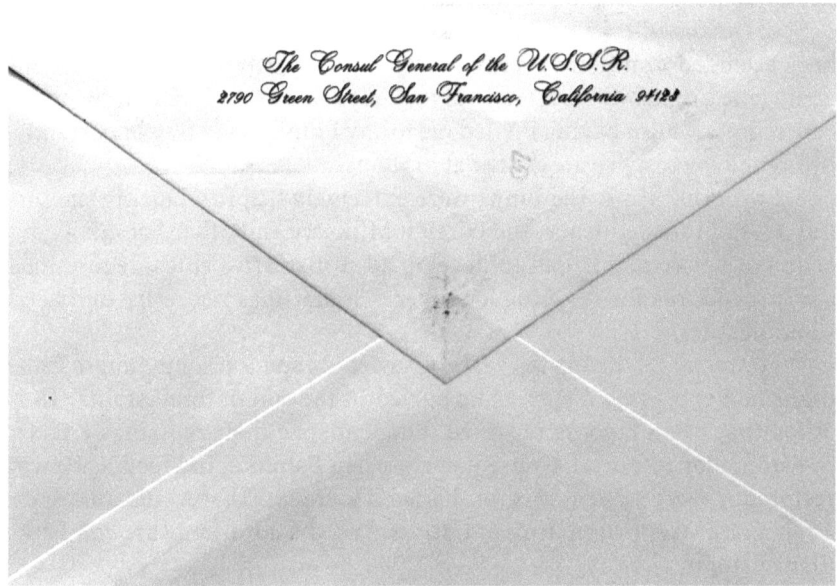

Consul General of the Union of Soviet Socialist Republics and Mrs. Valentin M. Kamenev."

The State Choir of Armenia was touring America. I, along with all other consular corps heads-of-post, was invited to attend their Los Angeles performance. A black-tie reception would follow. The name and address on the envelope in which my invitation came did not appear to be a pre-printed address label. Apparently, a typist had manually addressed my envelope. Mistakenly, Estonia had not been removed from the Soviet's master invitation list.

I was excited. I wanted to attend. It was the Soviet Union who did not recognize Estonia, not vice versa. The BAFL and other Baltic activists could have some fun with this explicit recognition of Estonia by the Soviet Consul General. At the very least, it was an opportunity to embarrass the Soviet Union while publicizing its illegal occupation of the Baltic States.

I wrote Jaakson, explaining why I thought it was a good idea to attend. I asked him if I could. He replied, "No." I telephoned him. He still said, "No." Even if I didn't attend, I wanted to acknowledge receipt of the invitation with a written response. I drafted different variations. None of them were used. I was told to ignore the invitation. Even today I smile ruefully as I imagine the look on the Soviet Consul General's face as I introduced myself and thanked him for his invitation. Perhaps Jaakson consulted with the State Department and was asked to nix my attendance.

For the most part I received the same invitations that all other heads-of-post received. However, after Estonia regained its independence, I realized that I and my Latvian and Lithuanian colleagues had been excluded from some events. For example, shortly after August 1991 an apologetic Finnish Consul General took me aside and offered profuse, sincere regrets for not having invited me to any Finnish events. Concurrently, he invited me to a private dinner at his house.

From that time, the Finns were extremely helpful. During the initial days of independence, the Foreign Ministry and other Estonian government departments had to develop administrative rules, regulations and procedures for running a country. Sometimes necessity outpaced promulgation.

For instance, during the years of Soviet occupation some émigré Estonians had expressed a wish to be buried in the soil of free Estonia. They asked that when Estonia regained independence their remains be taken to Estonia for re-burial. Consequently, when Estonian independence was restored, I received requests for official documents that would authorize an urn or casket originating in California to be admitted through Estonian customs.

There were no Foreign Ministry directives to follow. No one at the Estonian Embassy or the New York consulate could even tell me what information the still nonexistent documents should contain. I turned to the Finnish Consulate. "What do you do when an urn or casket is to be transported to Finland?" I was given step-by-step instructions and provided with forms that were almost ready to use.

While a few countries such as Finland had, before 1991, quietly avoided official contact with me and my Latvian and Lithuanian colleagues, other countries made a point of acknowledging our presence. I recall leaving an event at the home of the Belgian Consul General in either 1987 or 1988. I was about 100 feet from the Belgian's Hancock Park home when someone shouted my name. I turned. It was the Swiss Consul General. He was looking toward me. Paying no heed to the other departing consuls and guests, he roared a thunderous "Long live free Estonia!" in my direction.

The Written Word

"The pen is mightier than the sword." Words placed in the mouth of Cardinal Richelieu by a British playwright in 1839 have become a trite but nevertheless true saying. Magazine articles, newspaper op-ed pieces and letters to the editor by various Baltic activists were useful tools for expanding Estonia's visibility. So were books and scholarly articles by academics such as Rein Taagepera, Toivo Raun and Tõnu Parming.

I had written numerous short pieces for BAFL's newsletters. However, my first venture into writing for mass circulation publications materialized through the initiative of the minister of the Los Angeles Estonian Evangelical Lutheran Church. Pastor Rein Neggo introduced me to the sermons of Harri Mõtsnik—powerful sermons that centered on freedom and human rights, delivered from the pulpit in Estonia.

> Freedom is not an illusion, but an experience of reality. It is a vital need. It is not out of place to remember the valiant men and women who have chosen the noble path of self-sacrifice rather than self-interest and furthering their own careers; they have chosen the struggle for freedom as the only way of hope for the Estonian people, setting on one side the fear which they surely experience within and in the face of the totalitarian regime which confronts them. Truth is their guide along the way.

Quoting extensively from Mõtsnik's potent sermons, which had been translated into English in a publication of the émigré Estonian Lutheran Church, I wrote an article about him and Estonia's quest to regain independence. The article appeared in *The Lutheran Standard*. In 1987 this was America's largest circulation magazine for Lutherans.

In 1990 the Soviet Union enacted a law, ostensibly designed to implement a Soviet republic's guaranteed right to secede. The passage of that law generated favorable comments by some American political pundits. In response, I wrote an op-ed piece in which I argued, "The new law 'On the Procedure for Resolving Questions Connected with a Union

Republic's Secession from the U.S.S.R.' actually violates the Soviet Constitution, bestows all relevant secession decision making power on the central government, and invents a new, ad hoc, political unit." I concluded that "Charitably viewed, the newly enacted Soviet secession law constitutes false advertising. Analytically viewed, it is pure demagoguery."

I wasn't sure how to get what I had written published quickly, while the secession law was still topical. I contacted one of the editors of the *Los Angeles Times* whom I had met at Orange County's Protocol Ball. He suggested I submit my piece to the *Wall Street Journal*. That would give my article a larger, more relevant audience than his newspaper. He gave me the necessary contact information. My commentary was accepted and appeared as a *Wall Street Journal, European Edition* Opinion piece titled, "The Soviet Secession Law Is a Sham."

Speeches

In her narrative my mother notes my appointment as honorary consul. Then, before moving on to other, unrelated thoughts, she simply recounts that, "*Jaak delivered his first speech at the 1986 West Coast Estonian Days. He encouraged people to fight for our country and our freedom.*" The speech was delivered in Vancouver. My mother is very matter-of-fact. She does not mention the backstory—the excruciating, at times comical, process of how that speech evolved.

Estonian is my mother tongue. That is what we spoke at home. But I have never been taught Estonian, not even at a weekend "Estonian school." My Estonian grammar was, and still is, poor. While my pronunciation is good, my vocabulary is limited. I cannot always find the right words. I had to face the practical consequences of my deficiency when I began to prepare the Vancouver speech—a speech I was asked to deliver in Estonian.

I wrote the first several drafts in English. It began, "Once upon a time in the future, what will be the story of Estonia and her people? Will it be a tale of what once was and what might have been or will the story be a commemoration of accomplishments, told in independent Estonia?"

I asked my father, with his broken English but fluent Estonian, to translate what I had written into Estonian. Looking back, I now see that my turns of phrase may not have been the easiest to translate, especially for a non-professional translator.

While I lacked the ability to correctly structure a speech in Estonian, my Estonian was good enough to know if my father's translation reflected what I wanted to say. Frequently I did not think his translation was accurate. My father thought otherwise. This mutual incomprehension triggered many strenuous debates between us, my mother often serving as arbiter and peace-maker. It was a family process that would be repeated each time I had to deliver a speech in Estonian and each time I had to write a long letter in Estonian.

The Vancouver speech was delivered, not in 1986 as my mother's narrative states, but in 1987, more than a year after my appointment. However, it was my first major speech, delivered in Estonian in front of nearly 1,500 Estonians who had gathered in Vancouver for the opening of the West Coast Estonian Days.

Since 1952 West Coast Canadian and American Estonians had gathered every two years to celebrate Estonian culture, with some politicking on the side. Estonian visitors from the rest of Canada and America also attended. The festival site alternated between Vancouver, Seattle, Portland, San Francisco and Los Angeles. It was an honor to be asked to deliver the opening day keynote address. Jaakson was there. The President of the Estonian American National Council was there as were other Estonian dignitaries.

Cooperative Efforts

Certainly, my work as honorary consul was not a one-person effort. I relied, not only on members of BAFL but also numerous others in carrying out my work. In seeking to further the cause of Estonian, Latvian and Lithuanian independence, many people, regardless of nationality, engaged in a variety of activities, sometimes alone, sometimes with family, sometimes with ad hoc groups or with organizations.

One instance when my role as honorary consul seamlessly melded with the efforts of many others was in 1988 with the drafting and adoption of a Baltic Policy Statement. This was an effort that produced a final product that belonged to everyone. It was also an example of how, even with the differences of opinion that often existed when it came to tactics, Estonians, Latvians and Lithuanians could unite when the need arose. In doing so each nationality group was also able to unite their own internal, warring factions.

On October 28, 1988, John Zeroles, the State Department's Baltic Desk Officer, publicly challenged Balts to provide new ideas on Baltic issues. In a contemporaneous editorial, the *New York Times* called for "a constructive American response [to the current events in the Baltic States] rising above the dogma of those who see the Baltic states only as captive nations." The challenge by Zeroles and by the *New York Times* had special urgency given the anticipated December visit to the United States by Mikhael Gorbachev.

I spoke with Mari-Ann Rikken (Kelam) about the Zeroles challenge and the *New York Times* editorial. We agreed that a response was required. I suggested that we have a "brainstorming" session open to all interested parties. Mari-Ann volunteered the use of her house in Alexandria, Virginia. Time was of the essence. We agreed to meet on November 5 and 6 and sent out a general call for interested parties to attend.

I flew to Virginia. Others came from Toronto, New York, and other points in Canada and America. Some who couldn't attend in person sent comments. I don't recall the exact number of people present but I believe it was 20 or so. I had prepared a draft of talking points based on pre-meeting conversations with a number of Baltic leaders. We met. We discussed. We argued. We arrived at a consensus. I acted as the scribe, recording the accord. Following the meeting I circulated drafts of what we had agreed to and then, after getting feedback, by November 29 I was able to distribute a final version of our Baltic Policy Statement for signatures.

By December 6, with unheard of speed, all principal Baltic organizations had signed the document: American Latvian Association, Baltic American Freedom League, Estonian American National Council, Joint Baltic American National Committee, Lithuanian American Community of the USA and Lithuanian American National Council.

When I distributed the final Baltic Policy Statement my cover letter summarized how the document had been compiled.

> It should be emphasized that the Policy Statement does not belong to any one organization. Over two dozen people helped formulate it. These individuals included Lithuanians, Latvians, Estonians and non–Balts. They included academics, activists and representatives from the Baltic diplomatic corps. While some of these people may have wished to have a more action-oriented document and others may have wished to delete some items, it nevertheless reflects a consensus.

As far as I know, this document was the first written, unified statement of Baltic policy presented to the American government by all the principal Baltic organizations. The hope was that it would serve as a starting point for more specific policy proposals. To an extent it did. Today the document is worthy of nothing more than a short, historical footnote in a study of the American Baltic émigré experience or perhaps in a treatise on social dynamics. Yet, its existence was proof that internal squabbles could be overcome, that broad agreements could be reached and that it was possible to overcome organizational egos where no one person or organization would claim credit.

Consultation

The Estonian Consulate in New York was a physical reminder that America did not recognize the legality of the Soviet annexation of Estonia.

26. Flying the Flag

It was also a place where Estonian émigrés, other supporters of Estonia and politicians turned to for information and guidance about what was happening in Estonia.

In early June 1989 Jaakson asked Ilmar Heinsoo, the Estonian Honorary Consul General in Toronto, and me to meet with him and Aarand Roos at the Estonian consulate at 9 Rockefeller Plaza, New York. The meeting would take place on July 14 and 15. Heinsoo and I had met with Jaakson one-on-one whenever we happened to be in New York but we had never met as a group.

Jaakson did not tell us what prompted his call for a meeting. I suspect it was a combination of wanting our input concerning a myriad of decisions he had to make and a desire that we arrive at a consensus that would permit us to present a uniform, coordinated position concerning events taking place in Estonia.

The symbolic and actual manifestation of the continuity of the Estonian state was embodied in Ernst Jaakson, Consul General of Estonia in Charge of Legation in New York. Jaakson, second from right, is flanked on his left by Aarand Roos, Estonia's Consul in New York. I am on Jaakson's right. Next to me is Estonia's Honorary Consul General in Toronto, Ilmar Heinsoo. But for America's policy of not recognizing the legality of the Soviet annexation of Estonia, Latvia and Lithuania, this picture would not exist. The picture was taken on July 14, 1989, at the conclusion of a meeting held at the New York consulate (Estonian Ministry of Foreign Affairs, Archives).

The pro-independence activity in Estonia was reaching a crescendo. The National Independence Party and dozens of heritage clubs had increased their visibility and their activity. Preparations were also underway for elections to the Congress of Estonia—a body of representatives that would effectively constitute a freely elected parliamentary body. Estonian citizens, within and outside of Estonia were being registered to vote in preparation for the elections.

There was also the Popular Front, a group that did not always mix well with the more vocal independence groups. Outside this mixture there was the Communist Party, proceeding along its own, Moscow dictated, path.

In the United States, Jaakson was caught between pressures from a segment of the Estonian American community to be more activist while the American government was, as I understand it, urging him to maintain a lower profile. People wanted to show their support for the Estonian independence movement. They turned to the New York Consulate, applying for Estonian passports. Printing passports was expensive and the Estonian gold reserves that supported the consulate were close to exhausted.

We sat in Jaakson's 14th floor, Rockefeller Center office, the furnishings a time warp from the 1930s, and reviewed current events, covered the agenda items and exchanged ideas. Roos, Heinsoo and I engaged in some vehement arguments which Jaakson refereed. Some suggestions were given and some decisions were made, perhaps the most significant being to support the elections for the Congress of Estonia. We departed as friendly colleagues.

27

Visitors and Guests

"We were watching Estonia's rebirth."

Despite the Soviet Union's restrictive emigration policy, in 1980 Neeme Järvi was granted an exit visa. He was allowed to leave. At the time he was not yet an internationally renowned conductor but his achievements already included top prize at a prestigious Rome conducting competition. While living in America, Järvi conducted elite orchestras all over the world. His repertoire included pieces that promoted Estonia, compositions by Eduard Tubin and Arvo Pärt.

The one time I met Järvi, I sat next to him at an outdoor, summer dinner held in his honor at a Beverly Hills estate that was large even by Beverly Hills standards. The following evening, he would conduct the Los Angeles Philharmonic Orchestra at the Hollywood Bowl in one of its acclaimed "Symphony Under the Stars" performances. I marveled at the charisma Järvi exuded and the impact he had on the assembled group of Los Angeles's cultural elite. I envied the ease with which he wove Estonia into his conversations.

In the late 1980s the pianist Rein Rannap, known within Estonia for his patriotic rock themes, and his wife, soprano Katre Kõiva, defected to America while Rein was on a concert tour in Italy. Both were amazing, talented musicians. They lived in Los Angeles until Estonia regained independence. Their performances helped raise Estonia's profile even as they expanded their musical talents through advanced studies at the University of Southern California. On one occasion Rein performed at the consular corps' annual Holiday Ball, helping highlight Estonia to an international audience.

The Urb Brothers, Toomas and Tarmo, were well known in Estonia for their songs, reminiscent of the American folk singers of the 60s. Their roots were in my parents' hometown of Võru. They defected when Tarmo was warned that the KGB planned to assassinate him. His persistence in performing anti-Soviet songs had become too much for the authorities.

Both brothers came to Los Angeles. Through their music and in their interviews, they explored humanity's ongoing search for meaning and the need to expand the concept of civil and political human rights. I recall how everyone was spellbound when they performed at a small reception at my house—a common reaction. They generated a slew of favorable buzz for Estonia, especially within the entertainment industry—an industry that loves buzz.

Järvi, Rannap, Kõiva and the Urbs are a sample of the people who fled Estonia in the 80s and then, even as they started new lives, used their talents to advocate for Estonia's independence. While their advocacy usually did not generate major headlines, they educated their fans about Estonia and Estonians' desire to regain independence even as their presence infused fresh blood into the ranks of the activists outside of Estonia.

There was a group of visitors from Estonia whose presence did generate significant headlines. In 1985, when I applied for the honorary consul position, the thought of personally meeting any of these people was farfetched. But rapid changes were taking place. By 1987 I was greeting a steady stream of freedom fighters from Estonia, a number of whom had survived the gulags.

The *glasnost* era of "openness" eased travel prohibitions for those living under Soviet rule. This enabled some dissidents to travel outside Estonia. Others found themselves summarily expelled as "trouble makers." In either case, the results were the same. Leaders of the Estonian independence movement were able to wend through Europe and North America to seek political and moral support. Their "circuit" generally consisted of stops in Stockholm, Toronto, New York, Washington, D.C., Chicago, Los Angeles and San Francisco with occasional forays as far as Australia.

The initiative for these visits came from Estonia's National Independence Party, the first formally organized, non-communist political party in the Soviet Union. Émigré groups, including the Estonian American National Council, pooled their resources to finance the trips.

For those of us outside Estonia, the visitors were people we had observed and admired from a distance. To us, they were heroes. Spending time with these leaders of the Estonian independence movement was an education. Speaking with them was a reminder that the events we watched on television, read about in newspapers and magazines, and that were recorded on smuggled home videos, were real, not scripted. But we were also reminded, then and later, that they were human beings, not only with the strengths of our species but also with our shortcomings.

Their defiance of Soviet authority called for sacrifice, sometimes psychological, sometimes physical, sometimes both. Their actions had real consequences—consequences that could effectuate regime change. For

27. Visitors and Guests

some the pursuit of Estonian independence included imprisonment in gulags scattered throughout a frozen Siberia.

Nobel laureate Alexander Solzhenitsyn described life in the gulags in *One Day in the Life of Ivan Denisovich*:

> It looked sort of eerie all over, with the bare plain, the empty compound, and the moon gleaming on the snow. The guards had already gotten in place—ten paces away from each other and their guns at the ready. There was this black herd of prisoners, and in among them, in a black coat like everybody else, was that man, S-311, who'd worn golden shoulder straps in his time and been pals with a British admiral. And now he had to carry hods with Fetyukov.
> There's nothing you can't do to a man....
> ....
> The gruel was always thinner than in the morning—they had to feed you in the morning so you'd work, but in the evening they knew you just flopped down and went to sleep.
> He began to eat. He started with the watery stuff on the top and drank it right down. The warmth went through his body and his insides were sort of quivering waiting for that gruel to come down. It was great! This was what a prisoner lived for, this one little moment.

In 1987 Tiit Madisson was the first of a succession of former gulag prisoners to stop in Los Angeles on his tour of important American cities. He arrived a hero. He stayed at my house. Tiit had been a political prisoner from 1980 to 1986, sentenced for "anti-Soviet activities." Four of those years had been at the infamous Perm labor camp. Located in the Ural Mountains, it was favored by the regime for political prisoners considered especially dangerous. Inmates were housed in 24-hour cells. Perm was possibly the harshest political camp in the Soviet Union.

Following his release, Tiit resumed his anti-Soviet activities. As a result, he was again taken into custody. Shortly after being re-incarcerated, he was blindfolded, then led out of his cell, driven to the airport and put on board a plane. All of this took place in total silence and darkness—not a word was spoken. The blindfold was kept in place.

Tiit could hear the plane's engine as it took off to an unknown destination. Would he be shoved out of the plane somewhere over the Baltic Sea? Was he being taken to a new labor camp? After about an hour, the plane landed. His blindfold was removed as he was thrust out onto firm ground. He was in Sweden. He had been expelled.

Soon after he was dumped in Sweden the Swedish, Canadian and American Estonian émigré organizations financed a tour of principal North American cities where he could tell his story and the story of the Estonian independence movement.

I remember Tiit's interview with the editorial board of the *Orange*

County Register. During a multi-hour session, members of the editorial board asked him what life was like at the Perm labor camp. Tiit described the dire conditions and referenced other political prisoners who were there. He then mentioned, as a footnote, that in order to maintain their sanity he and the other prisoners would sometimes fantasize about where in the world they would most like to be. Their unanimous, first-choice fantasy destination—Disneyland, a place that was only a few miles from where our interview was taking place. Thanks to the Orange County Office of Protocol, I was able to arrange a Disneyland visit for Tiit.

Tiit's story is also a reminder that while some heroes remain heroes for their entire lives, others do not. In later years Tiit turned to fringe political activities and antisemitic attacks.

Another former prisoner who came to Los Angeles as a hero and remains one to this day was Lagle Parek. Lagle's father had been one of the roughly 10,000 Estonians deported by the Soviets during a single night in June 1941. He was taken as far as Leningrad, then shot. Lagle and the remainder of her family were seized in the subsequent 1949 mass deportations when nearly 3 percent of Estonia's population were herded into cattle cars and transported to Siberia. She was seven years old at the time.

Following Stalin's death, Lagle was repatriated to Estonia. She was an activist. In 1983, she was arrested and again imprisoned in a Siberian labor camp. There she became acquainted with political prisoners from other parts of the Soviet Union. An unintended consequence of the connections made in the gulags by Lagle and other dissidents was the creation of a rudimentary, Soviet Union–wide dissident network. During her time in the labor camps Lagle went on a series of hunger strikes in order to bring attention to events such as Human Rights Day. After each hunger strike, she would be placed in solitary confinement.

Following her release from the gulags, Lagle continued her anti-Soviet pursuits. She was a principal organizer of the August 1987 *Hirvepark–Deer Park* demonstration in Tallinn. Around 5,000 people participated in one of the first organized public protests to target the Estonian Communist Party and the Soviet occupation of Estonia.

The demonstration at *Hirvepark* was a catalyst for more demonstrations. It ignited what had been a smoldering independence movement into a national bonfire. Later Lagle became one of the founders and chairperson of the Estonian National Independence Party. When Estonia regained independence Lagle was named Minister of the Interior. Savoring a sense of poetic justice, she took over the offices where the KGB had interrogated her.

Unpretentious and unassuming yet charismatic, Lagle's 1989 visit to Los Angeles coincided with L.A.'s hosting the West Coast Estonian Days.

27. Visitors and Guests

Estonian dissidents who passed through Los Angeles generated publicity for the Baltic cause for independence. Pictured here from left are Juhan Simonson, President of the Estonian American National Council; Lagle Parek, Estonian dissident and multiple time gulag survivor; California Governor George Deukmejian; and me during the 1989 West Coast Estonian Days held in Los Angeles (Treiman family archive).

Lagle was a featured speaker at the closing event, held at the Sheraton Universal Hotel in Universal City. She worried briefly that the local Estonian community would look askance at her lack of a ball gown for the festival's black-tie, closing dinner. We both decided that a former political prisoner didn't need to wear a gown. Lagle's lack of formal attire only enhanced the inspirational message she delivered to the audience—an audience that included not only local Estonians but also the Governor of California.

Another one of my house guests was Heiki Ahonen. Heiki had been a member of Estonia's underground opposition since 1977. He was arrested and imprisoned in 1983. After his release he became another one of the organizers of the *Hirvepark* demonstration. The Soviets expelled him in 1988.

In 1972 Tunne Kelam wrote a memorandum to the United Nations in which he asked for international assistance in removing Soviet troops from Estonia. He followed this up with a steady flow of letters and memoranda. His name was familiar to the émigré Estonian community. At the time of his Los Angeles visit Tunne was a leader of the Estonian Citizens'

Heiki Ahonen speaking to a group of Baltic activists in my living room. Heiki had been a member of Estonia's underground opposition since 1977. He was arrested and imprisoned by the Soviets in 1983. After his release, he became another one of the organizers of the famous *Hirvepark* demonstration. The Soviets expelled him in 1988 (Treiman family archive).

Committee, registering Estonian citizens who would then elect representatives to serve in the Congress of Estonia. The Congress was Estonia's parallel, freely elected, alternate Parliament to the Supreme Soviet which ostensibly governed Estonia.

When Tunne was in Los Angeles, I invited him to accompany me to a reception where other members of the consular corps would be present. During the reception I saw the Chinese Consul General and introduced Tunne to him. The two engaged in an extended conversation about Estonia. The Chinese was remarkably current about Estonian events.

Trivimi Velliste was also well known to the Estonian émigré community. He had formed a society for the protection of Estonia's national monuments. By preserving the past, he sought to influence the future. Meticulously following the letter but not the spirit of Soviet law, he was a thorn the Soviets didn't know quite what to do with. Later, he would serve as Estonia's Foreign Minister and as a member of Parliament.

Mart Niklus was a political prisoner from 1958 to 1966, 1976, and 1980–1988. Because of his status as an Amnesty International Prisoner of Conscience, his reputation transcended the Estonian émigré community. President Reagan had placed the persuasive power of the American presidency behind efforts to free him. While Mart was in Los Angeles, we visited President Reagan's Century City post-presidency office so he could thank the former President personally.

27. Visitors and Guests

A month after Estonia regained its independence, my parents held an afternoon reception for Tunne Kelam, Chairman of the Executive Committee of the transitional Congress of Estonia, and Mari-Ann Rikken, a Baltic activist who lived in Virginia. As Mari-Ann told me, the people at the reception were "such a warm and friendly group" it "felt right" for Tunne and Mari-Ann to make the first public announcement of their intention to marry. In this picture, taken by Mari-Ann that evening after the reception, my parents joined them in a private celebration (Treiman family archive).

In Los Angeles, as at every stop on their circuit, each of our visitors was interviewed by the local media. In addition, they met key American politicians and spoke to the local Estonian community. Invariably their appearances would generate sympathetic articles and additional political support as they went from city to city.

* * *

One of my other house guests was a freedom fighter who had never served time in the gulags yet he lived under a death sentence imposed by the Soviet authorities. He lived in New York. His Dutch wife, Claire, had died five years earlier.

Eighty-three-year-old Ernst Jaakson was Estonia's Consul General in charge of Legation in New York—the man who had appointed me to the honorary consul position. Jaakson was the physical embodiment of America's policy of not recognizing the legality of the Soviet annexations of the Baltic States and the corollary of that policy, the legal continuity of the

In 1995 I joined in the celebration of Ernst Jaakson's 90th birthday at the Estonian House in New York. When Estonia regained independence in 1991, Jaakson, in recognition of his work, was appointed, on a short-term basis, Estonia's ambassador to the United States and its Permanent Representative to the United Nations. From 1993 he continued to work as Consul General in New York. According to the U.S. State Department, at the time of his death in 1998 Jaakson was the longest-serving diplomat in the world (photo by Alfred Treiman).

Estonian State. A tall, physically fit, handsome man who any Hollywood producer would have cast as a diplomat, Jaakson represented Estonia's interests from the consulate's rooms in Rockefeller Center.

Jaakson's first job with Estonia's Foreign Ministry was at the Estonian legation in Riga, Latvia in 1919. Later he worked at the Foreign Ministry's

27. Visitors and Guests

headquarters in Tallinn. From there Jaakson was posted to the United States, initially in San Francisco, then New York. He had served as Consul General in Charge of Legation in New York since 1965.

Jaakson's stay at my house was by happenstance. Born in Riga but with his family roots on the Estonian island of Hiiumaa, Jaakson had an affinity for the sea. Each year he would try to make time for a cruise. In November 1988 he was on a cruise ship destined for Alaska. His ship passed through the Panama Canal with a scheduled, brief docking at the Los Angeles port of San Pedro. I was to meet him on board.

When I arrived, a concerned ship's steward told me that Jaakson was seriously ill. As I entered his cabin, I could see that he was obviously weak. After a great deal of persuasion, he agreed to disembark and stay at my house to recuperate from a very bad case of the flu.

A week or so before Jaakson's arrival in Los Angeles I had received a series of video cassettes from Sweden, sent by my godfather, Arvo Horm. Their sometimes fuzzy, black and white images chronicled current protests in Estonia. I gave the cassettes to Jaakson and he watched the videos. They were so fresh he had not seen them or even heard of some of the filmed events.

As he recuperated, Jaakson spent two days lying on a couch in my den watching the videos. He viewed them again and again. I could see a physical and mental transformation take place. The content excited him and seemed to reinvigorate his belief that Estonia would regain independence. We were watching Estonia's rebirth.

I welcomed other house guests as well, persons such as William Hough, a 10th-generation American whose lineage dated back to Pennsylvania in the 1600s. Bill was the author of a 1985 *New York Law School Journal of International and Comparative Law* article on the doctrine of non-recognition of forcibly seized territory. This article was often cited by activists within and outside of Estonia to buttress their arguments. He was one of the most energetic activists for Baltic freedom anywhere.

Other guests included the precocious young Harvard economist Ardo Hansson, who would later be the Economic Advisor to the Estonian Prime Minister and later, Governor of the Bank of Estonia (Estonia's Federal Reserve); and from America's East Coast, Mari-Ann Rikken (Kelam), who was my principal source of news from Estonia and whose ability to think creative, positive thoughts made her a pleasure to work with.

* * *

There was one house guest who was a guest only because of a tragedy. Avo Piirisild, the person who had conveyed Valdis Pavlovski's suggestion urging me to apply for the honorary consul position, spent several weeks at my house. Both Avo and his wife Viivi were well-known Baltic activists. Avo was a former president of the Baltic American Freedom League. Viivi was one of BAFL's vice presidents and an active, outspoken journalist writing for the Estonian emigre press.

Two Estonians, Tauno Waidla and Peeter Sakarias, had deserted from the Soviet army while stationed in East Germany. They told a harrowing tale of their escape to West Germany. They sought political asylum in the United States and arrived in New York in January 1987. Waidla and Sakarias were greeted as heroes by the Estonian-American community. They came to Los Angeles, were feted and given assistance by the Estonian community. My father hired Waidla to work at Metex. Unfortunately, after about a week and a half, greatly disappointed, my father fired him. Waidla did not like to work.

The Piirisilds took in the pair. In return for room and board Waidla and Sakarias performed household chores and repairs. They left after about a year, insisting they were owed, as part of their compensation, a non-operational Triumph Spitfire automobile that belonged to the Piirisilds.

On the morning of July 12, 1988, Viivi telephoned me at my office. She was alone at home and scared. Avo was on a business trip outside of California. The day before she had received a postcard barren of any writing. There was only a picture of a coiled rattlesnake, ready to strike. She believed Waidla and Sakarias had sent the postcard.

Viivi told me she was afraid of what Waidla and Sakarias might do. Notwithstanding her imposing, heavy-set build, she feared for her life. From the postmark she thought they would arrive in Los Angeles in a couple of days. Viivi said she would call me to finish our conversation when she returned from her dental appointment.

I never spoke with her again. Waidla and Sakarias were already in Los Angeles. When Viivi returned home, they were waiting. They murdered her. On one of the appeals from the guilty verdicts rendered against each of them, the California Supreme Court in *People v. Tauno Waidla* 22 Cal4th 690, 710 summarized the official record of the killing:

> On Viivi's return, as she passed through the front door toward the living room, before she could even attempt to resist, Waidla and Sakarias set upon her, dispatched her toward death, and then dragged her to a bedroom where her body would subsequently be found. They throttled her, fracturing her larynx and hyoid bone; bludgeoned her several times about her head and face and neck with perhaps the butt of the head of a hatchet, delivering some blows with such force as to crush her skull, fracture her jaw and various facial bones with her teeth knocked back, and generally deform her features; chopped her three times around the top of her head perhaps with the edge of the head of a

hatchet, delivering one blow with similar crushing, fracturing, and deforming force to penetrate her skull completely, delivering the other two blows with less force and, evidently, prior post-mortem; and stabbed her four times in the left chest area perhaps with a knife, inflicting two wounds that were six inches deep in the environs of vital organs, one that was three inches deep, and one that was only one-half inch deep and, evidently, prior post-mortem. They caused her death through the combination of the throttling, bludgeoning, chopping, and stabbing, and may have done so through any one of such means, because each was potentially fatal in and of itself. Before they went off, with things in disarray but apparently with their hands washed, they took various items of the Piirisilds' personal property, including a purse, wallet, green jade earrings, black star sapphire pendant, and credit and telephone charge cards, all belonging to Viivi.

Avo was notified of Viivi's death and immediately flew back to Los Angeles. His modest North Hollywood home was unfit for human habitation. Blood was spattered on the walls, floors and ceilings. Avo wanted seclusion. He wanted to disappear. He came to my house, located on the edge of Los Angeles in a gated community.

Avo stayed with us until after Viivi's funeral. My wife Jean and I tried to nurture him but most of the time he sat alone in our backyard, his thoughts interrupted only when the investigating detectives came to talk and to deliver progress reports. Viivi's funeral was closed casket. Not even a skillful mortician could repair the wounds inflicted on her, making an open casket impossible.

Waidla and Sakarias had fled cross-country to the East Coast leaving a trail of stolen credit card charges. From there they slipped across the border to Canada. For whatever reason they returned to the United States and were apprehended in New York. From there they were extradited to California.

Waidla and Sakarias were tried separately in Los Angeles. Each was found guilty and sentenced to death. Subsequently, Sakarias' death penalty was overturned by the California Supreme Court but he remains in prison for life. Waidla remains on death row while various appeals of his death sentence continue to meander through the courts.

28

Los Angeles Marathon: A Story in Four Parts

Part 1. Los Angeles Marathon 1987

"'Estonia' was spelled perfectly."

In the 1980s there were parallel universes, 5600 miles apart, each populated by activists seeking identical goals. In Estonia, Soviet law permitted social societies organized to strengthen awareness of local culture and environment—"heritage clubs." Beginning with the second half of 1986 these heritage clubs began to proliferate as activists tested the law's boundaries.

Protecting Estonia's natural resources from the adverse effects of phosphate mining, preserving the environment from oil fuel products such as the aviation fuel dumped at the 800 or so Soviet military sites that pockmarked Estonia's landscape and cultivating historical memory by preserving old monuments commemorating the war of independence were technically permissible activities. Activists used the opportunities the letter of the law presented. Estonian heritage clubs became proxies for the independence movement.

While Estonians were busy organizing heritage clubs in Tallinn, Tartu, Pärnu, Võru and other cities, the City of Los Angeles was making plans for the running of the Second Annual Los Angeles Marathon, an event that offered opportunities for publicizing the quest for Estonian independence.

I received a letter from Tom Bradley, Mayor of Los Angeles. Dated July 14, 1986, the salient parts read:

Dear Consul Treiman:

The second annual City of Los Angeles Marathon will be held March 1, 1987, and will include, as a part of the race, the first L.A.'s the Place Friendship Cup Run, symbolizing the unity of nations through peace and brotherhood.

28. Los Angeles Marathon: Part 1 1987

As Mayor of Los Angeles, I would like to invite your country to send two runners to join in this prestigious event. We would like your Federation to select the runners based not only on their competitive qualities but with the spirit of friendship and cooperation between people and nations in mind. Every nation that enters the race will receive an L.A.'s the Place Friendship Cup trophy at the Mayor's Luncheon which will be held on Saturday, February 28th, the day preceding the race.

I sincerely hope your nation will be represented in the 1987 City of Los Angeles Marathon.

I was excited. The invitation was not only an acknowledgment of Estonia's continued existence by the mayor of America's second largest city, it presented opportunities for educating the public about Estonia. My enthusiasm was somewhat tempered by my experience with the 1984 Olympics. If I accepted Mayor Bradley's invitation, would there be a quick retraction, similar to that experienced by our local Estonian, Latvian and Lithuanian folk dancers when they were denied the right to participate in the opening ceremonies because their presence was deemed "too political"? I did not want a new lawsuit. What I wanted was a platform that would highlight Estonia's existence as an occupied country.

I decided to telephone the founder and President of the Los Angeles Marathon, Dr. William Burke. I wanted to clarify the scope of the invitation—did it really include Estonia? I did not personally know Dr. Burke or his wife, former Congresswoman and County Supervisor Yvonne Brathwaite Burke. By reputation each was a significant and respected political personality, not only in the Los Angeles African American community but also throughout California.

Though not a runner, Dr. Burke had previous sport management experience. He had been Commissioner of Tennis for the 1984 Los Angeles Olympics, supervising the participation of 35 countries in what at that time was a demonstration sport. I would soon find out whether his association with the 1984 Olympics was an ill omen.

I began my conversation with Dr. Burke by introducing myself and telling him about Estonia and the other Baltic States—how the Soviet Union had illegally annexed them during World War II and that the United States and many other countries had never recognized the legality of the annexations. I started to explain why, because of the occupation, it was unlikely that two runners from Estonia could participate as part of the Friendship Cup. Instead, we planned to select our Friendship Cup runners from Estonians who lived outside Estonia.

Before I could get too far into my explanation Dr. Burke interrupted. He was very much aware of the history of the Baltic States. He would be delighted if Estonia, Latvia and Lithuania could be represented in the competition. He saw no problem with our plan.

My conversation with Dr. Burke was a promising start. The Los Angeles

Marathon was young. The previous year had been its inaugural run. It was a hybrid public/private mix between the City of Los Angeles and the entrepreneurial Dr. Burke and his company. Possibly to our benefit, it did not have international accreditation. We did not have to worry about Estonia's status on the books of international sports' overlords.

For Bill Burke and the Los Angeles Marathon, the Friendship Cup was a convenient way to capture international awareness for their fledgling event. It was also a way to entice various communities in ethnically diverse Los Angeles to support the marathon. In reality, Friendship Cup runners would be part of the larger race and other than the token Friendship Cup trophy presented to each country the Friendship Cup required little additional work on the part of the organizers. Sponsors would pick up additional costs.

From my standpoint, Estonia's legal status as a country would be reinforced by having the City of Los Angeles officially invite two runners representing Estonia to participate. In addition, the race would be seen in person by an anticipated million people and would be viewed by countless more on television. There would be opportunities to expose them to Estonia and its runners.

Participation by Estonian runners would also help maintain enthusiasm within the émigré Estonian community. Finally, to the extent they heard about our participation, and I was pretty sure they would, the presence of two runners officially representing Estonia would be a show of solidarity with the Estonians working for independence in Estonia.

I spoke with Jaakson. He approved. I sent a letter to Mayor Bradley accepting his invitation and began a search for two runners. Aarand Roos, who had come to the New York Consulate from Sweden in 1982 to serve as consul and to assist Jaakson, was an athlete in his own right. He, other individuals and Estonian societies and sports federations in Australia, Germany, Great Britain and the United States sent me names of potential runners. Estonian newspapers in all parts of the world carried the story of our search.

I mailed enquiries to the recommended runners. They were in Europe, North America and Australia. I asked Heino Jõgis from San Francisco and Arno Niitme and Jüri Kalviste from Southern California to serve as a selection committee. Following a distinguished career, Jõgis had just retired from Standard Oil of California (Chevron). He was one of the most politically and culturally knowledgeable Estonians in America. Niitme had been an elite athlete in Estonia. In 1931–1932 he had been Estonia's decathlon champion. Kalviste was an academically oft-cited aircraft engineer with the Northrup Corporation who had run in the previous year's inaugural marathon. He was familiar with the mechanics of how the marathon operated. Aarand Roos and I served as *ex officio* members.

The committee members made their selection from the numerous, worldwide responses I had received. Their first choice was Jaan Peetri, an Estonian-Swedish judge from Lund, Sweden. He had the best marathon times from among all our candidates. With complimentary plane fare in hand from marathon sponsor Pan American Airways, he would fly to Los Angeles from Sweden. He would stay at my house.

Jõgis and Niitme then selected their fellow committee member Jüri Kalviste as the second runner. Kalviste was selected because of his running times and his prior experience with the Los Angeles Marathon.

Some of the runners who were considered but not selected for the Friendship Cup plus a few others, decided to also run the marathon. They included a mother—daughter team from Australia, Helen and Penelope Paabo; a husband-and-wife team from Canada, Valdur and Desiree Reinsalu; Siim Sööt, who as of 2023 is Estonia's Honorary Consul in Chicago; and Uve Sillat, Ain Rajala and Jüri Tint, all from Los Angeles. Thanks to Kalviste, most of our runners wore custom made T-shirts that pictured the Estonian flag. A few local Latvian and Lithuanian runners also ran the marathon but did so on their own account. We decided to hold an unofficial "Baltic Cup" competition among all the Baltic marathon runners.

In October I received the official list of participating countries. Appearing next to the name of each country was the name of the country's local head of post. My name was misspelled but "Estonia" was spelled perfectly. I secured press passes for two local Estonians, Gerdrud Änilane and Viivi Piirisild, both of whom reported for Estonian newspapers scattered throughout the world. I assumed their stories would also filter back to Estonia.

As we in California prepared for the marathon, a group of political prisoners were being released from Siberian gulags, including several Estonians. About the time of the prisoner release, the second general meeting of representatives from all Estonian heritage clubs was taking place in Tallinn. Their principal agenda item was to reach agreement on the clubs' cultural-political-social activities.

While political prisoners returned home to Estonia; as heritage club members debated strategy; in Los Angeles race-day neared. We were busy with pre-race events.

Leo Weiss, representing the Latvian community, and Kalviste, Peetri and I, representing Estonia, attended the mayor's pre-race lunch at the Biltmore Hotel. The Friendship Cup was featured during the lunch. Each country received a small trophy. Viivi Piirisild was there as a member of the press corps. Displaying her own inimitable audacity, she generated a

The Latvian, Leo Weiss (right), and I flank Los Angeles Mayor Tom Bradley. Each of us is holding a "Friendship Cup" that was presented to every country that sent an international representative to the Los Angeles Marathon. Estonia and Latvia receiving a cup was a positive statement by the city of Los Angeles and the Marathon organizers concerning the continued existence of Estonia and Latvia as countries (photograph by Viivi Piirisild).

photo-op. Viivi literally grabbed the Mayor of Los Angeles as he walked by and posed Leo Weiss and me with him, holding our respective Friendship Cup trophies.

An official pre-race dinner was held at Universal Studios. All runners were invited to attend. Helen and Penelope Paabo, our Australian mother-daughter duo, were interviewed on television and by the *Los Angeles Times*. A more intimate reception, just for the Baltic runners, was held by BAFL at the Latvian House the evening before the race.

On Sunday, March 1, about one million people lined the streets of Los Angeles to cheer 15,000 or so runners as they moved along the 26.2-mile course. First came the elite runners, competing for prizes. They were followed by a gradually thinning mass of weekend athletes, some running, others jogging, stumbling or walking. Countless more people watched on television. The day's high temperature was a pleasant 68 degrees

Fahrenheit. By the time the temperature reached that level, many of the runners had already completed the course.

With the help of the City of Los Angeles, the block between Plymouth Boulevard and Windsor Boulevard on the south side of Wiltshire Boulevard was reserved for onlookers from the Estonian community—an area that local Latvians and Lithuanians were also invited to use. (At the time the Latvian Honorary Consulate was vacant and the Lithuanian honorary consul general was caught in the middle of a discord within the Lithuanian community so I represented, to a degree, the entire Baltic community at the Marathon.)

Because the race ended at the Los Angeles Memorial Coliseum, the Estonian House, a little less than two miles away, was a convenient location for Baltic American Freedom League to hold a post-race celebration and awards ceremony. The winner of the Baltic Cup competition was the Latvian runner, Janis Lapkis.

The 1987 Los Angeles Marathon was prelude. In the next three years events would raise Estonia's world-wide profile; Estonia's participation in the Los Angeles Marathon would become more significant; and two parallel universes would meet.

Estonians, Latvians and Lithuanians gathered on Wiltshire Boulevard watching the marathon runners move past them. A local Estonian, Tõnis Rebane, is shown holding the Estonian flag. To his right is Viivi Piirisild. The man on his left is Avo Piirisild (Treiman family archive).

The runner closest to the woman holding the blue, black and white Estonian Flag is Juri Kalviste. Kalviste was one of the original organizers of Estonia's participation in the Los Angeles Marathon. The city assigned the block of Wiltshire Boulevard between Plymouth Boulevard and Windsor Boulevard to the Estonian community for the purpose of watching the marathon. Members of the Latvian and Lithuanian communities joined the Estonians at this location (Treiman family archive).

Part 2. Los Angeles Marathon 1988

"Please register me for the March 6, 1988 Los Angeles Marathon."

On August 15, 1987, a broadside "Notice to Residents of Estonia" was distributed throughout Estonia:

> A social organization with the name The Estonian Group for the Disclosure of the Molotov-Ribbentrop Pact (MRP-AEG) has been formed in Estonia. The primary goal of this group is to fight for the disclosure of the secret document signed in Moscow on August 23, 1939, by the governments of Stalin and Nazi Germany. The social representative of the group is Tiit Madisson of Pärnu—a

former political prisoner and president of the Pärnu Heritage Society. The names of the other members of the group will be announced in Tallinn on August 23. A rally will begin at 12 noon.... Our group hopes for massive participation at the rally.

As Estonians in Estonia prepared for what would become a historic demonstration at Tallinn's *Hirvepark–Deer Park*, in California Mayor Bradley invited me to submit the name of one runner to represent Estonia as part of the 1988 Los Angeles Marathon's Friendship Cup program.

As Mayor of Los Angeles, and on behalf of the people of the City of Los Angeles, I would like to invite your country to send a runner to Los Angeles to join in this prestigious event. For the first 30 countries accepting our invitation, we are able to offer one round trip ticket for your runner, travel originating from the nearest city serviced by Pan Am. In addition, we will provide four days hotel accommodations for one runner from each country accepting our invitation.

I accepted Mayor Bradley's invitation on August 17. The day before, in Estonia, Tiit Madison, the public face of the MRP-AEG planned demonstration, had sent a memorandum to the Executive Committee Chairman of the Soviet of People's Deputies of the City of Tallinn. Citing Soviet legal authority, he asked for assurances that no harm would come to the those participating in the upcoming demonstration.

On August 23 in Tallinn, The Estonian Group for the Disclosure of the Molotov-Ribbentrop Pact (abbr. MRP-AEG) will be organizing a rally and wreath-laying to commemorate the victims of Fascism and Stalinism.
The demonstrators will assemble in front of Tallinn Town Hall at 12 noon. From there they will move on to Harjumäe, where wreaths and flowers will be placed at the foot of the Linda monument.
Please ensure the security of the demonstrators, in accordance with Article 47 of the Constitution of the Estonian S.S.R.

On August 23, about 5,000 people congregated in Old Town Tallinn's *Raekoja Plats*–Town Hall Square to protest the Soviet occupation of Estonia. From there they moved on to the statue of Linda, the mother of Estonia's mythical national hero, Kalevipoeg. Flowers and wreaths were left at Linda's feet. The assemblage then pressed on to *Hirvepark*. This was the first open, unsanctioned, mass political demonstration in Estonia since the Soviet occupation began. Speeches were made. A petition drive was started to erect a monument to Stalin's victims.

As events in Estonia, Latvia and Lithuania continued to escalate, Aarand Roos, the marathon selection committee, BAFL and I prepared for Estonia's participation in the 1988 Friendship Cup, much as we had in the previous year.

I sent invitations to the Estonian societies and sports federations. Estonian newspapers were notified. The same selection committee convened. A few of the runners who had applied to run in the 1987 Friendship Cup were unable to come to Los Angeles in 1988; new applicants asked to be considered.

In November, while the selection committee was still considering who should represent Estonia, I received a letter forwarded to me from the East Coast. It began, "Please register me for the March 6, 1988 Los Angeles Marathon...." After providing background information about himself, the letter closed with the salutation, "From occupied Estonia, A. Pruvli."

I communicated with Aivar Pruvli. I told him he would have to run under the blue, black and white flag of independent Estonia. He responded, "I am Estonian!" He had no intention of seeking asylum in America, he would return to Estonia after the race. While he had never run the marathon, he had excellent times in the 1500 meters and half marathons. He also had extensive experience cross-country skiing. What seemed impossible for the running of the 1987 marathon was now a possibility. An Estonian from occupied Estonia was prepared to run in the 1988 Los Angeles Marathon, representing Estonia, not the USSR.

At about the time I received Aivar's letter, an "Open Letter to Mikhail

Estonians, Latvians and Lithuanians competed for the "Baltic Cup" within the larger marathon race. The Latvian-American runner Janis Lapkis won the Baltic Cup the first two years. Here he is running along Wiltshire Boulevard, just having crossed Plymouth Boulevard, "Latvija" stenciled on his shirt (Treiman family archive).

28. Los Angeles Marathon: Part 2 1988

Gorbachev" dated November 30, 1987, was published in the West. It had been smuggled out of Estonia by a dissident group. The lengthy letter laid out the inconsistencies between theory and practice of the Soviet Union's nationalities policy. The letter pointed out:

> The only hope for the preservation of the Estonian people lies in its secession from the "unified multi-national state" and the reinstatement of its national sovereignty. In theory, you should have nothing against this. But in reality...?
>
> Since the powers over which you preside still prohibit open discussion of these questions in Estonia, and since all attempts to do so are accompanied by the immediate repression of the involved parties, then we must present the following questions to you by way of Estonian organizations abroad and the international news media, in hopes that you will not avoid answering them.

The letter to Gorbachev appeared in New York in December. At about the same time, in Los Angeles, I wrote to Lesley Calise, Director of Community Relations for the Los Angeles Marathon. I informed her that our 1988 Friendship Cup runner lived in Estonia.

I had met Lesley earlier. I knew her knowledge about Estonia was limited. I included with my letter some background material including Aarand Roos's book, *Estonia: A Nation Unconquered*, and my *Lutheran Standard* article about Harri Mõtsnik.

Lesley reviewed my letter with Dr. Burke. He and the other marathon organizers approved of Aivar Pruvli's participation as Estonia's Friendship Cup representative. Pruvli was sent roundtrip air fare from Helsinki to Los Angeles.

Although mailed well in advance, the ticket arrived too late. Aivar received it two days before the marathon start date, not enough time to fly to Los Angeles and run the marathon. Disappointed, Aivar returned the ticket. Accompanying the ticket was a letter to Lesley Calise. He reported that while the Los Angeles Marathon was being run, he ran his own private marathon in Tallinn. His time had been 2 hours and 39 minutes. He wondered if it was possible to include his result in the official results.

Lesley showed Pruvli's letter to Dr. Burke who was so moved that he sent a reply to Aivar. "I honestly feel that your story, how you ran your own marathon in 2 hours and 39 minutes, is one of the most heart warming that I have ever heard. Please accept a finisher's medal and a runner's T-shirt. You have earned them."

The actual marathon took place as before. Estonians, Latvians and Lithuanians from the Free World ran the course under an overcast sky. They competed against the field but also against each other for the Baltic Cup. The Latvian, Janis Lapkis, won again. Afterwards there was a BAFL reception at the Estonian House. We all wondered, could a runner from Estonia actually participate next year?

Part 3. Los Angeles Marathon 1989

"...our parallel universes met."

Main stream media news about Estonia was limited in quantity, often incomplete and not always accurate. Reporters for the major newspapers, wire services and television networks were based in Moscow. Their opportunities to visit Tallinn were restricted, visiting other Estonian cities was out of the question. Stories were often based on second- or even third-hand sources. Original source news often became public through avenues outside main stream media.

First-hand reports arrived in the form of letters, memoranda and smuggled videos, usually sent to members of the émigré community. The reports would then be distributed among other community members and Western news outlets. The news outlets might or might not use the material. Sometimes news from these alternate sources would be consolidated and published as a pamphlet or a booklet.

One such 118-page, staple-bound booklet appeared in March 1989. It bore the unwieldy yet descriptive title, *Documents from Estonia, Articles, Speeches, Resolutions, Letters, Editorials, Interviews Concerning Recent Developments from April 1986 to March 1989*. It was compiled and edited by two activist Estonian-Americans, Michael Tarm and Mari-Ann Rikken (Kelam), and funded by the Estonian American National Council.

One document in the booklet, *A Letter from Estonia* dated December 2, 1988, described salient events in Estonia, events that were a backdrop to our preparations for the 1989 Los Angeles Marathon and which the outside world was beginning to call "The Singing Revolution."

> In this letter I want to give you a summary of all that's happened in Estonia, events that have truly been extraordinary for people over here. Actually, the ferment hasn't stopped yet; the processes continue.
>
> In early 1987 ... the Estonian people were made aware of a nearly catastrophic plan: to begin mining phosphorite in the Rakvere region, the most fertile agricultural area of Estonia.... According to scientists, this kind of mining project would cause a significant drop in ground water levels, as well as the pollution of these waters. The source of many of Estonia's large rivers ... lie in this phosphorite region....
>
> Our problems are not limited to phosphorite mining. Pärnu beach, Estonia's largest resort, has been closed because the pollution in the Gulf of Pärnu exceeds all permissible limits by a factor of hundreds; disease bacteria thrive in the waters....

28. Los Angeles Marathon: Part 3 1989

In 1987, a new era of national awakening began in Estonia. After 48 years, new hopes arose for democracy. The rally in Tallinn's Hirve Park on August 23, 1987 was a pivotal event.... The next big event was the commemoration of the Tartu Peace Treaty and the 70th anniversary of Estonian independence in Tallinn, Tartu and Võru....

In the Spring of 1988, the blue, black and white national flag was reintroduced at the meeting of the Estonian Heritage Society in Tartu.

With the events of Spring 1988 ... circumstances were favorable for the formation and open activity of many groups and organizations. The Estonian National Independence Party, the Free Independent Column No. 1 (in Võru), the "Word of Life" (religious group), Scouting organizations, and many other independent youth groups emerged. The Estonian Popular Front was created—a movement led by liberal Communists in support of *perestroika* and *glasnost*....

The dismissal of Karl Vaino [the much despised First Secretary of the Estonian Communist Party—J.T.] and the mass demonstration at the Song Festival grounds (with about 200,000 participants) seemed to indicate an inclination toward concession-making by the authorities.

In the summer of 1988, demonstrations were held in many areas under the blue, black and white national flag, patriotic songs from the independence era were sung, fiery speeches were made, and monuments to those who fell in the War of Independence were restored. In the fall, the Song Festival grounds were the site of a true festival of patriotic songs and speeches; the last speech of the president of the independent Republic of Estonia, Konstantin Päts, was read. There were about 300,000 participants—meaning one of every three Estonians was there. On October 1 & 2, the I. Congress of the Estonian Popular Front was held in Tallinn's Town Hall. They demanded the proclamation of Estonian as the official state language and the passage of a language law protecting the Estonian language. They demanded the prosecution of Stalinist criminals....

The cold winter brought an end to the heated emotions of summer. The first ill omens appeared on October 25 with the publication of the proposed amendments to the U.S.S.R. Constitution and the forthcoming election of deputies. If these proposals were to take effect, then all matters of the economy, construction, population makeup, state boundaries, trade relations, and thus all domestic and foreign policy would be decided by the U.S.S.R. Congress of People's Deputies and the U.S.S.R. Supreme Soviet....

The Supreme Soviet of the Estonian S.S.R. met on November 16. Because of pressure from both sides—from the Estonian people as well as from Moscow—they approved a declaration of Estonian sovereignty, took a stand on the federation agreement and on the amendments to the U.S.S.R. Constitution, and made some amendments to the Estonian S.S.R. Constitution. In essence, these resolutions represented a timid attempt to assert the authority of the Estonian government.

... Information explaining the situation in Estonia and the endeavors of its people is not printed.... People are once again being punished for expressing their views....

Any way you look at it, the current situation in Estonia is pretty tense, and there's no reason to be unduly optimistic. We can't help but ask: what are we guilty of? Of being born Estonian here in Estonia?....

Force reigns in Armenia; there are tanks in the streets.... It is still quiet in Estonia, Latvia and Lithuania. But for how much longer?

While conditions in Estonia may have been "pretty tense," our preparation for the 1989 Los Angeles Marathon was uneventful and routine—until it wasn't. The mayor's invitation arrived. I accepted. I told Jaakson and Roos. The selection committee was contacted. A search for runners began. Then, everything changed.

In late 1988 Peeter Tammoja and Toivo Rande of the Estonian Chamber of Commerce in Tallinn contacted me. Established in 1927, the Estonian Chamber was shut down during the Soviet occupation. Peter and Toivo were now re-establishing it as a private, voluntary business organization.

While not strictly within the purview of a business organization, some elite Estonian athletes were also associated with the Chamber. Tammoja and Rande told me that eight of them were prepared to run in the Los Angeles Marathon, representing Estonia. They would not seek the mandatory Soviet sports federation authorization to participate.

With General Secretary Mikhail Gorbachev's loosening of travel restrictions, leaving Estonia was not a primary issue. However, in order to enter the United States each runner needed a visa from the American Consulate in Leningrad. There were three prerequisites to their receiving a visa: an invitation, a guarantee, and an acceptable explanation as to why they were coming to Los Angeles. Was I able to help?

I spoke with my parents. They agreed that our family company, Metex, would invite Rande and Tammoja to Los Angeles. The purpose of their visit would be to explore commercial opportunities between Estonia and America as well as possible business avenues between Metex and Estonian companies. They would visit between February 23 and March 7, 1989, conveniently including the March 5 running of the marathon.

Inviting the two chamber of Commerce Members was straightforward, our stated reasons made sense. But, how to explain why eight elite Estonian athletes would accompany them? And, why would a company that manufactured honeycomb decorations be inviting elite athletes for a visit?

We added the real object of the invitation toward the end as an "inconsequential" afterthought: "In order to further economic ties and to introduce Estonians to Americans, an invitation is extended to the following people to participate in the Los Angeles Marathon." The invitation named Sirje Eichelmann, Meelis Minn, Kristjan Port, Enn Sellik, Aivar Tsarski, Toomas Turb, Rein Valdmaa and Meelis Veilberg.

28. Los Angeles Marathon: Part 3 1989

The invitation, signed by my father on Metex stationery, included a promise that "Our company and I personally guarantee that we will be responsible for not only your but the other invited person's living expenses during their stay in Los Angeles."

We continued to be concerned that adding athletes to an invitation whose objective was to explore business opportunities might be considered a stretch of logic, which it was. The American Consulate in Leningrad might deny their visa applications. I approached a good friend, Yuan-sen Hsia. Actually, Hsia and I were more like brothers than friends.

We first met at the University of Chicago. He now lived in Southern California. As a young child he and his mother fled from mainland China to Taiwan when the Communists came to power in 1949. Their escape was not dissimilar to my mother's experience when she left Estonia.

In Taiwan, Hsia and his mother reunited with his father, who had escaped earlier with Chiang Kai-shek. Hsia had come to America to study at the University of Chicago, working on his doctorate. Ultimately, he remained in the United States. He was involved with a variety of businesses. One of them was a shoe store.

Hsia and I brainstormed. Then, after some serious discussion, interrupted by occasional impromptu chuckles, Hsia and I concluded that his shoe store should sponsor, at least on paper, a symposium on sports training techniques and sporting gear. The Estonian athletes would be invited to participate in the symposium. We reasoned that shoes were a necessary piece of sports equipment so Hsia's store sponsoring a sports symposium should not raise eyebrows. We decided to overlook the fact that his store did not sell athletic shoes.

With Hsia's consent, given with a satisfied chuckle, on January 12, 1989, I sent a telegram to the American Consulate in Leningrad that supplemented my father's original invitation. The telegram offered an additional reason for the visit, namely, "To participate in a symposium dealing with isometric training techniques and sports equipment."

To buttress our credibility and to emphasize the need for quick action, I telephoned the American Consulate in Leningrad. I identified myself as Estonia's Honorary Consul in Los Angeles. I don't recall if my explanation to the consul I spoke with was completely honest. I think it was, pretty much. Regardless, the consul in Leningrad indicated a willingness to help. In fact, I had a feeling that he understood exactly what was happening. All the visas were issued within one day—an extraordinarily short time frame.

Lesley Calise, now with her new name, Lesley Fuller, was still the marathon's Director of Community Relations. I told her that athletes were coming from Estonia, ready to participate in the Friendship Cup. Lesley was delighted. She had read the Estonia-related material I had given her the previous year and she remembered Aivar Pruvli's attempt to run in that year's marathon. For the past year she had followed news reports about Estonia and had become a fan of the independence movement. She told Bill Burke and the marathon organizers about the coming Estonian athletes.

A short time later a disconsolate Lesley telephoned me. She was in the uncomfortable position of telling me that the Estonian runners would not be permitted to participate in the Friendship Cup. The organizers, i.e., Bill Burke, now took the position that Estonia was not a country and therefore it could not be represented in the Friendship Cup.

In an aside, Lesley explained that Burke and the City of Los Angeles were seeking international accreditation for the marathon. They wanted their "child" to be recognized as a serious sporting event. To accomplish this, they had to be accredited by TAC (The Athletic Congress), which did not recognize Estonia, Latvia and Lithuania as countries. According to TAC, none of the Baltic States existed, so no one could represent them. I

The Estonian marathon contingent arrived at Los Angeles International Airport in 1989. From left to right: Rein Valdmaa, Meelis Minn, Aivar Tsarski, Meelis Veilberg, Igor Pihela, Peeter Tammoja, Toivo Rande, Jaak Treiman, Sirje Eichelmann. Following my usual practice when meeting Estonians at the airport, I am holding a small Estonian flag. That was a practical way for arrivals to find me (Aivar Tsarski family archive, taken by Aivars Jerumanis).

28. Los Angeles Marathon: Part 3 1989

Near the Los Angeles Memorial Coliseum, the elite runners, including the Estonian contingent, move toward the front of the starting line and get ready for the start of the race (Aivar Tsarski family archive, taken by Aivars Jerumanis).

wrote to TAC and spoke with their representative on the telephone, all to no avail.

Although the Estonian athletes could not participate in the Friendship Cup, they could run in the marathon, which was open to all comers. Their presence, even outside the Friendship Cup parameters, would effectively make them ambassadors for Estonia, so long as they were identified as Estonian.

The Estonians came. One evening, a week before the start of the marathon, I met Peeter Tammoja and Toivo Rande along with six of the eight invited athletes at Los Angeles International Airport: Sirje Eichelmann, Enn Sellik, Meelis Veilberg, Rein Valdmaa, Meelis Minn and Aivar Tsarski.

They spent their first night at a Holiday Inn near the airport. No doubt they felt right at home—the hotel had the charm of a building designed by someone who admired the Soviet school of architecture.

The next morning, we split the contingent and assigned the runners to the homes of different members of the local Estonian community who had volunteered to share their houses. The same community that had been traumatized by Viivi Piirisild's murder and had sworn they would never again house strangers, Estonian or not, reverted to their traditional

After the race, the runners came to the Estonian House, located just under two miles from the finish line. Here, from left, Meelis Veilberg, Sirje Eichelmann, Enn Sellik, Meelis Minn, Aivar Tsarski and Rein Valdmaa pose before going to the Estonian House (Aivar Tsarski family archive, taken by Aivars Jerumanis).

A group shot taken on the Estonian House stage during the post-race celebration (Aivar Tsarski family archive, taken by Aivars Jerumanis).

hospitality. The runners were welcomed into their homes. Sirje Eichelmann and Aivar Tsarski stayed with my parents. Enn Sellik was my house guest. The remaining visitors were welcomed into other homes.

The day of the marathon, Sunday, March 5, 1989, was warm and sunny. The temperature was 73 degrees Fahrenheit. As before, the marathon started at Exposition Park, next to the Los Angeles Memorial Coliseum.

All the runners who had come from Estonia had been classified as "elite," meaning they started the race ahead of the pack of 19,000 non-elite participants. In addition to being in front, elite runners also had a special holding area where they could warm up before the start. I walked with our runners into the elite holding area. By happenstance we passed the Soviet runners. I broke into a smile when I saw their shocked faces as the Estonians walked by. "What are you doing here?" "We came to run in the marathon!" was the simple response. After a very brief chit-chat, the Estonian runners moved on.

For two weeks in March parallel universes met. The Estonian independence movement in Estonia and the Estonian independence movement in the United States became one in the suburbs and streets of Los Angeles.

Our runners performed well. Sirje came in seventh among the women. Rein Valdmaa came in 18th among the men. Following tradition, after the race there was a celebration for all the Baltic runners at the Estonian House. The Estonian runners were the center of attention. Could they come again next year? Could they do even better, vying for the top prizes?

Aivar Tsarski, Enn Sellik, my mother, Sirje Eichelmann and Arno Niitme, at my parents' home (photograph by Alfred Treiman).

Part 4. Los Angeles Marathon 1990

Joy and Disappointment

On February 10, three weeks before the running of the 1990 Los Angeles Marathon, the Congress of Estonia, a grass roots Parliament freely elected by an overwhelming majority of the population, issued its "Declaration on the Authority and Legal Competence of the Congress of Estonia." In a direct challenge to the Supreme Soviet of the Estonian SSR and to the Soviet Union, the declaration stated that "the supreme power of the State in Estonia is held by the people" and that "only the Congress of Estonia is authorized to represent and to express the will of the citizenry of the Republic of Estonia."

On March 11, 1990, a week after the Los Angeles Marathon, Sajūdis, the anti–Soviet, democratic force in Lithuania, acting through its Supreme Council, passed the "Act of the Re-Establishment of the State of Lithuania"—their own Declaration of Independence from the Soviet Union.

Powerful political changes were taking place in the Baltic States, often daily. Even so, the outcome was not inevitable. Lithuanians and Latvians would die, there would be an attempted coup in Russia, there would be a face-off at an Estonian television tower.

In the meantime, in the sunny, palm tree stippled, sprawling basin surrounded by ocean, mountains and desert that is Los Angeles, the 1990 marathon was about to start. A year after her seventh-place finish Sirje Eichelmann returned to Los Angeles determined, on her second try, to come in first. She came on her own, by herself. This was a personal challenge.

She registered as an Estonian, not as a Soviet runner. Again, she stayed at my parents' home. Lesley Fuller, now with the enhanced title of the Los Angeles Marathon's Director of Communications and Public Affairs, continued to be a fan of Estonia.

The day of the marathon, Sunday, March 4, was cooler than in 1989. The air temperature at the start was a marathon perfect 62 degrees Fahrenheit with occasional light rain. Nineteen elite runners, including Sirje, were set to start in front of 20,000 runners lined up behind them.

Muhammad Ali was present. He gave a short speech from the starting platform. Then, after a false start that was to everyone's amazement contained, the starter's gun sounded and the runners were off. Sirje positioned herself in the middle of the pack of elite runners. After an hour or so she

28. Los Angeles Marathon: Part 4 1990

The official poster for the 1990 Los Angeles Marathon (photograph of the poster, Margus Välja. Treiman family archive).

took the lead. As in previous years, the marathon course started at Exposition Park, next to the Los Angeles Memorial Coliseum, zig-zagged a circular route through Los Angeles and finished at the peristyle end of the Coliseum.

Radio and television booths were located near the finish line. The runners' progress was broadcast through loud speakers. This was the area from which I followed the race. As Sirje continued to maintain her lead, the announcers took notice. They saw that she was more than a one-mile flash. They identified her as a Soviet runner. I was discombobulated. I was irritated.

I rushed to the official broadcast booth and voiced my objections, telling the broadcasters that Sirje was an Estonian runner, representing Estonia. My protestations were unavailing. The announcers would only identify Sirje as Estonian if the organizers told them to.

I looked for Bill Burke. Fortunately, I could not find him. Instead of Burke, I found Lesley Fuller. She knew why I was upset. On her own initiative, without looking for Dr. Burke, she ordered the announcers to identify Sirje as Estonian, not Soviet. They did so. For the last quarter of the race the announcers referred to her as the Estonian runner.

Sirje maintained her lead until mile 22.5 when an American runner passed her. Sirje came in second. She was referred to as the Estonian runner. Later, a celebration took place at the Estonian House, full of exuberance and joy. We reveled in the changes that had taken place, in Los Angeles and in Estonia, since 1987 when Jaan Peetri from Sweden was Estonia's marathon representative.

That evening, after I had returned home, I received a telephone call from Lesley. She asked if I had been told there was a press conference scheduled for the next morning. It was supposed to feature the marathon's top three men and top three women finishers. I told her that neither Sirje or I knew anything about it.

Lesley told me when and where the press conference was scheduled. I told her Sirje and I would be there. As the second-place finisher they would have a hard time preventing her from participating, especially with the press present. Although Sirje's English was more than adequate, she and I agreed that I would be her translator.

Next morning, Sirje and I drove to the press conference site. We arrived exactly on time. As we walked in, the other athletes were already seated on a stage in front of a bevy of reporters. Sirje took a vacant seat alongside the other runners. I sat behind her, ready to interpret. When Bill Burke saw us, he was as shocked as the Soviet runners had been the previous year when they saw the Estonian athletes.

Since no one present was conversant in Estonian my translations expanded Sirje's short responses, made in Estonian, to questions directed to her. I wove into Sirje's answers historical background, references to the Soviet occupation of Estonia and current information about the efforts to regain independence. Lesley stood in the back of the room, watched quietly and listened, not sure if she would still have a job when the press conference ended.

Near the end of the press conference, I dropped any pretense that I was translating. I explained what Sirje and the Estonian athletes had done the previous year and challenged the position taken by the marathon organizers. When I finished, Bill Burke took the microphone. Lesley and I each held our breath. We didn't know what to expect.

To our relief, Dr. Burke transformed into the person I had spoken with in 1987. He gave a rousing speech supporting not only an open-door policy for Estonian runners but also Latvian and Lithuanian runners. He concluded by saying that runners from the Baltic States could always participate in the Los Angeles Marathon.

Lesley kept her job. She also took her place in the pantheon of unrecognized heroes who, each in their own way, helped Estonia regain independence.

There was a frustrating aspect to the press conference. With one exception, the only people who understood what had transpired were Lesley, Bill Burke, Sirje and me. Except for a reporter for a small suburban newspaper, the *Pasadena Star-News*, the assembled sports writers were either clueless or uninterested. After the press conference, the *Pasadena Star-News* reporter took Sirje and me aside and asked a series of intelligent, to-the-point questions.

Announcement of the official results took several months. Top finishers were required to take a drug test. The order of finish would not become official until the drug test results arrived. The day before the official results were to be publicly announced a dejected Lesley called me. In a subdued voice she told me that Sirje's test was positive. She had been disqualified. The subsequent media reports referred to Sirje as the "Soviet runner." This time, I did not try to correct them.

Sirje denied using any prohibited substances. In retrospect, her denial has some credibility. For several years following the 1990 Marathon there were news stories that described the sloppiness of TAC's testing procedures, procedures that were still in their infancy. Also, given TAC's vehement opposition to recognizing Estonia, Latvia and Lithuania, it is not outside the realm of possibility that Sirje's results were falsified. On the other hand, most TAC tests were properly done and accurate. Sirje had grown up in the Soviet sports system where doping was a common practice. Who can tell where the truth lies?

A postscript: Ten years later, on March 5, 2000, I experienced closure. Jane Salumäe, from independent Estonia, took first place at the Los Angeles Marathon, officially.

29

Conversations with American Presidents

"Mr. President, we have taken way too much of your time."

I have been fortunate. Because of my position as honorary consul I have been privileged to meet uncommon people, including American Presidents. I spoke with one President while he was in office and two after their terms ended: George H.W. Bush, Ronald Reagan and Gerald Ford.

President Bush

I met President Bush in the Roosevelt Room of the White House on April 4, 1990. He had invited 14 Baltic-Americans, drawn from the leadership of the Baltic American Freedom League and Joint Baltic American National Committee, for a personal conference. The topic was America's Baltic policy. I was part of the BAFL delegation.

It was a time of rapid global change. Although a year had passed since the Tiananmen Square protesters were quashed, their Goddess of Liberty—the spirit of freedom—was alive in Europe. During the fall and winter of 1989, a series of mass demonstrations took place throughout Eastern Europe. In Poland, the Polish people restored "Republic of Poland" as their country's name and discarded "People's Republic." The Berlin Wall fell.

Three weeks before our White House meeting Lithuania's Supreme Council declared the re-establishment of Lithuanian independence. In March 1990 Estonia held free elections that established the Congress of Estonia, with Tunne Kelam as chair of its executive body. Latvia and Ukraine also held free elections.

President Bush feared that chaos would result if the Soviet Union disintegrated. His policy was reactive—go slow rather than be proactive. The Bush Administration's lodestar was stability—stability rather than transformation; cohesion rather than support of human rights. I was one of

29. Conversations with American Presidents

many Balts who were unhappy with the administration's reluctance to visibly support the national aspirations of the Baltic States or the other nationalities the Soviet Union had enveloped and colonized.

In August 1990 Professor J. Arch Getty reviewed a recently published book, *Soviet Disunion*, in the *London Review of Books*. I took exception to a number of Getty's assertions and responded in a long letter which, to my surprise, the *LRB* ran, unedited (except for misspelling "Jaak" as "Jack"). To understand the unhappiness of many Balts with President Bush's Soviet nationalities policy, replace the name "Getty" with "Bush" as you read my response:

> [Getty] presumably believes that, but for Soviet power, a majority of the remaining 97 nationalities would also be at each other's throats. Mr Getty's assertion ignores the recent history of co-operation between many of the nationalities.... On what facts does Mr Getty base his hyperbolic conclusion that the Soviet nationalities are filled with hate for each other, and his equally frail corollary that "all the nationalities are blaming each other for their current problems"? Most blame the Soviet system. Only a few blame each other.
>
> Mr Getty suggests that assimilation is preferable to rampant nationalism. His suggestion may be correct as an abstract proposition, but his analysis assumes facts which simply do not describe Soviet reality. "Assimilation" implies a voluntary adoption of a different culture. The voluntary element has been, and largely continues to be, missing in Soviet nationalities policy. When Russian culture is imposed by force and native culture is destroyed, when native populations are exterminated and Russians are brought in as replacements, when Russian is mandated as *the* language, when street signs are changed to Russian by Moscow's edict, when all official and scholarly communications must be in Russian—what kind of moral imperative does such assimilation by fiat carry? In this context, perhaps the nationalism of the non-Russians, used as a vehicle for maintaining traditions and freedom of choice, is not such an unsavoury concept....
>
> Mr Getty ignores the impact of Russian chauvinism. The thrust of the Soviet empire has been at least influenced by the Russian version of Kipling's "White Man's Burden," just as it has been fueled by a belief that more territory is better for its own sake.... Mr Getty's image of the Soviet Union as a boiling, hate-filled cauldron of nationalities which only Soviet power can keep from spilling over reflects a blind acceptance of Moscow's political rhetoric.
>
> Why are we so scared to see democracy given a chance? Would removal of Soviet power from its ethnic colonies result in self-annihilation by those nationalities? I submit that the answer is no—not if democratic institutions are permitted to replace Soviet power. When was the last time that democratic nations went to war with each other?

The White House had asked attendees to agree on one opening statement. A discussion would follow. The JBANC prepared a possible statement as did I for BAFL. Tony Mazeika, a firebrand even among activists, and I sat next to each other on our flight from Los Angeles to Washington, D.C. Tony and I reviewed what I had written and made revisions. We became more and more indignant about the Bush policy as our plane got closer and closer to Washington. We made more and more revisions. My proposed statement reflected our indignation. It was not a model of diplomatic finesse.

We had a roundtable meeting the evening before our White House appointment. My proposed opening statement, reflecting BAFL's position, was read to the group. This was followed by a reading of JBANC's proposed statement, which was clearly more conciliatory. The consensus was to use JBANC's statement.

In retrospect, the decision was perhaps tactically wise. As the iconic song writer, folk singer and social activist Pete Seeger had lyricized, borrowing from the Book of Ecclesiastes, there is "A time to cast away stones, and a time to gather stones together; a time to embrace, and a time to refrain from embracing."

After passing through security and entering the White House we were escorted into the Roosevelt Room, directly across from the President's Oval Office. In 1902, when the West Wing was added to the White House, the President's office was in the space now occupied by the Roosevelt Room. That room had been the site of much history, including President Kennedy's press briefings during the Cuban Missile Crisis.

We sat around a large rectangular conference table with rounded corners. The room was windowless; the table was in the middle. Called the Fish Room by Franklin Roosevelt it was renamed the Roosevelt Room by President Richard Nixon to honor both Theodore and Franklin Roosevelt.

After we were seated, key members of the White House staff, the Cabinet, the State Department and National Security Council entered and sat behind us. As far as I could tell, only the White House chef and the Vice President were missing. The President entered last, into a full room.

Our opening statement was read and then, during the course of our 70-minute meeting we offered comments and asked questions. President Bush responded. Secretary of State James Baker interposed occasional comments. The rest of the Administration's attendees sat, watched and listened.

We presented a five-point agenda. Three of the five points related to the recent Lithuanian declaration of independence. The previous night we had agreed on who was going to say what. When it was my turn, I urged President Bush to engage in strong Presidential advocacy to persuade Gorbachev to negotiate with Vytautas Landsbergis, Chairman of the Supreme Council of Lithuania.

Our meeting lasted considerably longer than the scheduled half hour. Afterwards we were told the President's office was happy with how the

29. Conversations with American Presidents

To Jaak Treiman
With appreciation and best wishes, *George Bush*

The April 1990 meeting between the leadership of Baltic American Freedom League, Joint Baltic American National Committee and President George H.W. Bush took place in the Roosevelt Room of the White House. When President Bush entered, he suggested that photos be taken before we began the substantive part of our meeting. He indicated how we should line up for the pictures. My picture happens to look more informal than the typical photo-op picture because I was confused by the President's indication of where the line for pictures was supposed to start. President Bush, noting my confusion, came and pulled me towards him as the photographer snapped the picture (White House photograph).

meeting went. While I no longer remember many of the details of that meeting, I do recall that during its course Mari-Ann Rikken (Kelam) remonstrated that Tunne Kelam, who was in Washington and was waiting for us on the sidewalk next to the White House, had not been invited to attend. Mari-Ann referred to Tunne's status as chair of the executive body of the Congress of Estonia and used the word "President." President Bush avoided a direct response by saying he did not realize Estonia had elected a President.

The next day a portion of our delegation met with future Secretary of

State Condoleezza Rice. At the time she was the National Security Council's Soviet and Eastern Europe Affairs Adviser. That meeting was more informal, did not include the Presidential entourage, lasted about an hour and a half and consisted of an unscripted give-and-take discussion.

Our meeting with President Bush was chronicled by both the American and Baltic press. When the BAFL contingent returned to Los Angeles we held a well-attended meeting of the Baltic community at the Latvian Community Center and reported on what had taken place.

President Reagan

A little more than two months after the April White House meeting with President Bush I met President Ronald Reagan.

Mart Niklus had spent a combined 18 years imprisoned in the gulags. He had been an Amnesty International Prisoner of Conscience. President Reagan had taken up his cause. Niklus was now in Los Angeles as part of the campaign to acquaint Americans and Estonian-Americans with conditions in Estonia. This was the same Mart Niklus I had spoken with on the telephone during the 1988 BAFL Awards Banquet.

In addition to meetings with the press and with the Estonian community, Niklus wanted to personally thank President Reagan for having advocated his release from the gulag. A meeting with the former President was arranged.

After he left office, President Reagan had returned to California. He worked from an office in Century City, a conglomeration of mostly high-rise buildings located about 12 miles from downtown Los Angeles. The Century City complex was built on the former backlot of the 20th Century–Fox studios. President Reagan and his wife Nancy (or, I should say, their respective foundations) had rented the 34th floor penthouse of one of Century City's smaller buildings—a space where the Bruce Willis classic movie *Die Hard* had just finished filming. Reagan's wife and her staff used one half and he and his staff worked from the other half. Bernhard Nurmsen, President of the Los Angeles Estonian Society, accompanied Niklus and me.

Our meeting lasted about half an hour and went smoothly. We shook hands and then talked while standing, forming a half circle in front of President Reagan. Niklus thanked the President for his support. In addition to telling a few jokes Reagan spoke knowledgeably about the Baltic States. Near the end of our meeting, he returned to his desk and offered each of us a handful of jellybeans from a jar.

Less than a month after escorting Mart Niklus to President Reagan's office I received a telephone call, I don't remember from whom, saying that

29. Conversations with American Presidents

From left: President Reagan, Mart Niklus, Jaak Treiman, Bernhard Nurmsen. Mart Niklus was imprisoned in the Soviet gulags for a combined 18 years. He had been an Amnesty International Prisoner of Conscience. President Reagan was aware of his case and every time there was a meeting between the U.S. representatives and Soviet representatives, the Niklus case would be brought up. Niklus wanted to personally thank Reagan for his assistance. Bernhard Nurmsen, President of the Los Angeles Estonian Society and active in the Republican Party, arranged the meeting (Ronald Reagan Foundation).

Lennart Meri would be meeting President Reagan on July 26. Could I also be there? At the time, Meri was Estonia's Foreign Minister, designated as such by the Popular Front—a sort of transitional appointment as the Soviet Union was crumbling but before the restoration of Estonian independence. Following the restoration, he would become Estonia's first President since World War II.

I was the first to arrive at Reagan's office. Shortly afterwards Meri arrived, accompanied by an American lawyer, Jennik Radon, and his Estonian assistant, Anu Lehmann (Part). I did not know Meri, Radon or Lehmann. Meri and I barely had time to shake hands before we were escorted in to see Reagan.

During the Niklus meeting Reagan looked just as I had seen him on television—healthy, charismatic and alert. During the Meri meeting, less than a month later Reagan still joked and spoke coherently but it felt as though he was reciting memorized lines. He did not look healthy. His

From left: Jennik Radon, Ronald Reagan, Lennart Meri, Anu Lehmann (Part), Jaak Treiman. The meeting was arranged by Jennik Radon. Meri would become Estonia's first President following the reacquisition of independence. We all left the meeting with a pocketful of jelly beans, Reagan's favorite candy (Ronald Reagan Foundation).

disclosure that he had been diagnosed with Alzheimer's disease did not occur until much later, November 1994. Perhaps he was just having a bad day.

I don't recall what we talked about. The meeting's main purpose seemed to simply be the act of meeting and speaking with Reagan. The meeting rather than the content of the meeting was important. It would raise Meri's profile and increase his credibility within and outside of Estonia—something that had political value both in Estonia and in the United States.

After about half an hour the meeting ended. Again, I left with a handful of jellybeans. Once outside the office I wanted to talk with Meri. The feeling seemed mutual. However, he was shuttled back to the car by Radon before we could do anything other than shake hands.

President Ford

My meeting with President Gerald Ford took place on April 2, 1998, long after the convulsions of the late 1980s and early 1990s had subsided.

29. Conversations with American Presidents

Following his Presidency, President Ford liked to spend his summers in Colorado and his winters in Rancho Mirage, near Palm Springs, California. When I, along with my parents, went to Rancho Mirage to present him with a medal on behalf of the Estonian President, I anticipated that a few pictures would be taken, brief pleasantries would be exchanged and I would then present President Ford with his award. I assumed we would then leave. It all went as anticipated until I had presented him with the award. Instead of bidding us goodbye, President Ford asked us to sit and we began an extended conversation (Gerald R. Ford Presidential Foundation).

Lennart Meri was now in his second term as President of Estonia; Tunne Kelam was Deputy Speaker of Parliament.

The meeting with President Ford was my most satisfying Presidential meeting and, thanks to my mother, the most memorable. It took place at President Ford's winter residence at Rancho Mirage, California, not far from Palm Springs.

From Võru to Stockholm, from Stockholm to Sydney, from Sydney to Los Angeles—a memorable moment in my parents' lives was meeting and speaking with an American President, Gerald Ford (Gerald R. Ford Presidential Foundation).

President Meri wanted to award America's 38th President a medal that acknowledged the support he had given Estonia and the other Baltic States while he was President. In the face of strong opposition, Ford had the United States sign the 1975 Helsinki Final Act of the Conference on Security and Co-operation in Europe—the Helsinki Accords. The civil rights portion of the Accords turned out to be of inestimable value in the struggle for Baltic independence.

President Meri could not come to California to make the presentation. Neither could Estonia's ambassador to Washington, Kalev Stoicescu. Stoicescu adopted a trickle-down theory and asked me to make the presentation. I called President Ford's office, asking for an appointment. While I was on the phone, I had a sudden inspiration. I queried if I could bring my parents. I was told "of course." With some excitement, the three of us made the two-and-a-half-hour drive from Los Angeles to Rancho Mirage.

We arrived a little early. As we waited, I looked at my parents and thought of their life in Estonia, their escape, our stay in Sweden, the journey through America on the way to Australia and our return to America.

29. Conversations with American Presidents

The three of us were now about to meet and talk with a former President of the United States—a memorable capstone to our journey.

After a short wait, we were escorted into President Ford's spacious office. I made the presentation. A few pictures were taken. The formalities completed, President Ford asked us to have a seat.

We engaged in a delightful conversation. He told us how the support he had received from the Latvians in Michigan had been crucial in securing his election to Congress. I told him how some of us had had misgivings about the Helsinki Accords because of our fear that it would dilute if not void America's nonrecognition policy. I also told him that in retrospect I could see how wrong my misgivings had been. The Accords had been a powerful weapon in the hands of the dissidents, not only in the Baltic States but throughout the Soviet Union. They used it as a weapon to reveal to the world how the Soviet Union was trampling basic human rights.

We continued to exchange stories when, after about 45 minutes, from the corner of my eye, I could see my mother becoming nervous. A few fidgety minutes later, she broke off our conversation, stood up and said apologetically, "Mr. President, we have taken way too much of your time." She was concerned that we were imposing on President Ford by continuing our conversation. Notwithstanding the President's protestations, we took our leave. Outside, I somewhat gently suggested to my mother that when one meets a President, it is the President who decides when the meeting should end.

30

Reconnecting with Family

"They were familiar strangers."

My mother fled Estonia when she was 25 years old. For the next 46 years she knew nothing about her family or friends. She did not know when her father, Samuel, died. She did not know when her younger brother, Aleks, was sentenced to a labor camp. Neither did she know that her childhood playmate, Verner with the runny nose, had been killed during the war. My mother did not know of marriages and births, uncles and aunts, nieces and nephews. My father was equally bereft.

The "Iron Curtain" was a product of Soviet isolationism, engineered by Stalin and continued, in varying degrees, by his successors. Sealing the Soviet population from the West included erecting communication barriers. Radio, and later television broadcasts from outside the Soviet Union, were jammed. Soviet functionaries reviewed and censored private letters.

Even after the Stalinist reign of terror ended, there were potential negative consequences for anyone in Estonia who had contact with people in the West. Letters, especially from the West, were screened and noted. Those who received such letters could lose their freedom or their job, or at the very least, forfeit privileges or advancement opportunities.

For refugees in the West, maintaining contact with relatives living behind the Iron Curtain generated anxieties not only about their relatives' safety but about their own safety. The assassination of high visibility targets such as Stalin's rival, Leon Trotsky and the Czechoslovak patriot, Jan Masaryk, were examples that the lowest of low-profile refugees took notice of. The letters my parents received from East Germany in the early 50s—letters that urged them to return to Estonia, fueled more concern about safety. Someone knew where they were even after they had moved from Sweden to Australia to America. Who was keeping track of them, and why?

The fears that permeated the thoughts of many refugees may at times have been exaggerated but nevertheless, in their minds the fears were real.

30. Reconnecting with Family

The Soviet barriers to communication, while not absolute, were barriers that neither my parents or many other refugees tried to penetrate.

When Soviet political life began to liberalize and visitation opportunities materialized, there was also the matter of principle or at least, perceived principle. Even as some émigré Estonians were beginning to visit Estonia, my father insisted he would never return if he had to travel there with a Soviet visa. He would not acknowledge the right of the Soviet Union to exercise sovereignty over Estonia by asking the Soviet Union's permission to step onto Estonian soil.

For a mixture of these reasons, my parents did not try to communicate with anyone in Estonia. My mother's younger brother Aleks had tried to find my mother through an enquiry with the Red Cross. My parents were aware of the enquiry but never responded—an omission that saddened them and I suspect, at least with respect to my mother, grew into regret as the years passed. Apparently, my mother's older sister Rosilda also had tried to find my mother shortly after the war ended.

Mother: *On my 71st birthday, January 21, 1989, I received an unexpected present—a letter from Võru. It was not from my oldest brother, Kalju or from my sister Rosilda or my younger brother, Aleks. It was from Kalju's son, who had not even been born when I left. The letter was dated December 8, 1988. It was signed "Mati."*

The letter began, "I don't know if I have sent this letter to the right person but I believe you are the same Valli who is my father's sister. If this is so, then it would be amazing if, after so many years, you were to respond."

Mati had gotten my address through my mentor when I first went to Tallinn, Miss Oja. She had relatives who lived in Canada. A young man from Canada who belonged to the student society Põhjala, to which Alfred also belonged, had provided our address when he visited Võru.

My mother's explanation of how Mati came to have her address is ambiguous. I never asked her for clarification. Now, more than thirty years later, responding to my enquiry, Mati's daughter Jaana offers this account, as told to her by Mati and supplemented by my mother's half-sister, Hilja:

> Mati got your mother's address from Aunt Hilja who heard it from a person in the village whose name was Matvere. Matvere had an acquaintance in another village who had the address. How that acquaintance got the address we don't know.

I suppose if my mother's account is supplemented with the information Jaana offers, and a few inferences are added, one might be able to reconstruct the chain of information which gave Mati my mother's address. On the other hand, perhaps we should just shrug and accept, in Jaana's words, "If something is destined, one way or another, it will happen."

Mother: *I replied at once to Mati's letter. "Yes, I really am your father's sister." Alfred and I talked. We concluded that given all the changes taking place in Estonia, we should visit. I told Mati we wanted to visit. We applied to the Soviet Consulate in San Francisco for a visa. We received it in June and left for Estonia that same month.*

Over the years the rationale for not communicating with friends and relatives living in Estonia grew weaker. Earlier fears of harm decreased. Some of my parents' friends traveled to Estonia and returned with stories that kindled old memories of places, friends and family.

My parents had listened to the dissidents who traveled through Los Angeles and spoke about changes that were taking place. I suspect having Sirje Eichelmann and Aivar Tsarski stay at their home when they competed in the 1989 Marathon helped solidify their decision to visit. My parents recognized that real changes were happening. Mati's letter was the final push they needed to reconnect with family.

Mother: *We flew to Helsinki. From there we took a boat to Tallinn. When we arrived, it took a long time to clear customs. Once our papers were inspected and once we had retrieved our luggage, we saw a crowd of people waiting to welcome us. We had never personally met any of them yet we were connected to each. They were familiar strangers. We had met Mati and his wife Ilme only by mail and telephone.*

We bridged the decades of separation and easily re-united. There were introductions. We learnt names. We hugged through cascades of tears. My older brother Kalju was absent. He was waiting for us at his home. My younger brother, Aleks, was not there. He had been arrested and sentenced to serve 20 years plus 5 years of internal exile. He had served 12½ years in Vorkuta, possibly the worst labor camp in the Gulag system. Then, he was one of the recipients of the mass amnesties that eventually followed Stalin's death. Aleks returned to Estonia and died in 1984, five years before our visit. At least he was buried in Estonian soil.

We left the Tallinn port area. The next control point we had to pass was in Old Town. As he checked our papers the guard asked where we were staying. I started to explain that we were going to Võru. Ilme poked me in the ribs and took the lead. A special permit was required in order to travel outside of Tallinn. Ilme had the gift of speech. I couldn't hear what she told the guard but we soon had our permit. We began our ride to Võru.

After a drive of three or so hours we arrived in Kasaritsa, a small village in Võru County. This is where my older brother, Kalju lived. Along with Kalju, about twenty people were waiting to welcome us. More introductions. More hugs. More tears. I was told that my sister Rosilda's health was not good. We would see her the next day. When we did, we both burst into joyful tears.

30. Reconnecting with Family

Mati took us to where he lived. It was an apartment in a complex of five-story buildings on the edge of the town of Võru. Each building was identical. No elevator. We had to walk up the stairs to the fifth floor. Halfway I had to stop to catch my breath.

My parents visit and their stay with Mati, Ilme and their daughters, Jaana and Jane generated some pre-arrival bureaucratic movement in Võru. In the Soviet Union, all city housing belonged to the government. Places to live were distributed to residents by municipal authorities. Generally, people had no choice in the housing they were given. As told to me by Jaana, here is the backstory to my parents' return to Estonia:

> Your parents coming to Estonia gave us the chance to get a new apartment. Our usual home was an apartment directly above a bookstore. That building was being repaired. The city assigned us temporary, emergency quarters in an old, run-down building. "Temporary" tended to be permanent.
> We shared the kitchen in our temporary quarters with our neighbors—two old men whom life had bypassed and who loved their alcohol. There was no running water. We could not wash. To keep bedbugs from infesting our beds, we put each bed footing into a cup filled with water.
> The old house had a long, windowless, barracks style corridor with multiple doors leading to adjoining rooms. One of the rooms was a shared, dry toilet. The smell from the toilet was compounded by the strong smells from the slaughterhouse that was next door. The house was especially odoriferous during the summer.
> When it was certain that Valli and Alfred were coming, my mother and father went to the city government. They described our living conditions and then asked the officials, "Is this how you want Estonians from abroad to see how Estonians in Estonia live?" On the morning of May 27, my mother's birthday, she was given keys to a new apartment.
> The apartment was in a new district. The inside of the apartment was not yet complete. A lot of the materials needed to finish the interior had been stolen by the builders. The interior work that had been completed was shoddy. We quickly started work on finishing the interior. By the time your parents arrived, our fifth floor apartment was ready for guests. We had our own toilet, washing facilities and even hot water!

Mother: *We visited my stepsister [half-sister], Hilja. She lived in the same house where I had once lived for a short time. It used to be an old, windowless, community grain house that father remodeled into a home after we moved from the old courthouse. It had three rooms and a kitchen. From the outside it still looked like a grain house but its windows were proof that there was life inside.*

Wherever we went, the surrounding countryside was desolate. The Matson's large farm, so full of life with its many family members, was abandoned, overgrown with weeds. My childhood friend Verner had died during

Some years after my maternal grandmother Maria died, Samuel remarried. My mother's half-sister, Hilja, was the product of that second marriage. Here, Hilja and my mother stand by the front door to Hilja's house (author's photograph).

the war. His brother Oskar, an agronomist with whom I worked in Ravila, had also died. I didn't know what had happened to the rest of the family.

The beautiful Võru farms that I remembered were abandoned and overgrown with weeds. Everything was as I had left it, except worn and uncared for—a state of progressive decay. I wondered how one could restore life and joy. The school house stood on the other side of the river, lonely. I didn't see any children. I didn't see anyone walking.

I remembered sitting quietly next to my father as he fished in the Pärli-jõgi—the Pearl River. The river still flowed but it lacked the joy and the power of my youth. Even so, it still lived up to its name. Its swirling, iridescent waters continued to glisten as though it was a string of unclasped pearls winding through fields and forests. The Eomoisa mill was still there, where the farm girls' clothes were dyed and wheat was ground. I was able to gather up a small bag of wheat to take home.

We spent time at Kalju's house. It was such a loving, homey feeling to sit there, next to my brother. His smiling face and his optimism never faded.

30. Reconnecting with Family

My mother, during her last visit to Estonia, gazed at the wall of Hilja's house, a house she had lived in for a time when she was growing up (author's photograph).

I looked at Kalju and remembered how he lost the fingers on his left hand. It happened when he was 19 years old. He and two friends were walking in the forest. They found a strange looking package. Kalju was curious. He wanted to know what was inside. He poked. It exploded. The fingers on his left hand were shattered, his stomach imbedded with grenade fragments. He was placed in a horse-drawn cart and taken to the Võru city hospital. There was little hope. I cried and prayed every day. In three weeks, Kalju was able to come home.

Kalju did not let the accident affect his life. He liked to mold beautiful things out of wood. He gave me a small, wooden flag holder with an Estonian flag to give to Jaak for his birthday. He presented me with a wooden flower vase. Kalju and his wife Linda had turned a small cottage into a beautiful home.

We went into the town of Võru. Again, we had the joy of seeing old friends and relatives. We hugged and observed with curious wonder the footprint Time had left on each of us. More visits followed. Everyone wanted to welcome us. We looked at old sites. The house where I had lived in Võru no longer existed. A bomb had dropped on it during the war. A new house had still not been built in its place.

We went to the cemetery, took flowers, lit candles. We remembered those who were no longer with us. Before we knew it, it was time to leave. We wanted to spend a day in Tallinn where we could see the Song Festival [One of the world's largest choral events, it has been held every five years since 1869; sometimes more than 30,000 voices perform simultaneously on stage.] *Then we would go by boat to Helsinki and the flight home to Los Angeles.*

There was a lot to think about. Where do we belong? Is it where we were born, grew to adulthood and now, after many years, have returned? Or is it California, where we have built our lives? Life requires material as well as emotional support. We are attached to Estonia, our homeland, even as our day-to-day life is in California, where we live and also have roots.

Our visit to Estonia after so many years was an experience in contrasts. We could compare the freedom and the material benefits of democracy and the free world versus the stagnation and lack of material benefits of dictatorship and communism. It appeared that the era of communism was coming to an end. We hoped so, never to return. Truth and justice go hand-in-hand. May that be Estonia's guiding light. May Estonia keep its identity as a nation, and continue to survive.

While my parents were in Estonia, they invited Mati and Ilme to visit. My parents returned home during the first few days of July. Mati and Ilme arrived in California less than two weeks later. Their visit was part of the reconnecting process that Mati's letter to my mother initiated. They stayed with my parents for about a month and a half. My parents had sold our family business, Metex, earlier that year. Now, in retirement, they had time.

My parents wanted to show Mati and Ilme what life in a democracy was like. Even more, I think, they wanted to connect and to catch up—catch up with family history, catch up with happenings in Võru during the past 45 plus years, catch up with life in Estonia since their departure to Sweden. As they were catching up, my parents introduced Mati and Ilme to their friends and neighbors—Estonian and American and drove them up and down the state, showing them the sites.

Mother: *We invited Mati and Ilme to visit us in California. They did so from July 10 to August 28, 1989. We wanted to introduce them to life in the free world. We wrote the required invitation letter.*

On our end, the paperwork was easy. Mati and Ilme did not have it so easy. They had to work hard to get permission from the government. Buying plane tickets was also a challenge. After our return to California, we spoke with Mati and Ilme on the telephone. For them, using the telephone was like running an obstacle course.

To telephone us they first had to go to a central office in Võru and place an order. They would be given a date and approximate time when

30. Reconnecting with Family

they could make the call. Then they had to return to the central office on the assigned date and wait for their name to be called on a loudspeaker. They would then go to a designated telephone. They were able to talk only for the number of minutes they had ordered. When time expired the call was shut off.

My mother goes on to quote from a letter Mati and Ilme sent my father and her that described their preparation for visiting California:

> An invitation to visit California! First, we had to acquire a second passport—one for overseas trips. This was in addition to our internal passport for use in Estonia and within the Soviet Union. In 1989 few people in Estonia had a passport for international travel. Next, we needed an American visa. The closest American Consulate was in Leningrad (Petersburg). We waited in line outside the consulate entrance for two days and nights before it was our turn to enter.
>
> Next, we had to go to a currency exchange in Tallinn. We arrived in the morning but it wasn't our turn until evening. Only then were we able to exchange any money. The exchange rate was very bad.
>
> The next morning, we went to buy plane tickets. This is where the real nonsense started. We were told, "Come back tomorrow." "Come back in a week." "There are no tickets." "Come back in a few hours." Eventually we were able to get tickets and begin our travel to the Moscow airport. Our driver was a commercial truck driver who delivered goods between cities. We went in his vehicle. Everything went smoothly in Moscow. Our flight was uneventful.
>
> In Los Angeles there was the pleasure of seeing you both again but disappointment that when we arrived our luggage did not. We assumed it was lost forever. But, wonder of wonders! The next morning our luggage was at your front doorstep. That was unbelievable!

Mother: *Alfred and I greeted Mati and Ilme at the Los Angeles airport. We let them rest for a few days. They swam in our backyard pool and we enjoyed the California sunshine. They saw our neighborhood. We drove to the Estonian House and showed them the rooms, the stage and the kitchen. Because it was summer vacation time, there were no people to meet there. We took them to Disneyland and to the Los Angeles Zoo. We celebrated Jaak's birthday with Ilme making one of her specialties, a Napoleon cake. We visited with Estonian friends. There was time for a little shopping.*

We wanted to show Mati and Ilme California, with its ocean, mountains and deserts. We drove north towards San Francisco, the Pacific Ocean on our left. We saw whales and seals. Mati was busy recording everything with a video camera Alfred had bought for him. He has those videos to this day. We stayed at Mammoth Lakes in the Sierra Nevada Mountains. We drove through miles and miles of desert. All of us admired the California scenery. Before we knew it, it was time for them to leave.

During the two years following Mati and Ilme's visit, more seismic changes took place in Estonia. In March 1991 a referendum in favor of independence received overwhelming support. On August 20, 1991, Estonia declared the restoration of independence, a declaration the Soviets formally recognized on September 6. Elections were held in 1992. A freely elected Parliament convened. Lennart Meri took office as President on October 6, 1992.

Through numerous letters and occasional telephone calls my parents stayed connected with Mati and Ilme. In 1992 my parents invited them to send their daughter Jaana and a friend to visit. (Jaana's sister had recently married and therefore could not come.) What was originally planned as a 10-week stay was extended into a six-month visit. Jaana had just turned 16. The friend who accompanied her, Ingrid Pall, was two years younger. They left for California on June 22. Two days earlier, on June 20, Estonia had issued its own currency, the kroon.

Mother: *Alfred and I thought it would be a good educational experience if Mati and Ilme's daughter, Jaana, stayed with us for an extended period. She could go to school here and experience life in California. We thought that if she came alone, she could easily become homesick. It would be more fun for her to come with a friend. We bought tickets for Jaana and her relative, Ingrid. They arrived in Los Angeles in June 1992. There was time for the girls to get used to their new environment before school started.*

We took a couple of weeks to drive to northern California. We tried to show them as much as possible—San Francisco, Mammoth Lakes and the Eastern Sierras, the desert. At home we had a swimming pool where the girls could swim. I hired an English teacher so it would be a little easier for them at school. When school started, I drove the girls to school in the morning and brought them back at the end of the day. The girls were energetic and did well.

Soon Christmas was upon us and it was time for the girls to return home to Estonia. I hope that living in the free world was beneficial, helped broaden their worldview and that they acquired something valuable to remember. They also saw and heard how the fight for Estonia's freedom took place in America—how Estonians, Latvians and Lithuanians united in a common cause. Alfred and I were left with a feeling that we had helped open a window to the free world for two young persons.

Now, as I write these words, the girls have grown into young women. Jaana has three children, all smart and talented. She works in a small southern Estonian school. She wants to make her school the best in Estonia. I look at her and I have confidence in Estonia's future.

31

Independence Restored

"...these ends required new beginnings."

Mother: *Alfred and I had visited many countries around the world, in Europe and in Asia. One day as we looked at a globe, our eyes paused on Turkey. We looked at each other. Alfred said, "Alright. Turkey it is." He telephoned our travel agent. We were told the next group tour left in August. We reserved a spot and ordered our plane tickets. In a few weeks, we flew to Turkey.*

The year was 1991. My mother doesn't mention the reason she and my father were looking at the globe, considering what country to visit. My father's 80th birthday was approaching. It would fall on a Thursday, August 22. My mother wanted to celebrate with a big party that weekend.

My father was not a fan of parties, large or small, especially when he was the center of attention. My parents compromised. Instead of a birthday party they would celebrate his birthday by visiting a country they had not yet been to. They picked Turkey. That is why they weren't in Los Angeles on August 20, the day Estonia declared its independence to be restored.

Mother: *After we arrived in Turkey, we rested for a day. Then our bus tour began. At one stop in western Turkey, I sat near the columns that surround the historic trade center of Agora Ephesus. A middle-aged man must have heard me say something. He asked me my nationality. I told him I was Estonian. He congratulated me. I must have looked confused. He happily informed me that Estonia was now independent!*

We looked for English language newspapers, found some, and read more details about the independence declaration. As we continued our tour, many people congratulated us, especially the Kurds. More than one Kurd told us, "Our turn is next."

Our trip to Turkey came to an end. When we returned to Los Angeles Jaak met us at the airport. His first words were, "Estonia is free." He had tried to contact us with the news. Unfortunately, we had left each place just before he telephoned. We told him we had heard. We were sorry that

237

we had not been able to be with our son and friends on the day Estonia regained independence. *That was disappointing.*

Even before my parents left for Turkey dramatic changes were taking place within the Soviet Union. The changes, as though powered by a centrifuge, gained more and more speed, disintegrating everything in its path. Boris Yeltsin had resigned from the Communist Party in 1990. He was now President of the Russian Republic while Mikhail Gorbachev held the newly designated position of President of the Union of Soviet Socialist Republics.

On August 18, while my parents were in Turkey, a coup was launched by hardliners in the Soviet government who opposed Gorbachev's policies of *glasnost* and *perestroika*. Gorbachev was forcibly isolated while vacationing in the Crimea. On August 19, tanks surrounded the building that housed the Soviet government. Yeltsin raced to the tanks and then, in what the BBC called "one of the abiding images of modern Russian history," spoke to the soldiers and the gathered crowds. The *Los Angeles Times* described the scene:

> The crowd raised nervous cheers as Russian President Boris N. Yeltsin, once again their hero and the focus of their hopes, clambered to the top of one of the dozens of armored vehicles encircling his government's building.
>
> "Hang on! Hang on!" the people chanted as Yeltsin used as a podium one of the tanks dispatched by the self-styled State Committee on the Emergency Situation to cow him and his followers.

At 11:02 pm on August 20, the Estonian Supreme Soviet, in a move endorsed and joined by the executive organ of the Congress of Estonia, proclaimed Estonia's independence from the Soviet Union. The Supreme Soviet of the Latvian SSR made a similar declaration.

Boris Yeltsin responded immediately. He issued decrees that recognized Estonia's and Latvia's independence. According to the *New York Times*, "The prompt declarations were considered a direct consequence of the support the three republics gave to Mr. Yeltsin's opposition to the coup. They were the only Soviet republics to issue declarations of support for the Russian leader on the day of the coup."

Fearing another coup attempt in Moscow, Estonia, Latvia and Lithuania sought swift recognition of their declarations of independence. They addressed appeals to 42 governments. While Iceland was the first country to formally recognize Estonian independence, others did not act as quickly. The *New York Times* reported that although Mr. Meri cited encouraging responses to his appeal from Denmark, Germany and Italy, there is a muted undercurrent of dissatisfaction here over the apparent unwillingness of the United States and Europe to complicate further their relations with Moscow by recognizing Baltic independence.

Finally, on September 2, 1990, the United States belatedly joined the flood of countries recognizing the reacquisition of independence by

31. Independence Restored

Estonia, Latvia and Lithuania. After decades of demonstrations, after attending a myriad of political meetings and signing an infinite number of petitions, after dreaming so many dreams, I wanted my parents to know their efforts had blossomed, their dreams had become reality. I didn't know how much world news was available in the far reaches of Turkey.

I telephoned distant villages where, according to their itinerary, they were supposed to be staying. Most of the time I heard ringing on the other end of the line but no one answered. When someone did, I was told my parents' tour had "just left." I faxed innumerable newspaper clippings. My faxes disappeared into an unknown void.

I kept missing them but my worries were needless. When they came home my parents said that even in Turkey's farthest corner, they had heard about Estonia regaining its independence. What my parents did miss was a huge celebration, one that even my father, with his aversion to parties, would have enjoyed. The Los Angeles Estonian, Latvian and Lithuanian communities combined for a mammoth victory celebration. We picked the largest, readily available auditorium—the social hall at the Lithuanians' St. Casimir Catholic Church.

This was where we had celebrated the Baltic Wave in 1989—the human chain that stretched from Tallinn to Riga to Vilnius. St. Casimir was where we helped the Lithuanians celebrate their National Day each year. This was where, in rotation with the Latvian Community Center and the Estonian House, we joined each year to commemorate the Baltic Deportations of 1941 and 1949.

The press, radio and television were all present, transmitting the joy of the occasion along with the speeches and music. The mood was sublime; the party was huge. The *Los Angeles Times* offered this description:

"Now I know how David felt after he slew Goliath," [Danute] Mazeika exulted as news spread that President Bush had finally decided to offer official U.S. recognition to the Baltic states of Latvia, Lithuania and Estonia.

As word spread here that the three tiny nations were officially independent in the world's eyes, Mazeika and thousands of other Baltic-Americans jammed phone lines, fired off telegrams and cobbled together hasty celebrations from the living rooms of suburban homes throughout Southern California....

In Los Feliz, hundreds poured into the parish hall of St. Casimir's Roman Catholic Church for an impromptu Baltic festival, filling the air with champagne toasts....

But even then, even with the celebratory laughter and back-slapping, even as we reminisced about battles won and lost, there was an understanding that much remained to be done. World War II may have finally ended for Estonia, Latvia and Lithuania but the end we celebrated, the end of one-party governance, the end of an irrational economic system, the end of a ruling elite who refused to recognize the worth and dignity of human beings—these ends required new beginnings.

How does one renew a country? How does one build a new society, a society that values the traditions of the Magna Carta, the universality of the Bill of Rights, the equality that underlies the Declaration of the Rights of Man, the optimism of the Universal Declaration of Human Rights?

Epilogue

Jaak: My father lived another 18 years following Estonia's restored independence; my mother for another 21 years. They continued to lead active lives, with neither the burdens nor the joys of running Metex—the business that had been an inseparable part of our lives since Australia and which they had sold in 1989.

No longer required to devote their time and energy to Metex, my parents increased their participation in the activities of the Los Angeles Estonian Society. Even after my father's death, my mother continued to make the 90-mile round trip drive from her home to the Estonian House so she could participate in the monthly meetings of the senior citizens club.

Following the restoration of independence, my father eagerly followed the resurrection of his student society *EÜS Pōhjala*. He continued to maintain and expand the *Pōhjala* contacts he had preserved while we lived in Sweden, Australia and America. Each summer my father and I paid homage to the Treiman and Uibo family heritage by going fishing in California's Eastern Sierra Mountains.

My parents continued to travel, visiting China and Italy, Argentina and New Zealand and many destinations in between. For some reason, they never returned to Australia. Their only return visit to Sweden was in 1980 for the worldwide gathering of Estonians, the Esto Festival.

Following their 1989 trip my parents returned to Estonia four more times as a couple, including a joint celebration of 90th birthdays with my mother's older brother, Kalju, and my father. Unfortunately, that was the only time I was able to be in Estonia with both of my parents.

Following my father's death on May 8, 2009, at age 97 from complications arising from emphysema (he did not stop smoking until he was in his 80s), my mother continued to live in a two-story house that had been their home since 1996. The house was not far from the Reagan Presidential Library, a place my parents liked to take visitors. This was also the house where she had cared for my mostly bedridden father during the last year of his life.

After my father's death my mother returned to Estonia two more

My father and Kalju, my mother's oldest brother, celebrated their 90th birthdays together. I joined my parents for that visit. While my parents were in Estonia they shared memories with me, including showing me the spot where, when they both happened to be in Võru, they would bicycle to meet each other while they were dating. They stood on that spot as I took this picture (author's photograph).

When my mother visited Mati and Ilme, she would invariably use their backyard sauna. Here, she and Ilme are returning to the main house after a spell in the sauna. The Estonian sauna is not to be confused with American steam baths. There are a variety of different saunas but generally they are based on dry heat generated by water thrown on hot rocks. Steam baths are not as hot as saunas and use moist heat generated from boiling water. Estonians also like to thrash themselves with freshly cut birch twigs while in the sauna. Alternate dips into cold water following a stint in the sauna adds an appropriate, refreshing climax to the experience (author's photograph).

times. I accompanied her both times. Her final visit was in September 2012 after she had been diagnosed with kidney cancer. She visited family—the quick and the dead, saw her childhood home, looked at other memory filled sites and visited long-time friends. Following her return to California she continued to enjoy life, a little slower but active and alert. We drove to Los Angeles County's neighbor, Orange County, to help celebrate her best friend Erika Anton's 90th birthday.

One morning not long after we had celebrated Erika's birthday and a few weeks before Thanksgiving I made my regular twice-daily telephone call to my mother. There was no answer. After several more unsuccessful attempts I asked her neighbor, to whom I had given a key while my father was bedridden, to check. She did and found my mother lying conscious on the bedroom floor, where she had fallen.

At the hospital she had a pin placed to repair her broken hip followed by a move to a convalescent home for physical therapy. She received visitors and made friends with some of the other patients. For Thanksgiving, Jean, now my ex-wife but still a friend, and I took her to Jean's brother's lakefront house for a family dinner and get-together. Her granddaughter Samantha and her great granddaughters Avery and Zoe were present. So were many members of the McLeod clan—Jean's family lineage. My mother had known many of the gathered adults for more than thirty years and the children all their lives. Five days later, on December 2, 2012, she died peacefully.

My mother concluded her narrative by offering a lyric to the strength, determination and perseverance of all Estonian people but words that are especially apropos to her, my father and their generation of refugees:

During return trips to Estonia, my father would borrow Mati's fishing gear and go fishing. To his delight, sometimes he caught a fish; size did not especially matter (photograph by Mati Uibo).

> Estonians are strong. We have weathered much and stood firm. Estonia's long-term survival depends on how well we maintain our national identity. Truth and justice go hand-in-hand.
> Estonians are as strong as oak trees. We bend but we don't break. The old take their leave. Alfred was 97 when we left him in God's care. He told me I would live to be as old as he. I am 93. If his prediction comes true, I will live another four years. I will continue to see Estonia's heyday. Be strong, Estonia! Bend but don't break.

In early 2009, as my mother cared for my dying father, I put my own thoughts about them and their compatriots on paper. In February, as the Los Angeles Estonian community celebrated the traditional Independence Day, I gave my usual, brief greeting and read what I had written:

Completing the circle, my mother shows me the hospital where I was born. We stood next to what had been the entrance. The building is now vacant, replaced by a modern hospital facility (photograph by Mati Uibo).

Thank You

"You had no name except 'refugees' or 'displaced persons.' You survived the carnage and political turmoil of World War II and its aftermath to leaven the lives of everyone you touched. You were a precursor to the Vietnamese, Cambodians, Cubans, Hmong, Tibetans, Sudanese and others who would find refuge on foreign shores.

"General George Patton likened you to locusts. A British official called you 'the scum of Europe.' The United States War Department described you as 'people who pushed, screamed, clawed for food, smelled bad, who couldn't and didn't want to obey orders.'

"You fled the bloody steppes of Ukraine, the ruins of Warsaw, the ashes of Dresden. You were uprooted from the shores of the Baltic and the Adriatic. Sometimes carrying infants, you walked, trudged, crawled and limped to escape the atrocities of Stalin, Hitler and Mussolini. Others sailed makeshift vessels that were prey to submarines, aircraft and mines.

"You had an instinct for survival, mingled with fear, courage and a desire for freedom and peace. Many of you were young; some recently married; others recently widowed, whether by death or by labor camp, the difference was abstruse. The anchor of family, friends and neighbors were a memory. You lacked food and shelter. You tried to avoid bombs, bullets, disease and marauding soldiers. You were wise, brave, altruistic and stubborn. You were also foolish, suspicious and self-centered. You were human; you were survivors.

"When you reached the British or American lines you were placed in camps and politely labeled 'displaced.' Some of you reached Sweden or other mostly friendly shores. You yearned for home but rejected cajolements to return. When the fighting stopped you realized that peace on the battlefields did not mean war's end. There was a Cold War. To return home meant death, prison or living a life shorn of the right to make choices.

"When you were finally permitted to leave the displaced persons camps, many of you gained entrance to America, Canada, Australia or other places whose language and customs were as strange to you as you were to your hosts. You arrived with little other than your clothes, your memories and a resilience grounded in stubbornness. You saw an opportunity to pursue your vision of a new, better life, for yourself and most importantly, for your children and grandchildren.

"In your new homes, you met compatriots, earned a living, raised families and pledged new allegiances while maintaining your and your children's roots. You spoke of liberty and justice, not as abstract concepts but as absolutes. You began a new life—as day laborers, as fruit pickers, as maids, as apprentice mechanics. You suffered insults and discrimination, real and perceived. You cautiously accepted the warmness and generosity that were also a part of your welcome to new shores. From your first, menial jobs you advanced to better positions even though many of you were never able to resume your original occupations. You sacrificed so your children would not have to.

"As years passed your children, neighbors and coworkers identified you with certain traits. You were formal. You were strict, or at least you liked to think you were. Except when it came to food for guests, you were frugal—not stingy or cheap but frugal.

"You valued education. You expected your children and grandchildren to be educated. You supported these expectations financially even as you scrimped on money for yourself. You adapted, in your broken new tongue, to the values and culture of your new home but you also instilled your children with your homeland's culture. Your stories were a constant reminder of the importance of truth, liberty, self-sufficiency and human dignity even if on occasion your deeds failed to match your words.

"Some of you became well known—Madeleine Albright; Jonas Mekas;

Tom Lantos; Hannah Arendt. The vast majority of you gained renown on a smaller scale. You were recognized and respected in your work and home communities because of your quiet steadfastness, integrity and modesty. All of you were, and those of you who are still with us are, extraordinary. Thank you!"

Further Readings

Perhaps some of the people or events mentioned in this book piqued your interest—the famine in Russia, the British role in Estonia's War of Independence, the Kellogg-Briand Pact? Or, perhaps my father's reaction to the policies of Australia's Labor Party aroused your curiosity? Here is a list of books and a few articles that can provide a starting point for those wishing to find out more about a particular subject.

This list is not comprehensive. There are dozens of excellent works on some of the subjects I mention, subjects such as the Russian Revolution. On the other hand, while there is a shortage of English language material about some Estonia-related subjects I have mentioned, even here there are often additional, excellent reference sources.

Print editions of a few of the listed books are rare or are difficult to find. However, some of these rare or difficult to find books, such as *Letters from the Shores of the Baltic*, are accessible through Google Books and other Internet sources and are freely downloadable.

I have not listed books for certain significant time periods and events. For example, there are no suggested readings that deal with the internal political events that took place in Estonia during the 1920s and 30s. If a topic was not mentioned by my parents or me in the text, I have not, for the most part, offered any readings for it.

Australia

Beilharz, Peter. *Transforming Labor: Labor Tradition and the Labor Decade in Australia*. United Kingdom, Cambridge University Press, 1994.

Birškys, Betty. *The Baltic Peoples in Australia: Lithuanians, Latvians, Estonians*. Australia, AE Press, 1986.

Campbell, Ernest William. *History of the Australian Labour Movement: A Marxist Interpretation*. Australia, Current Book Distributors, 1945.

Macintyre, Stuart. *Australia's Boldest Experiment: War and Reconstruction in the 1940s*. Australia, NewSouth Publishing, 2015.

Neumann, Klaus. *Across the Seas: Australia's Response to Refugees: A History*. Australia, Black Incorporated, 2015.

Persian, Jayne. *Beautiful Balts: From Displaced Persons to New Australians*. Australia, NewSouth Publishing, 2017.

Chicago 1968

The Czech Black Book. Prepared by the Institute of History of the Czechoslovak Academy of Sciences. United Kingdom, Pall Mall Press, 1969.
Farber, David. *Chicago '68.* University of Chicago Press, 1994.
Report of the National Advisory Commission on Civil Disorders. U.S. Government Printing Office, 1968.
Rubin, Jerry. *Do It!: Scenarios of the Revolution.* Simon & Schuster, 1970.

Cold War

Andrew, Christopher, and Mitrokhin, Vasili. *The Sword and the Shield: The Mitrokhin Archive and the Secret History of the KGB.* United Kingdom, Basic Books, 2000.
Applebaum, Anne. *Iron Curtain: The Crushing of Eastern Europe, 1944-1956.* Anchor Books, a division of Random House, 2013.
Morgan, Michael Cotey. *The Final Act: The Helsinki Accords and the Transformation of the Cold War.* Princeton University Press, 2020.
Redihan, Erin Elizabeth. *The Olympics and the Cold War, 1948-1968: Sport as Battleground in the U.S.-Soviet Rivalry.* McFarland, 2017.
Westad, Odd Arne. *The Cold War: A World History.* Basic Books, 2017.

Estonian Awakening (1850-1918)

Haltzel, Michael H. *Russification in the Baltic Provinces and Finland, 1855-1914.* Princeton University Press, 1981.
Lieven, D.C. B. *Empire: The Russian Empire and Its Rivals.* Yale University Press, 2002.
National Movements in the Baltic Countries During the 19th Century: 7th Conference on Baltic Studies in Scandinavia: Papers.
Zelnik, Reginald E. *Law and Disorder on the Narova River: The Kreenholm Strike of 1872.* University of California Press, 1995.

Estonian Community in America

Estonians in America, 1945-1995: Exiles in a Land of Promise. United States, Estonian American National Council, 2016.
Pennar, Jaan, Tönu Parming, Reane P. Peter. *The Estonians in America, 1627-1975.* United States: Oceana Publications, 1975.

Estonian Culture

Harris, E. Howard. *Literature in Estonia.* Boreas Publishing Company, 1947.
Holmes, Ramona. *Resilient Voices: Estonian Choirs and Song Festivals in World War II Displaced Person Camps.* Routledge, 2021.
Kärner, Karin Annus. *Estonian Tastes and Traditions.* Hippocrene Books, 2005.
Koiva, Enn O. *Using Estonian/American Based Culture Models for Multicultural Studies: An Innovative Approach to Studying the Multi-cultural, Multi-ethnic Experience.* United States Office of Education, Ethnic Heritage Studies, 1979.
Kreutzwald, Friedrich Reinhold, et al. *Kalevipoeg: The Estonian National Epic.* Estonian Literary Museum, Kunst, 2011.
Kurrik, Juhan. *Ilomaile: Anthology of Estonian Folk Songs with Translations and Commentary.* Canada, Maarjamaa, 1985.
Paulson, Ivar. *The Old Estonian Folk Religion,* tr. N.p., n.p.
Paulson, Ivar, Juta Kõvamees Kitching, and H. Kõvamees. *The Old Estonian Folk Religion.* Indiana University Press, 1971.

Piirisild, Viivi. *The Estonian Cookbook*. Estonian Women's Club of Los Angeles, 1976.
Puhvel, Madli. *Symbol of Dawn: The Life and Times of the Nineteenth-Century Estonian Poet Lydia Koidula*. Estonia, Tartu University Press, 1995.

Estonian History, Pre-1850

Clemmesen, Michael Hesselholt, Niels Bo Poulsen, and Anna Sofie Schoning. *The Great Northern War: New Perspectives*. University Press of Southern Denmark, 2018.
Eastlake, Elizabeth. *Letters from the Shores of the Baltic*. J. Murray, 1842.
Lisk, Jill. *The Struggle for Supremacy in the Baltic, 1600-1725*. Funk & Wagnalls, 1968.
Murray, Alan V. *Crusade and Conversion on the Baltic Frontier 1150-1500*. Taylor & Francis, 2017.
Roberts, Michael. *The Swedish Imperial Experience 1560-1718*. Cambridge University Press, 1984.
Schildhauer, Johannes. *The Hansa: History and Culture*. Edition Leipzig, 1985.

Estonia Occupied

Applebaum, Anne. *Gulag: A History*. Doubleday, 2003.
Kukk, Kristi, et al. *Soviet Deportations in Estonia: Impact and Legacy: Articles and Life Histories*. Estonia, Tartu University Press, 2007.
Laar, M. *War in the Woods: Estonia's Struggle for Survival, 1944-1956*. Compass Press, 1992.
Misiunas, Romuald J., and Taagepera, Rein. *The Baltic States, Years of Dependence, 1940-1980*. University of California Press, 1983.
Oksanen, Sofi. *Purge*. United States: Black Cat, 2010. (Fiction.)
Parming, Tönu, and Elmar Järvesoo. *A Case Study of a Soviet Republic: The Estonian SSR*. Westview Press, 1978.
Taagepera, Rein. *Softening Without Liberalization in the Soviet Union: The Case of Jüri Kukk*. University Press of America, 1984.

Estonia War of Independence

Agar, Captain Augustus V.C. Willington Shelton Commodore. *Baltic Episode: A Classic of Secret Service in Russian Waters*. Hodder and Stoughton, 1963.
Bennett, Geoffrey. *Cowan's War: The Story of British Naval Operations in the Baltic, 1918-1920*. Collins, 1964.
Dunn, Steve R. *Battle in the Baltic: The Royal Navy and the Fight to Save Estonia and Latvia 1918-20*. Seaforth Publishing, 2020.
Graham, Malbone W. *The Diplomatic Recognition of the Border States: 2. Estonia*. University of California Press, 1939.
Tallents, Stephen George. *Man and Boy*. Faber & Faber, 1943.

Finland, Winter and Continuation Wars

Edwards, Robert. *White Death: Russia's War on Finland 1939-40*. Weidenfeld & Nicolson, 2006.
Jakobson, Max. *The Diplomacy of the Winter: An Account of the Russo-Finnish War, 1939-1940*. Harvard University Press, 1961.
Lunde, Henrik O. *Finland's War of Choice: The Troubled German-Finnish Coalition in World War II*. Casemate Publishers, 2011.
Nenye, Vesa. *Finland at War: The Continuation and Lapland Wars 1941-45*. Osprey Publishing, 2016.
Uustalu, Evald. *For Freedom Only: The Story of Estonian Volunteers in the Finnish Wars of 1940-1944*. Canada, Northern Publications, 1977.

Los Angeles Marathon

Greenwood, Noel. *L.A. Marathon: The First Ten Years*. Los Angeles Times, 1995.

Los Angeles 1984 Olympics

D'Agati, Philip. *The Cold War and the 1984 Olympic Games: A Soviet-American Surrogate War*. Palgrave Macmillan, 2013.
Llewelly, Matthew P., John Gleaves, and Wayne Wilson. *The 1984 Los Angeles Olympic Games: Assessing the 30-Year Legacy*. Routledge, 2015.

Non-recognition

Hathaway, Oona A., and Scott J. Shapiro. *The Internationalists: How a Radical Plan to Outlaw War Remade the World*. Simon & Schuster, 2017.
Hiden, John, Vahur Made, and David J. Smith. *The Baltic Question During the Cold War*. Taylor & Francis, 2008.
Hough, William J. H. *The Annexation of the Baltic States and Its Effect on the Development of Law Prohibiting Forcible Seizure of Territory*. New York University Law School, 1985.
Pacy, James S., and James T. McHugh. *Diplomats Without a Country: Baltic Diplomacy, International Law, and the Cold War*. Greenwood Press, 2001.
Mälksoo, Lauri. *Illegal Annexation and State Continuity: The Case of the Incorporation of the Baltic States by the USSR: A Study of the Tension Between Normativity and Power in International Law*. Netherlands, Martinus Nijhoff, 2003.

Political Activism

Ainso, Sirje Okas. *The Story of BATUN 1966–1991: Baltic Appeal to the United Nations*. United States, Sirje Okas Ainso, 2018.
Baltic Bulletins 1982–1992. United States, Baltic American Freedom League, n.d.
Kalm, Arne. *Baltic Musketeers in the U.S. Congress: A Brief History from an Estonian's Perspective of the First Baltic Resolutions in the U.S. Congress, 1961–1966*. Estonia: Aade Publishers, 2015.
Zake, Ieva. *American Latvians: Politics of a Refugee Community*. Transaction Publishers, 2010.
Zake, Ieva. *Anti-Communist Minorities in the U.S.: Political Activism of Ethnic Refugees*. Palgrave Macmillan, 2009.

Refugees

Aun, Karl. *The Political Refugees: A History of Estonians in Canada*. McClelland and Stewart, 1985.
Bethell, Nicholas. *The Last Secret: The Delivery to Stalin of Over Two Million Russians by Britain and the United States*. Basic Books, 1974.
Ehin, Charles. *Coming Home: The Reconciliation of an Estonian Family Torn Apart by War*. Lakeshore Press, 2011.
Epstein, Julius. *Operation Keelhaul: The Story of Forced Repatriation from 1944 to the Present*. Devin-Adair Company, 1973.
Genizi, Haim, and Genîzî, Ḥayyîm. *America's Fair Share: The Admission and Resettlement of Displaced Persons, 1945–1952*. Wayne State University Press, 1993.
Nasaw, David. *The Last Million: Europe's Displaced Persons from World War to Cold War*. Penguin, 2021.
Portes, Alejandro, and Rube'n G Rumbaut. *Immigrant America: A Portrait*. University of California Press, 1996.

Shephard, Ben. *The Long Road Home: The Aftermath of the Second World War*. Anchor Books, 2012.
Silabriedis, J., and B. Arklans. *"Political Refugees" Unmasked!* Latvia S.S.R., Latvian State Publishing House, 1965.
Vesilind, Priit. "Return to Estonia." *National Geographic*, v. 157, No. 4, April 1980.
Wyman, Mark. *DPs: Europe's Displaced Persons, 1945-51*. Cornell University Press, 2015.
Yang, Jia Lynn. *One Mighty and Irresistible Tide: The Epic Struggle Over American Immigration, 1924-1965*. W.W. Norton, 2021.
Zucker, Norman L., and Naomi Flink Zucker. *Desperate Crossings: Seeking Refuge in America*. M.E. Sharpe, 1996.

Russian Revolution and Civil War

Davis, John P. *Russia in the Time of Cholera: Disease under Romanovs and Soviets*. Bloomsbury Academic, 2018.
Katkov, George. *Russia, 1917: The February Revolution*. Greenwood Press, 1979.
Kerensky, Alexander. *Russia and History's Turning Point*. Duell, Sloan and Pearce, 1965.
Luckett, Richard. *The White Generals: An Account of the White Movement and the Russian Civil War*. Routledge & Kegan Paul, 1971.
Mawdsley, Evan. *The Russian Civil War*. Pegasus Books, 2007.
Pipes, Richard. *The Russian Revolution*. Knopf, 1990.
Robien, Louis comte de. *The Diary of a Diplomat in Russia, 1917-1918*. Praeger Publishers, 1970.
Ulam, Adam B. *The Bolsheviks: The Intellectual and Political History of the Triumph of Communism in Russia*. Harvard University Press, 1998.
Weissman, Benjamin M. *Herbert Hoover and Famine Relief to Soviet Russia: 1921-1923*. Stanford University Press, 1974.

Singing Revolution

Kelam, Tunne. *Estonia's Way to Freedom*. Estonia, Epp-Ed, 2005.
Laar, Mart, and Tunne Kelam. *Estonia: Almost Extinguished, Successfully Reborn*. Estonia, Pro Patria Institute, 2017.
Lieven, Anatol. *The Baltic Revolution: Estonia, Latvia, Lithuania and the Path to Independence*. Yale University Press, 1994.
Šmidchens, Guntis. *The Power of Song: Nonviolent National Culture in the Baltic Singing Revolution*. University of Washington Press, 2014.
Vesilind, Priit, James Tusty, and Maureen Tusty. *The Singing Revolution: How Culture Saved a Nation*. Estonia, Varrak Publishers, 2008.

Sweden

Blair, Alan, and Per Olov Enquist. *The Legionnaires: A Documentary Novel*; translated from the Swedish by Alan Blair. United Kingdom, Cape, 1974.
Olsson, Lars, *On the Threshold of the People's Home of Sweden: A Labor Perspective of Baltic Refugees and Relieved Polish Concentration Camp Prisoners in Sweden at the End of World War II*. United States, The Center for Migration Studies, 1997.
Veedam, Voldemar, and Carl B. Wall. *Sailing to Freedom*. Thomas Y. Crowell, 1952.

World War II

Buttar, Prit. *Between Giants: The Battle for the Baltics in World War II*. Osprey Publishing, 2013.

Grooss, Poul. *The Naval War in the Baltic 1939–1945*. Seaforth Publishing, 2017.
Hiden, John, and Thomas Lane, eds. *The Baltic and the Outbreak of the Second World War*. Cambridge University Press, 2003.
Koburger, Charles W. *Steel Ships, Iron Crosses, and Refugees: The German Navy in the Baltic, 1939–1945*. Praeger, 1989.
Mertelsmann, Olaf. *The Second World War and the Baltic States*. Belgium, Lang, Peter GmbH, 2014.
Moorhouse, Roger. *The Devils' Alliance: Hitler's Pact with Stalin, 1939–1941*. Bodley Head, 2014.
Piirimäe, Kaarel. *Roosevelt, Churchill, and the Baltic Question: Allied Relations During the Second World War*. Palgrave Macmillan, 2014.
Weiss-Wendt, Anton. *Murder Without Hatred: Estonians and the Holocaust*. Syracuse University Press, 2009.
Weiss-Wendt, Anton. *On the Margins: Essays on the History of Jews in Estonia*. Hungary, CEU Press, 2017.

Index

Abrams, Elliott 152
Across the Pacific 95
"Act of the Re-Establishment of the State of Lithuania" 214
Adelaide 103, 112
Agora Ephesus 237
Ahonen, Heiki 189, *190*
Alaska Gold Rush 34
Alexandria, Virginia 182
Ali, Muhammad 214
American Civil Liberties Union 160
American consulate, Leningrad 208, 209, 235
American Dream 9, 117, 138
American Embassy, Canberra 106, 115
American Express 132
American Latvian Association 168, 170, 182
American Museum of Natural History 84, 85, *86*
Americans (song) 118
Amnesty International 153, 190, 222, *223*
Anderson, Leo 170, 172
Anderson, Robert 157
Änilane, Gerdrud 199
Anschluss 36, 38, 42
Anton, Erika 243
Antsla, Estonia 30
Antsla Home Economics School 38
Antsla Manor House 38
Army, service in 140–145
The Athletic Congress (TAC) 210–211, 217
Auckland, New Zealand 95, 100, 101
Australia 43, *64*, 70, 74–75, 80, 90, 91, *93*, *94*, 95, 100, 101–116, 118, 120, 124, 131, 132, 186, 198, 199
Australian National Airways *113*
Azrael, Jeremy 137

Baker, James 220
Baltic American Freedom League (BAFL) 145, 146–154, *157*, 158, 160, 162, 168, 181, 200, 203, 205, 218, 219, 220, 222
Baltic barons 18
Baltic Cup 199, 201, *204*, 205
Baltic Deportation Day 149
Baltic Desk Officer 181
Baltic Freedom Award 152–154
Baltic Freedom Day 146, 148, 149, *150*
Baltic Policy Statement 181–182
Baltic Sea 17–18, 55, 187
Baltic Tribunal 172
Baltic Wave 152, 239; *see also* Baltic Way
Baltic Way 154; *see also* Baltic Wave
Baltic World Congress 172
Barauskaite, Danute *see* Mazeika, Danute Barauskaite
basic training, US Army 141–142
Belgian Consul General, Los Angeles 179
Berlin, Irving 118
Berlin Wall 146, 218
Biltmore Hotel 122, 199
Black Captains 50; *see also* Nikkar
Black Sea 11, 18
Blackstone Rangers 137–138
Blakis, Ansis 148
Bloch, Marc 136
Bloody Sunday massacre 19
Blue Mountains, Australia *113*
Bolsheviks 19, 20, 33
M/S *Boogabilla* 115–120
Boy Scouts 32, 35, 124, *125*
Bradley, Tom 196–197, 198, *200*, 200, 203
Braukis, Yanis 156–157, *157*, 158, 161
Brisbane, Australia 103, 112, 116
SS *Britannia* 76, 77
British 19, 20, 74, 149, 152
British Legation, Stockholm 74
Brown, Doris 127
Brown, Ervin 127
Buccaneer Enterprises *123*
Burbank, California 123, 145

255

256 Index

Burke, William 197–198, 205, 210, 216–217
Burke, Yvonne Brathwaite 197
Bush, George H.W. 218–222, 239

Cabramatta, Australia 107–109
"California living" 91, 93
Calise, Lesley see Fuller, Lesley Calise
Canada 43, 164, 173, 181, 195, 199, 246
Canberra 112
Canoga Park, Los Angeles 133, 145
The Career of Class 104
Carter, Jimmy 155–156
Catch-22 142
Cekanauskas, Vytautas 171, 201
Century City, Los Angeles 190, 222
Chicago, Illinois 136–139, 165, 186
Chicago Seven 138
Children's Encyclopedia 112
China 67, **69**, 159, 164, 209, 241; *see also* Taiwan
Chinese Consul General, Los Angeles 190
The Chronicles of the Catholic Church in Lithuania 153
Chudovo 11, 13, 15, 19, 21
Churchill, Winston 42, 73
Coffey, Sheila 174
The Cold War and the 1984 Olympic Games 156
Cole's 103
Colorado Springs **126**
comic books 112
Commission on Civil Rights, United States 160
Committee on International Relations, University of Chicago 136
Communist Party 104, 110, 114, 172, 184, 188, 207, 238
Communists 42, 43, 73, 104, 106, 110, 146, 155, 160, 209, 234
Congress of Estonia 184, 190, **191**, 214, 218, 221, 238
Continuation War 55
Convention Relating to the Status of Refugees, United Nations General Assembly 7
Courts and Boards 142
Crumrine, Avery 244
Crumrine, Zoe 244
Czechoslovakia 36–37, 139

Dabsys, Tadas **151**
D'Agati, Philip 156
Daley, Richard 138
Damusis, Saulius 148
The Death and Life of Great American Cities 136

Declaration of Independence (Lithuania) 214, 220
Declaration of Independence (United States) 117
declaration of sovereignty (Estonia) 175, 207
Defense Production Act of 1950 131
Democracy in America 117
Democratic National Convention 137, 138–139
demonstrations 9, 135, 144, 146, **147, 148**, 154, 155, **157**, 188, 207, 218, 239
Denmark 131, 172, 238
Department of State, U.S. 75, 152, 159, 160, 165, 166, 167, 168, 171, 172, 178, 181, **192**, 220
deportations 37, 42, 44, 73, 110, 116, 188, 239
Deukmejian, George **189**
Die Hard 222
Diplomats Without a Country 174
Disneyland 188, 235
displaced persons (DPs) 50, 74
Dr. Strangelove 118
Documents from Estonia 206
Dominican Republic 74
draft 140–141
SS *Drottningholm* 82–84
Du Bois, W.E.B. 118
Dutton, Leslie 147

East Valley Family YMCA 133
Ecclesiastes, Book of 220
Eichelmann, Sirje 208, **210**, 211, **212**, 212, **213**, 213, 214–217, 230
Eisenhower, Dwight **126**
Emmanuel, Kitty 95
Encino, California 145
entry questionnaire **16–17**
Eomoisa dam **28**, 28–29
Eomoisa mill **28**, 28, 232
Ericsson Telephone Factory 67
Estonia: A Nation Unconquered 205
Estonia, Manifest 20
Estonian Aid Center 57, 58
Estonian American National Council 181, 182, 186, **189**, 206
Estonian Chamber of Commerce 208
Estonian Citizens' Committee 189–190
Estonian Consulate, New York 77, 85, 88, 165, 167, **168**, 169, 170, 178, 182–184, 191, 193, 198
Estonian Consumers' Co-Operative 52
Estonian Embassy, London 74
Estonian Embassy, Stockholm 74, 164; *see also* Estonian Legation, Stockholm

Estonian Embassy, Washington, D.C. 164–165, 178
The Estonian Group for the Disclosure of the Molotov-Ribbentrop Pact (MRP-AEG) 202, 203
Estonian House (Los Angeles) 201, 205, *212*, 213, 216, 235, 239, 241
Estonian House (New York) 192
Estonian House (Sydney) 102, 110
Estonian Legation, Stockholm 75; *see also* Estonian Embassy, Stockholm
Estonian Maritime Union 75
Estonian National Independence Party 146, 184, 186, 188, 207
Estonian News Service **21**
Estonian Relief Committee 102
Estonian World 50
Eu, March Fong 174
European Parliament 172
Exodus, Book of 7
Exposition Park, Los Angeles 213, 215

Falklands War 149
Faust 71
Feudal Society 136
Fiji 99–100, 110
Finnish Consul General, Los Angeles 178
Flaming Arrows Scout patrol 126
flying fish **96**, 96, 97
"Flying the Flag" 172, 173–184
folk costumes **40**
folk university 39–40, 42
Fontana, Barbara Oseguera 169
Ford, Gerald 218, 224–227
Fort Belvoir **141**, 142–145
Fort Ord **141**, 141
Fox, Samantha 244
Friendship Cup 196–198, 199–200, **200**, 203–205, 209–211
Fuller, Lesley Calise 205, 209, 210, 214, 216, 217

Galbraith, James 136
The Gathering Storm 42
Gdansk shipyards 146
General Pact for the Renunciation of War 36; *see also* Kellogg-Briand Pact; Paris Peace Pact
Germany (East) 127, 152, 194, 228
Germany (Nazi) 36, 42, 50, 55, 64, 82, 154, 202
Germany (West) 110, 164, 194, 198, 238
Getting Here: An Odyssey Through World War II 82
Getty, J. Arch 219
Gibson, Kirk 154

glasnost 172, 186, 207, 238
Glenwood Elementary School 124
gluing machine 144–145
God Bless America 118
"Goddess of Liberty" **148**, 218
Golding, William 136
Gorbachev, Mikhail 172, 181, 204–205, 208, 220, 238
Gothenburg, Sweden 70, **76**, 76, 77, 81, 82
Gotland, Sweden **65**, 66
government-in-exile 49, 51, 174–175
Grant Park, Chicago 138
Great Britain 72, 101, 164, 198
Great Depression 36, 37
Greene, Graham 169
"Group of Estonian Artists" **63**
gulags 110, 146, 153, 186, 187, 188, **189**, 191, 199, 222, **223**, 230
Gulf of Finland 18, 50–51, 54, 55, 57
Gulf of Tonkin 140

Hägersten, Stockholm 61, 62
Hallmark Greeting Cards 132
Hanko, Finland 57, 59
Hannaford, Peter 148, 149
Hannaford Public Relations Company 147, 148–150
Hansson, Ardo 193
Hara Bay, Estonia 50
Hargreaves, Katie 95
Harjumäe 203
Hawke, R.I.J. 152
Hawkeye Pierce 144
Hayden, Tom 138
Hegel, Georg Wilhelm Friedrich 136
Heinsoo, Ilmar 168, **183**, 183, 184
Heller, Joseph 142
Helsinki 51, 55, 57, 58, 59, 86, 174, 205, 230, 234
Helsinki Accords 226, 227
Helsinki Declaration 151
Helsinki-86 153
Hendrix, Jimi 118
heritage clubs 184, 196, 199, 203, 207
Hiiumaa 52, 193
Hilton Hotel, Chicago 138
Hirvepark (*Deer Park*) 188, 189, **190**, 203
Hitler, Adolf 7, 37, 64, 245
Hoffman, Abbie 138
Holiday Inn 211
Hollywood Bowl 185
Hollywood Way, Burbank 123, 132, 133, 145
Holy Mai 25
honeycomb decorations 67–69, 80, 102, 104, 105 128–133

Index

The Honorary Consul 169
honorary consuls 165–166, 170
Horm, Anne-Mari 61, **70**, 70–71
Horm, Arvo 44, 52, 61, **63**, 65, 66, 69, 90, 91, 125, 193
Horm, Maarja 61, 62, **63**, 70
Hough, William 193
Hsia, Yuan-sen 209
Huguenots 7
Huittinen, Kaapro 51
human rights 44, 146, 147, **148**, 179, 186, 188, 218, 227
human rights conferences 147, **151**, 152
Human Rights Day 188

illness 13, 16, **21**, 21–22, 24, 25–26, 34, 90–91
Immigration Act of 1924 75
International Olympic Committee (IOC) 158, 159, 160
International Parade 156–160
International Refugee Organization 74
Iron Curtain 9, 146, 228
Israelites 7
Ivan III (Tsar) **21**
Ivangorod Fortress 21

Jaakson, Claire 191
Jaakson, Ernst 165, 166, 167–172, 173, 174–175, 178, 181, 183–184, 191–193, 198, 208
the Jaansons 110
Jackson, Mahalia 137
Jacobs, Jane 136
JAG *see* Judge Advocate General's Corps
Janson, Marta 167
Japan 19, 36, 91, 94, 132, 160
Järvi, Neeme 185, 186
JBANC *see* Joint Baltic American National Committee
Jenolan Caverns 112, 113
Jõgis, Heino 198, 199
John H. Francis Polytechnic High School 126
Johnson, Lyndon 138, 140
Joint Baltic American National Committee (JBANC) 149, 182, 218, 219, 220, **221**
Judge Advocate General's Corps (JAG) 142–143

Kaiv, Johannes 77, 78, 85, 88, 164–166
Kalevipoeg 18, 20, 203
Kalviste, Jüri 198, 199, **202**
Kamenar, Paul 152
Kamenev, Valentin 177
Karja Street, Võru 33, 34

Kasaritsa, Võru County 230
Kasarmu Street, Võru 47
Katoomb, Australia 112
Kelam, Mari-Ann Rikken 181–182, **191**, 193, 206, 221
Kelam, Tunne 146, 189–190, **191**, 218, 221, 225
Kellogg-Briand Pact 36; *see also* General Pact for the Renunciation of War; Paris Peace Pact
Kennedy, John F. 220
Kerensky, Alexander 19, 33
Kerouac, Jack 90
Keynes, John Maynard 136
KGB 60, 174, 185, 188
King, Martin Luther 138
Kivikasukas 156, 157, 158, **161**, 162
Kodumaa—Homeland (publication) 172
Kodusaar, Kalju 34
Kodusaar, Leena 34
Koidula, Lydia 18
Kõiva, Katre 185, 186
Kojelis, Juozas 147–148, 160
Kojelis, Linas 160
Köleri Street, Tallinn 42, 44
kookaburra birds 108
Kõpp *see* Võru Higher Elementary
Kõpp, Johan 80, 81, 110
Kõpp, Maria 80, 81, 110
Korean War 128, 131
Korol *see* Võru Higher Elementary
Kose, Estonia 40
Kõvatu, Jaana 229, 231, 236
kümmel 12
Kummelnäs refugee camp 51
Kuril Islands 160
Küün, Captain 85, 87

Labor Party (Australia) 74, 104, 107, 114, 116, 131
Laid, Eerik 78, 81
Laid, Milvi 62
Lake Placid, New York 159, 160, 162
Lake Shore Drive, Chicago 138
"Landing Permit" 74
Landsbergis, Vytautas 220
Lapkis, Janis 201, **204**, 205
Laretei, Heinrich 74, 78
Lasnamäe, Tallinn 42, 43
Latvian Community Center 153, 222, 239
Laur, Ernst 58–59, 166, 167, 168, 172
learning English 111–112
Leaves of Grass 118
Leek, Tiiu 158–159
Lefcoe, George 136
Lehmann, Anu Part 223, **224**

Index

Lenin, Vladimir 19
Leningrad 21, 55, 64, 188, 208, 209, 235; see also Petrograd; St. Petersburg
A Letter from Estonia 206–208
letters from East Germany 127
Liberik 81
The Life and Adventures of Robinson Crusoe 112
liikva 24
Lincoln Memorial 144
Linda, statue of 203
Linkhorst, Aksel 65, 69, 75, 78, 81
Lithuania, re-establishment 214
Lithuanian American Community of the USA 182
Lithuanian American National Council 182
Loksa, Estonia 50
London 74, 76, 77–78
London Review of Books 219
"Long live free Estonia!" 179
Lord of the Flies 136
Los Angeles, conferences 146–147, *151*, 152–154, 157
Los Angeles Consular Corps 175, 177, 185, 190
Los Angeles Daily Journal 160
Los Angeles Dodgers 154
Los Angeles Estonian community 125, 167, 169, 171, 244
Los Angeles Estonian Evangelical Lutheran Church 179
Los Angeles Herald Examiner 160
Los Angeles Induction Center 141
Los Angeles Marathon 196–217
Los Angeles Memorial Coliseum 156, 201, *211*, 213, 215
Los Angeles Olympic Organizing Committee (LAOOC) 156–162
Los Angeles Olympics 155–162, 197
Los Angeles Philharmonic Orchestra 185
Los Angeles Times 153, 172, 175, 180, 200, 238, 239
Los Angeles, visitors 146, 187–195, 222–224, 235–236
Lund, Sweden 199
The Lutheran Standard 179, 205

Maasep family 110
MacArthur Park, Los Angeles 122
Madis 52
USS *Maddox* 140
Madisson, Tiit 146, 187–188, 202
magic fan 67–69, 104
Mammoth Lakes, California 235
Manchester, England 75, *76*, 76, 77, 78, 79

Manchuria 19, 36, 91, *94*
Manton 103
maps 14, 54, 72, 89
SS *Marine Phoenix* 75, 93–101
Mark, Heinrich 51
Marx, Karl 116, 136
Masaryk, Jan 228
MASH 144
Matson, Verner 27, 228, 231–232
Matson Line 94, 95
Matulaitis, Jonas 148
Mazeika, Anthony 148, *157*, 219–220
Mazeika, Danute Barauskaite 148, *151*, 239
McCarthy, Eugene 138
McHugh, James T. 174
Meie Kodu–Our Home 102
Melbourne, Australia 103, 112
Meri, Lennart 223–224, *224*, 225, 226, 236, 238
Metex *123*, 128–133, 136, 144–145, 194, 208, 209, 234, 241
Michigan Avenue, Chicago 138
Midway, Chicago 137
Military Occupational Specialty (MOS) 142
mink factory 67
Minn, Meelis 208, *210*, 211, *212*
Mr. Smith 99–100
Mr. Smith Goes to Washington 118
Molotov-Ribbentrop Pact 37, 64, 154; see also Stalin-Hitler Non-Aggression Pact
Monáe, Janelle 118
Mormon Tabernacle Choir 118
Moscow (city) 15, 56, 60, 202, 206, 235, 238
Moscow coup 238
Moscow Olympics 156
motivation for coming to America 116–118
Mõtsnik, Harri 179, 205
Muld family 81
Munamägi (Egg Mountain), Estonia 33
Munich Conference 36, 42
Myer Emporium 103

Narva, Estonia 13, 21–22, 32, 33
Narva Castle *21*
Narva River *21*
National Commission on Foreigners (Sweden) 72–73
National Independence Party 146, 184, 186, 188, 207; see also The Estonian Group for the Disclosure of the Molotov-Ribbentrop Pact
Neggo, Rein 179

New York 82–88, 89–90, 186
New York Law School Journal of International and Comparative Law 193
New York Times 181, 238
SS *Nicaragua* 75–80, 85, 87–88
Nicholas II (Tsar) 19
Niguliste Children's Clinic 46–47; *see also* Tallinn Pediatric Outpatient Clinic
Niitme, Arno 198, 199, *213*
Nikkar *see* Black Captain
Niklus, Mart 146, 152–154, 190, 222–223, *223*
Nixon, Richard 138, 220
NKVD 60, 65, 116
nonrecognition policy 10, 163–166, 168, 171, 227
Norfolk, Virginia 75, 85–88
North Atlantic 82, *83*
North Hollywood, Los Angeles 126, 195
North Sea 76, 77
Norwegians 78, 79
"Notice to Residents of Estonia" 202–203
Nurmberg, Heino 148
Nurmberg, Maie 148
Nurmsen, Bernhard 222, *223*
Nurse Toover 53

Obama, Barack 118
Office of the Historian, U.S. State Department 75
Oja, Miss 38–39, 229
Okun, Herbert S. 152
Olds, Reginald B. 167, *168*
Ole, Eduard *63*, *64*, 69
On the Road 90
One Day in the Life of Ivan Denisovich 187
1980 Winter Olympics 159
1944 mass exodus 50, 65, *66*
"Open Letter to Mikhail Gorbachev" 204–205
Operation Barbarossa 55
Orange County, California 175, 243
Orange County Office of Protocol 188
Orange County Register 187–188
Oseguera, Pepe 169
Otepää, Estonia 34

Paabo, Helen 199, 200
Paabo, Penelope 199, 200
Pacific Palisades, California 169
Pacy, James S. 174
Pago Pago 95, 97–99
Pall, Ingrid 236
Palm Springs, California *225*, 225

Pan American Airways 199
Parek, Lagle 146, 188–189, *189*
Paris Peace Pact *see* General Pact for the Renunciation of War; Kellogg-Briand Pact
Pärlijõgi (Pearl River) 23, *24*, 28–29, 232
Parming, Tõnu 152, 179
Pärnu, Estonia 196, 202, 203, 206
Parramatta, Australia 103
Part, Anu *see* Lehmann, Anu Part
Pasadena-Star News 217
Päts, Konstantin 207
Pavlovskis, Valdis 149–150, *151*, *157*, 168
"Peace in our time" 36
Peetri, Jaan 199, 216
Pell, Eugene 152
People's Department for Trade 44
"*perestroika*" 172, 207, 238
Perkonitis 156, 158, 161, 162
Perm labor camp 187, 188
Pershing Square, Los Angeles 122
Perti, Mr. 110
Petersons 110
Petrograd 21, 22; *see also* Leningrad; St. Petersburg
phosphate mining 206
Pihela, Igor *210*
Piirisild, Avo 148, 154, 168–169, 193–195, *201*
Piirisild, Viivi 148, *157*, 194–195, 199–200, *201*, 211
Pindi Church 47
Pirukas *124*
Põhjala ("Estonian Students Society, Nordic") 43–44, 122, 229, 241
Poland 37, 64, 164, 218
political issue 159–162
Poom, Ida 81
Poom, Oskar 122
Popular Front 184, 207, 223
Port of Los Angeles 121
Port of New York 84, 85
Port of Tallinn 56, 57, 230
Portland 181
Prague Spring 139
Prisoner of Conscience 152, 190, 222, *223*
Protocol Ball 175, 180
Provincial Assembly 19–20
Pruvli, Aivar 204, 205, 210
Punchbowl, Australia *111*, 111–112, 114

Queens, New York *84*, 85
A Question of Trust: The Origins of U.S.-Soviet Relations, the Memoirs of Loy W. Henderson 22
quota system 75

Index

Radio Free Europe 151
Radio Liberty 151
Radon, Jennik 223, *224*, 224
Raekoja Plats—Town Hall Square 203
"*Rahva ülikool*" 40
Railway Review 19
Rajala, Ain 199
Rancho Mirage *225*, 225, 226
Rande, Toivo 208, *210*, 211
Rannap, Rein 185, 186
Raun, Toivo 179
Ravila 37, 39, 40–41, 42, 60, 232
Ravin, Jean *see* Treiman, Jean Ravin
Reagan, Nancy 222
Reagan, Ronald 118, 148, 149, 150, 153, 160, 168, 190, 218, 222–224, *223*, 224
Reagan Presidential Library 241
Red Cross *21*, 21–22, 32, 34, 82, 229
refugee stages 8–9
refugees 8, 9, 21, 51, 60, *65*, 72–73, 117, 147
Rei, August 65, 125
Reinsalu, Desiree 199
Reinsalu, Valdur 199
Republican Party 125, 138, *223*
Rice, Condoleezza 221–222
Riga 192, 193, 239
Rikken, Mari-Ann *see* Kelam, Mari-Ann
Rockefeller Center, New York 84, 85, 164, 183, 184, 192
Ronimois, Hans 52
Roop 81
Roopa Avenue, Tallinn 56
Roos, Aarand 167–168, *183*, 183–184, 198, 199, 203, 208
Roos Island, Võru 44
Roosevelt, Franklin D. 73, 175, 220
Roosevelt, James 175
Roosevelt, Theodore 220
Roosevelt Room 218, 220, *221*
Rõuge, Estonia 23, 25, 29, 30, 38
Rubin, Jerry 138
Russian Civil War 19, 33, *94*
Russian Revolution 13, 15–16, 91
Russification 18, 219
Russo-Japanese War 19
Ruut, Dr. 110

saccharine 51
St. Casimir Catholic Church 154, 239
St. Petersburg 15, 18, 21, 43, 55; *see also* Leningrad; Petrograd
Sajūdis 214
Sakarias, Peeter 194–195
Salt Lake City, Utah 91
Salumäe, Jane 217
Salvation Committee 19–20
Samoan islands 97–99
San Fernando Valley 122, 126, 145
San Francisco 75, 76, 89–95, 105, 165, 166, 167, 181, 186, 193, 198, 230, 236
San Francisco Estonian community 93
San Pedro, California 121, 122, 193
Sänna 23, 25–26, 29, 30, 32, 36, 38, 40
Santa Claus 109
Sarv, Roland 110
sauerkraut 34–35
sauna *243*
Scalmer, Sean 104
Scanlan, John D. 152
Scheel, Klaus 65
Schiffman, Mark 158
Schmuul, Rudolf 65
Seattle, Washington 181
Seeger, Pete 220
Selg, Aleksander 74, 77–78, 79, 87, 101–102, 103
Sellik, Enn 208, 211, *212*, 212, *213*
Sheraton Universal Hotel 189
Shore, Astra 166, 171
Sillat, Uve 199
Simonson, Juhan *189*
Singer automobile *113*
"The Singing Revolution" 206
The Singleton Argus 101
Siniveer 51–52
Sirk's School 35
Skunk Works 128
Slitebaden Hotel, Gotland 66
Smith, Doug 153–154
smog 122
"socialist paradise" 106
Soe, Jane 231, 236
Solzhenitsyn, Alexander 187
song festival 18, 207, 234
Soom, Aleks 51
Sööt, Siim 199
The Souls of Black Folk 118
South Kimbark Avenue, Chicago 137
South Pacific 89, 95, 96
South Side of Chicago 136–138
Southern Hemisphere 101, 121
Soviet Consulate General, San Francisco 175–178, 230
Soviet Council of Ministers 110
Soviet Disunion 219
Soviet Embassy, Copenhagen 172
"The Soviet Secession Law Is a Sham" 180
Soviet Union 9, 10, 36, 37, 49, 50, 55, 64–65, 72, 73–74, 104, 116, 125, 131, 151, 153, 154, 155–156, 163–165, 172, 175, 178, 179–180, 186, 187, 188, 197, 214, 218–219, 223, 227, 228, 229, 231, 235, 238

Index

Spanish Civil War 36, 38
Special Processing Detachment 143
Spindulys 156–162
Spindulys, et al. v. Los Angeles Olympic Organizing Committee 155–163
Stalin, Joseph 7, 37, 64, 73, 116, 188, 202, 228 245
Stalin-Hitler Non-Aggression Pact *see* Molotov-Ribbentrop Pact
Stanford University 91
State Choir of Armenia 177
Statement of Non-interest 160
Stepanovicius, Julkionas 153
Stewart, Potter 117
Stockholm, Sweden 51, 55, 60–71, 75, *76*, 76, 77, 80, 81, 121, 186
Stoicescu, Kalev 226
The Story of Robin Hood and his Merry Men 112
Sun Valley 123–127, 145
Supreme Soviet, Estonia 190, 207, 214, 238
Supreme Soviet, U.S.S.R. 163, 165
Surbrunnsgatan, Stockholm 60, 62
Suursaar, Johannes *52*
Suva, Fiji 95, 99, *100*, 104
Sweden 18, 43, 50–53, 60–71, 72–76, 78, 80, 82, 89, 95, 102, 106, 110, 164, 187, 193, 199, 241, 246; relationship with Moscow 72–74
Swiss Consul General, Los Angeles 179
Switzerland 164
Sydney 95, 101, 110, *111*, 121

Taagepera, Rein 152, 179
Taiwan 159, 209
Tallinn 17, 37, 38, 42–45, 46–47, 50, 52–53, 56–57, *63*, 66, 122, 154, 172, 188, 193, 196, 199, 203, 205, 206, 207, 208, 230, 234, 235
Tallinn Pediatric Outpatient Clinic 42–43, 110; *see also* Niguliste Children's Clinic
Tallinn Town Hall 203, 207
Tamberg, Dick 93
Tamberg family 91–93, *94*, 108, 111
Tammoja, Peeter 208, *210*, 211, *212*
Tamula Lake 33
Tarm, Michael 206
Tarto, Enn 154
Tartu, Estonia 35, 40, 56, 196, 207
Tartu Peace Treaty 13, 20, 207
Tartu University 37, *39*, 43, 48, 52
Tartu University library 48
Teder, Maria *see* Uibo, Maria Teder
Teder, Mrs. 110

Teutonic Order 17, *21*
Tiananmen Square *148*, 218
Tint, Jüri 199
Tocqueville, de Alexis 117
Tohver, Dr. 110
Tondi, Tallinn 37
Toomingas 78
Toronto, Canada 167, 168, 182, *183*, 186
Toytex 104, 106, 109, 110, *111*, 112, *113*, 116, 129, 131, 132
Trapper John 144
Treiman, Eduard 33, 34
Treiman, Elfriede 34
Treiman, Jaan 33, 34
Treiman, Jakob 34
Treiman, Jean Ravin 195, 244
Treiman, Linda 33–34, 44
Treiman, Lisa 34
Treiman, Richard 33, 37, 44
Treiman, Rudolf (Rudi) 33, 34
Trotsky, Leon 33, 228
Truman, Harry 131
Tsarski, Aivar 208, *210*, 211, *212*, 212, *213*, 230
Tubin, Eduard 185
Turkey 237–239

Ueberroth, Peter 156
Uibo, Aleksander *12*, 13, 15, 30, 32, *39*, 103, 228, 229, 230
Uibo, Hilja 38, *39*, 55, 103, 229, 231, *232*, *233*
Uibo, Ilme 30, 134, 230, 231, 234–235, 236, *243*
Uibo, Kalju *12*, 13, 15, 25, 26, 30, *39*, 46, 49, 229, 230, 233, 241
Uibo, Linda 233
Uibo, Maria Teder *11*, 12–13, 15–16, 19
Uibo, Mati 30, 134, 229, 230, 231, 234–235, 236
Uibo, Rosilda *12*, 13, 15, 25, 30, 32, *39*, 46, 49, 229, 230
Uibo, Samuel *11*, 11–13, 15–22, 23–25, 27–31, *39*, 49, 60, *232*
Universal City, Los Angeles 189
University of California at Berkeley 93
University of Chicago 136–139, 209
University of Southern California 136
University of Sydney 104
Unruh Civil Rights Act 158–160
Ural Mountains 34
Urb, Tarmo 185 -- 186
Urb, Thomas 185 -- 186
Urb Brothers 185–186
Uustalu, Evald 81
Uustalu, Vilja 58, 67, 69, 81

Index

Vahtrik, Dr. 110
Vaino, Karl 207
Valdmaa, Rein 208, *210*, 211, *212*, 213
Vancouver 180–181
Vardys, Stanley 152
Veeroja, Imre 34
Veeroja, Õje 34
Veeroja, Velli 34
Veilberg, Meelis 208, *210*, 211, *212*
VEKSA—*The Society for the Development of Cultural Ties with Estonians Abroad* 172
Velliste, Trivimi 146, 190
Venckus, Jurate *157*
Verdugo Mountains 126
Veske, Aleksander 65, 78, 81
Vietnam War 138, 140, *141*
Viljandi, Estonia 44
Vilnius 153, 154, 239
Vladivostok *94*, 103
von Habsburg, Otto 172
Võõpsu 34
Vorkuta 230
Võru, Estonia 11, 15, 23–31, 32–35, 36, 37, 44–45, 46–47, *48*, 53, 55, 185, 196, 207, 229, 230–234, *242*
Võru Estonian Youth Sport League 35
Võru Higher Elementary 35
Võru hospital 53

Waidla, Tauno 194–195
Wall Street Journal 180
war in the Baltic 54–55
Washington, D.C. 144, 172, 186, 221
Washington Legal Foundation 160
Washington Monument 144
Washington Post 154
Weiss, Leo 199, *200*, 200
Weiss, Ruth I. 82–83
Welles, Sumner 164, 166
West Coast Estonian Days 180–181, 188, *189*
Westlake, Los Angeles 122
White House 144, 149, 160, 218, 219–221
Whitman, Walt 118
Willis, Bruce 222
Winter War 37, 55, 59
World-Wide Estonian Days 1980 *70*

Yalta Conference 73
Yeltsin, Boris 238
Yippies 138
Young Men's Christian Association 35
Young Women's Christian Association 58

Zeroles, John 181

www.ingramcontent.com/pod-product-compliance
Lightning Source LLC
Chambersburg PA
CBHW032034300426
44117CB00009B/1059